DIRECTIONS IN
CATHOLIC SOCIAL ETHICS

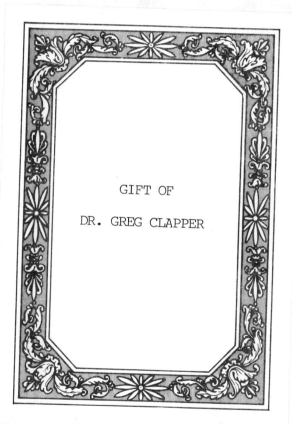

Books by Charles E. Curran Published by the
University of Notre Dame Press

Directions in Fundamental Moral Theology
Critical Concerns in Moral Theology
American Catholic Social Ethics: Twentieth-Century Approaches
Moral Theology: A Continuing Journey
Transition and Tradition in Moral Theology
Issues in Sexual and Medical Ethics
Catholic Moral Theology in Dialogue
New Perspectives in Moral Theology

Directions in
Catholic Social Ethics

CHARLES E. CURRAN

UNIVERSITY OF NOTRE DAME PRESS
NOTRE DAME, INDIANA 46556

Library of Congress Cataloging in Publication Data

Curran, Charles E.
  Directions in Catholic social ethics.

  Includes index.
  Contents: The changing anthropological bases of
Catholic social ethics — A significant methodological
change in Catholic social ethics — American Catholic
social ethics, 1880-1965 — [etc.]
  1. Christian ethics—Catholic authors—Addresses,
essays, lectures. 2. Social ethics—Addresses, essays,
lectures. 3. Church and social problems—Catholic
Church—Addresses, essays, lectures. 4. Catholic
Church—Doctrines—Addresses, essays, lectures. I. Title.
BJ1249.C816 1985   241'.02   84-28079
ISBN 0-268-00853-1 (pbk.)

Manufactured in the United States of America

In my twenty-fifth year of teaching
I remain ever grateful
to those who taught me at the following institutions

Nazareth Hall
St. Andrew's
St. Bernard's
Gregorian University
Academia Alfonsiana

Contents

Introduction

There has been an increased interest in the last few years in Roman Catholic social ethics. This interest has been sparked by a greater involvement of the Roman Catholic Church itself in social issues both in this country and abroad. The changes that have occurred and the directions in which both the theory of Catholic social ethics and the practice of the church should go call for greater study and analysis.

This book consists of essays, most of them previously published, which center on this theme of the changing directions in Catholic social ethics and in the social mission of the church. No attempt is made to present a totally systematic Catholic social ethic, but the different studies gathered together in this book try to indicate how and why Catholic social ethics and the social mission of the church should function. This book consists of theological reflections on Catholic teaching and practice in the social area, but it is not Catholic in a narrow sense. The Catholic tradition and its practice are always seen in relationship to the world and to all other people living in this world. Perspectives coming from other Christian traditions are employed to help understand, analyze, and criticize the Catholic tradition.

Since the encyclicals of Pope Leo XIII at the end of the nineteenth century a body of Catholic social thought has been developed in the official teaching of the popes and the universal church. The opening chapters analyze the changes that have occurred in this official Catholic teaching and its consequences for the Catholic Church's self-understanding of its own social mission. Attention is also paid to what has transpired here on the American scene. Too often in the past Catholic social ethics even when it was discussed and written about in this country did not give enough importance to the American tradition and experience. One chapter examines both the most significant figures and approaches to social ethics on the American Catholic scene, while another chapter reflects on and analyzes the practice of community organizations in the thought and work of Saul Alinsky. A most delicate question facing not only the Catholic Church but all churches and all citizens is the role of religion and the churches in working for political and social change in the United States. Religious pluralism and the separation of church and state are two prominent realities affecting social and political life in this country. Any adequate study of Catholic social ethics and practice in the United States must deal with this constitutional issue.

It would be impossible to study all the particular issues which are prominent and important today. In developing my understanding of what Catholic social ethics and the social mission of the church should be, the earlier chapters in this book touch on many specific problems. The later chapters discuss in some detail three important issues in social ethics — peace and war, population control, and the right to health care.

I am grateful to John Ehmann my editor at the University of Notre Dame Press for suggesting this volume. It was his idea to bring these studies together in one volume in order to provide a more in-depth and focused discussion of this important question. I have prepared one new study for this volume which appears as Chapter Two. The other chapters have already appeared in my recent works published by the University of Notre Dame Press, but some changes and updatings have been made for this volume. Again I renew my thanks to the staffs of the Mullen Library and the Department of Theology of the Catholic University of America for their help in my research and writing. I am particularly appreciative of Mary Zielinski Hellwig's efforts in typing part of this manuscript and other projects. Mark O'Keefe prepared the index.

I appreciatively acknowledge the permission of the following periodicals and publishers for allowing me to use in this volume materials which first appeared in their publications: *The Thomist*, for "The Changing Anthropological Bases of Catholic Social Ethics"; Fordham University Press, for "American Catholic Social Ethics, 1880-1965," which was published in *Thought*; Seabury Press, for "Social Ethics: Future Agenda for Theology and the Church," which appeared in *Towards Vatican III: The Work That Needs to Be Done*, eds. David Tracy with Hans Küng and Johann B. Metz; *The Jurist*, for "Religion, Law and Public Policy in America"; *Le Supplément*, for "An Analysis of the American Bishops' Pastoral Letter on Peace and War"; *Journal of Religious Ethics*, for "Roman Catholic Teaching on Peace and War in a Broader Theological Context"; Fordham University Press, for "Population Control: Methods and Morality," which originally appeared in *Human Life*, ed. William C. Bier (1977).

1. The Changing Anthropological Bases of Catholic Social Ethics

For one hundred years there has existed a body of official Catholic Church teaching on social ethics and the social mission of the church. There was a social teaching within the Catholic Church before that time, but from the pontificate of Leo XIII (1878-1903) one can speak of a body of authoritative social teaching worked out in a systematic way and often presented in the form of encyclicals or papal letters to the bishops and to the whole church. The purpose of this chapter is to point out some of the changing anthropological emphases in this body of social teaching, thereby proposing an approach which can and should be employed in Christian social ethics today. The limitation of our discussion primarily to the official body of papal teaching should not be construed as failing to recognize the other theological approaches within the Catholic community. However, the teaching of the hierarchical magisterium has a special degree of authority about it and historically has served as a basis for much of Catholic social teaching during the last hundred years. Also by limiting the discussion to this particular body of teaching it is possible to place some realistic perimeters on the study.

Until a few years ago Catholic commentators were generally reluctant to admit any development within the papal social teaching.[1] The popes themselves gave the impression of continuity and even went out of their way to smooth over any differences with their "predecessors of happy memory." Often Catholic commentaries on the papal teaching were uncritical—

5

merely explaining and applying the papal teaching. John F. Cronin, one of the better known commentators on Catholic social teaching in the United States, while reminiscing in 1971, recognized his failure to appreciate the historical and cultural conditionings of this teaching and the importance of a proper hermeneutic in explaining it.[2] In the area of church and state relations and religious liberty the historically and culturally conditioned aspect of the papal teaching was clearly recognized somewhat earlier.[3] In the last few years more scholars have realized the development and change which have occurred in Catholic social teaching.[4] Especially since the decade of 1960s this development has become so pronounced that no one could deny its existence.

This study will concentrate on anthropology, but it will be impossible to treat all aspects of anthropology. Two anthropological aspects will be considered in depth. The first section on the personal aspects of anthopology will trace the development culminating in an emphasis on the freedom, equality, and participation of the person. Some of the important methodological consequences of such an understanding of the human person will also be discussed. The second section on the social aspects of anthropology will show the greater importance given to the social dimensions of existence especially in terms of private property and of the approach to socialism.[5] The third section will evaluate the social teaching of Pope John Paul II in the light of these changing anthropological bases.

I. Personal Aspects of Anthropology

Octogesima adveniens, the apostolic letter of Pope Paul VI written on the occasion of the eightieth anniversary of *Rerum novarum*, proposes an anthropology highlighting the freedom and dignity of the human person which are seen above all in two aspirations becoming ever-more prevalent in our world—the aspiration to equality and the aspiration to participation.[6] Freedom, equality, and participation are the significant characteristics of the anthropology of *Octogesima adveniens*.

The differences with the writings of Leo XIII are striking.

The church at the time of Leo was fearful of freedom and equality and looked on the majority of people as the untutored multitude who had to be guided or directed by their rulers.[7]

Pope Leo condemned the "modern liberties." Liberty of worship goes against the "chiefest and holiest human duty" demanding the worship of the one true God in the one true religion which can easily be recognized by its external signs. Liberty of speech and of the press means that nothing will remain sacred, for truth will be obscured by darkness, and error will prevail. There is only a right and duty to speak what is true and honorable and no right to speak what is false. A like judgment is passed on liberty of teaching. Finally liberty of conscience is considered. The only true meaning of the freedom of conscience is the freedom to follow the will of God and to do one's duty in obeying his commands. At best the public authority can tolerate what is at variance with truth and justice for the sake of avoiding greater evils or of preserving some greater good.[8] Leo XIII was certainly no supporter of civil liberties and the modern freedoms.

Leo XIII not only did not promote equality as a virtue or something to be striven for in society, but he stressed the importance of inequality. Inequality is a fact of nature. There are differences in health, beauty, intelligence, strength, and courage. These natural inequalities necessarily bring about social inequalities which are essential for the good functioning of society. In short, the inequality of rights and of power proceed from the very author of nature. Leo had a view of society as a hierarchical organism in which there are different roles and functions to fulfill, but in which all will work for the common good of all.[9]

According to Leo:

> In like manner, no one doubts that all men are equal one to another, so far as regards their common origin and nature, or the last end which each one has to attain, or the rights and duties which are thence derived. But, as the abilities of all are not equal, as one differs from another in the powers of mind or body, and as there are many dissimilarities of manner, disposition and character, it is most repugnant to reason to endeavor to confine all within the same measure, and to extend complete equality to the institutions of civil life.[10]

Inequalities and some of the hardships connected with them will always be part of human existence in a world which is marked by the presence of original sin. To suffer and to endure is the lot of people. People should not be deluded by promises of undisturbed repose and constant enjoyment. We should look upon our world in a spirit of reality and at the same time seek elsewhere the solace to its troubles.[11]

Leo XIII likewise does not call for the active participation of all in social and political life, but rather he has a very hierarchical view of civil society which follows from the inequalities mentioned above. Leo's favorite word for the rulers of society is *principes*. The very word shows his hierarchical leanings. The citizen is primarily one who obeys the divine law, the natural law, and the human law which are handed down by the *principes*. Leo even quotes the maxim *qualis rex, talis grex* (as the King, so the herd — the people), which indicates the power of the ruler over all the citizens in practically every aspect of life.[12] The citizens are called by Leo the untutored multitude who must be led and protected by the ruler.[13] At best, authority appears as paternalistic, and the subjects are children who are to obey and respect their rulers with a type of piety.[14] Leo was fearful of the liberalistic notion of the sovereignty of the people, which really meant that the people no longer owed obedience to God and God's law in all aspects of their public and private lives.[15]

In this authoritarian and paternalistic understanding there is no distinction between society and the state which had been present in classical thought but then lost during the period of absolutism. Leo's theory is that of the ethical society-state in which the total common good of the society is entrusted to the rulers. Society is constructed from the top down with the ruler guarding and protecting the untutored multitude from the many dangers of life just as the father has the function of protecting and guiding his children in the family.[16]

Leo's denial of liberty, equality, and participation can be somewhat understood in the light of the circumstances of the times in which he lived. The pope was an implacable foe of a liberalism which in his mind was the root cause of all the problems of the modern day. Liberalism substitutes foolish license for true liberty. The followers of liberalism deny the existence of any divine authority and proclaim that every human being is a law unto oneself. Liberalism proposes an independent morality in which the human being is freed from the divine law and authority and can do whatever one wants. Leo consequently attacks those forms of government which make the collective reason of the community the supreme guide of life in society. They substitute the decision of the majority for the rule of God. God and God's law are totally removed from society.[17]

Behind Leo's fear of equality lurks the same individualism present in liberalism. For Leo society is an organism. Human beings are by nature social and called to join together in political society for the common good. To live in society is not a restriction on individual human freedom, for by nature all of us are social. Each one has a different function to play in the hierarchically structured organism which resembles the organism of the human body with all its different parts, but each functioning for the good of the whole. Leo fears an understanding which sees society merely as a collection of equal individuals, for this would destroy any social fabric and true social ordering. Participation is also looked on as a threat, for this could readily be confused with the demands of liberalistic license and destroy the organic unity of a society in which each person has one's God-given function to perform. In the context of Leo's understanding of the untutored multitude there could be little or no room for participation.

In general Leo rightly recognized some of the problems of liberalism and individualism. However, his only solution was to turn his back totally on all the developments which were then taking place in the modern world. At the very least Leo lacked the prophetic charisma to sort out the good from the bad in the newer developments which were taking place in the nineteenth century and to find a place for the legitimate demands of liberty, equality, and participation.[18] The picture emerges of a static and hierarchically structured authoritarian society governed by the law of God and the natural law under the protection and guidance of a paternalistic ruler who directs all to the common good and protects his subjects from physical and moral harm.

This explanation of Leo's approach shows the tremendous

gulf which exists between his understanding of anthropology and that proposed by Pope Paul VI in *Octogesima adveniens*. However, one can trace some of the major lines of the development which occurred from Leo XIII to Paul VI.

Even in Leo XIII there are some aspects pointing in a different direction, but they are found mostly in his 1891 encyclical *Rerum novarum* on the rights of the worker. In his political writings Leo especially argues against a totalitarian democracy with its emphasis on majority rule and its lack of respect for divine and natural law, but he always upheld the basic rights of individual human beings which might be abused because of the totalitarian democracy. In *Rerum novarum* he stresses even more the rights of the individual worker, and his approach is less authoritarian and paternalistic. In *Rerum novarum* Leo recalls, while pointing out the danger of socialism, that the human being is prior to the state and has natural rights which do not depend on the state.[19] The right to private property is based on our nature as rational and provident beings. Every individual has the right to marry. Marriage is older than the state and has its rights and duties independently of the state.[20] The state has an obligation to intervene to protect the rights of the workers, for public authority must step in when a particular class suffers or is threatened with harm which in no other way can be met or avoided.[21] Moreover, workers themselves have the right to organize into unions and associations to promote their own rights and interests.[22] Here appears the basis for participation in the shaping of one's own destiny.

In *Rerum novarum* Leo repeats his teaching on inequality. The condition of things inherent in human affairs must be borne with. These conditions include natural differences of the most important kinds — differences in capacities, skills, health, and strength. Unequal fortune is a necessary result of unequal conditions.[23] However, Leo appears to admit a basic equality of all to have their rights recognized and protected by the state. In fact the poor and badly off have a claim to special consideration.[24] As one would expect, Leo upholds the rights of the individual against socialism. In tension with his other emphases Leo's writing show differing degrees of recognition of some freedom, equality, and even of incipient participation as anthropological concerns.

Pope Pius XI (1922-1939) remains in continuity with his predecessor Leo XIII. Liberalism lies at the root of the problems of the modern world. The principal cause of the disturbed conditions in which we live is that the power of law and respect for authority have been considerably weakened ever since people came to deny that the origin of law and of authority was in God, the creator and ruler of the world. Liberalism has even fathered socialism and bolshevism. Pius XI insists on the importance of natural law and a hierarchical ordering of society based on it. In *Quadragesimo anno* on the fortieth anniversary of Leo's encyclical *Rerum novarum* Pius XI continues the discussion of justice and the economic order, insisting on the dignity and rights of the individual and also on the social nature of human beings. Here again the two extreme approaches of individualism and socialism are rejected on the basis of an anthropology which recognizes the dignity and rights of the individual as well as the social aspects of the human person.[25]

However, contact with different forms of totalitarianism brought to the fore an emphasis on the defense of the rights, dignity, and freedom of the individual. (There has been much discussion in the last few decades about the relationship of the Catholic Church to fascism, nazism and communism. Without entering into the debate, it is safe to generalize that the Catholic Church was much more fearful of the left and showed itself more willing to compromise with the right.) Pius XI defends the transcendental character of the human person against materialistic and atheistic communism. Communism is condemned for stripping human beings of their liberty and for robbing the human person of dignity.[26] Now the church becomes the protector of human freedom and dignity. In *Non abbiamo bisogno* Pius XI even defends the freedom of conscience with the recognition that he is speaking about the true freedom of conscience and not the license which refuses to recognize the laws of God.[27]

The development continues in the pontificate of Pope Pius XII (1939-1958). The historical context of the struggle against totalitarianism remains, but the significant role of Christian Democratic parties in Europe adds an important new dimension. In his Christmas radio message in 1944 Pope Pius XII insisted on the dignity of human beings and on a system of government that will be more in accord with the dignity and freedom of the citizenry. This emphasis on the dignity and freedom of the human being also calls for greater participation and active involvement of all. The human being is not the object of social life or an inert element in it, but rather is the subject, foundation, and end of social life.[28]

In the light of these historical circumstances and of a theoretical insistence on the centrality of the dignity of the human person, Pius proposed an understanding of the state remarkably different from that of Leo XIII. As John Courtney Murray lucidly points out, Pius XII abandoned Leo XIII's ethical concept of the society-state and accepted a juridical or limited constitutional state. For Leo there is no distinction between society and the state, for the state is hierarchically ordered, with the rulers having the function of guarding and protecting the illiterate masses in every aspect of life. By emphasizing the dignity, freedom, and responsibility of the individual person Pius XII clearly accepts a limited view of the state which sees it as only a part of society with a function of defending the rights of human beings and of promoting the freedom of the people. The state has a limited juridical role and does not act as the parent who guides the entire lives of one's children. No longer is the state understood in terms of the relationship between *principes* and the untutored multitudes. The rulers are representatives of the people, and the people are responsible citizens.[29]

Despite these significant changes in the importance of the dignity of the person and the recognition of limited constitutional government, Guzzetti still detects an air of the aristocratic about Pius XII's approach.[30] Also on the matter of inequalities in society Pius advances over Leo, but still insists that natural inequalities of education, of earthly goods, and of social position are not obstacles to brotherhood and community provided they are not arbitrary and are in accord with justice and charity.[31]

The short pontificate of John XXIII (1958-1963) with its convocation of the Second Vatican Council had a great impact on Roman Catholicism. In the area of social ethics John in his two encyclicals *Mater et magistra* and *Pacem in terris* defends human dignity in the midst of the ever-increasing social relationships and interdependencies which characterize our modern world. *Pacem in terris* gives the most detailed statement in the papal social tradition of human rights based on the dignity of the person but also adds the corresponding duties, thereby avoiding the danger of individualism. The dignity of the human person requires that every individual enjoy the right to act freely and responsibly. The dignity, freedom, and equality of the human person are highlighted and defended, but many of the assumptions of an older liberalistic individualism are not accepted.[32]

There is one fascinating development even within John's own writings. The papal social tradition consistently emphasized that life in society must be based on truth, justice, and love. John XXIII repeated the importance of this triad in *Mater et magistra* in 1961.[33] However, in 1963 in *Pacem in terris* a fourth element was added: a political society is well ordered, beneficial, and in keeping with human dignity if is grounded on truth, justice, love, and freedom.[34] Even in John there was only a later recognition of the fundamental importance of freedom alongside truth, justice, and love.

From the first encyclical of Leo XIII on the question of economic ethics there was some recognition for participation and responsibility, especially in terms of the workers' right to form organizations and unions to promote their own interests. John XXIII recognizes there is an innate need of human nature calling for human beings engaged in productive activity to have an opportunity to assume responsibility and to perfect themselves by their efforts. Participation of workers in medium-size and larger enterprises calls for some type of partnership.[35]

Two documents of the Second Vatican Council are most significant for our purposes—the Declaration on Religious Freedom and the Pastoral Constitution on the Church in the Modern World. It was only at the Second Vatican Council that the Roman Catholic Church accepted the concept of religious liberty—a concept which was anathema to Leo XIII. However, the council is careful to show that its acceptance does not stem from the tenets of an older liberalism and indifferentism. Religious liberty is the right, not to worship God as one pleases, but rather the right to immunity from external coercion forcing one to act in a way opposed to one's conscience or preventing one from acting in accord with one's conscience. The basis for religious liberty is stated very distinctly in the opening paragraph—the dignity of the human person which has been impressing itself more and more deeply on the conscience of contemporary people and a corresponding recognition of a constitutional government whose powers are limited. A limited government embraces only a small part of the life of people in society, and religion exists beyond the pale of the role of civil government.[36] The council brings out all the implications of a limited constitutional government which in principle had been accepted by Pius XII. The Roman Catholic Church thus became a defender of religious liberty even though in the nineteenth century the papacy stood as the most determined opponent of religious liberty.

The dignity of the human person serves as the cornerstone of the Pastoral Constitution on the Church in the Modern World—*Gaudium et spes*. The first chapter of the theoretical part one of the document begins with the dignity of the human person and its meaning and importance. Authentic freedom as opposed to license is championed by the conciliar document. In earlier documents there was a great insistence on the moral law as the antidote to any tendency to license. Now the emphasis is on conscience—the most secret core and sanctuary of the human person where one hears the call of God's voice. The shift from the role of law, which is traditionally called the objective norm of morality, to conscience, which is called the subjective norm of human action, is most significant in showing the move to the subject and to the person. Of course the document stresses the need for a correct conscience, but the impression is given that truth is found in the innermost depth of one's existence.[37]

Gaudium et spes gives much more importance to equality than some of the earlier documents. Inequalities are still recognized, but now the existence of inequalities appears in subordinate clauses with the main emphasis being on equality. For example: "True, all men are not alike from the point of view of varying physical power and the diversity of intellectual and moral resources. Nevertheless, with respect to the fundamental rights of the person, every type of discrimination, whether social or cultural, whether based on sex, race, color, social condition, language or religion, is to be overcome and eradicated as contrary to God's intent."[38] "Moreover although rightful differences exist between men, the equal dignity of persons demands that a more humane and just condition of life be brought about. For excessive economic and social differences between the members of the one human family or population groups cause scandal, and militate against social justice, equity, the dignity of the human person as well as social and international peace."[39]

There is also a call for responsibility and participation. The will to play one's role in common endeavors should be encouraged. The largest possible number of citizens should participate in public affairs with genuine freedom.[40] A greater share in education and culture is required for all to exercise responsibility and participation. The active participation of all in running the economic enterprise should be promoted.[41] The juridical and political structure should afford all citizens the chance to participate freely and actively in establishing the constitutional basis of a political community, governing the state, determining the scope and purposes of different institutions, and choosing leaders.[42]

In the light of this line of development the teaching of Pope Paul VI in *Octogesima adveniens* on the eightieth anniversary of *Rerum novarum* does not come as a total suprise: "Two aspirations persistently make themselves felt in these new contexts, and they grow stronger to the extent that people become better informed and better educated: the aspiration to equality and the aspiration to participation, two forms of man's dignity and freedom."[43] Such an anthropology stressing freedom, equality, and participation should have significant methodological consequences for Christian social ethics.

Historical consciousness

Before considering the methodological consequence of this new anthropology, historical consciousness, which affects both anthropology and methodology, should be considered. Historical consciousness, which is very pronounced in *Octogesima adveniens* but clearly absent from the documents of Leo XIII, gives great significance to historical conditions, growth, change, and development, and has often been contrasted with a classicist approach. In the area of methodology the classicist approach emphasizes the eternal, the universal, and the unchanging and often employs a deductive methodology. The historically conscious approach emphasizes the particular, the individual, the contingent, and the historical, and often employs a more inductive methodology.[44]

The importance of historical consciousness becomes very evident in the deliberations of the Second Vatican Council on religious freedom. Pope Leo XIII had condemned religious liberty. Perhaps the most pressing question facing the fathers of Vatican II was how to reconcile Leo's condemnation with the acceptance of religious liberty less than a century later. John Courtney Murray in his writings on religious liberty provided a solution. One has to interpret Leo in the light of the circumstances of his own day. Leo was struggling against a Continental liberalism with its denial of any place for God in society and its acceptance of an omnicompetent state with no recognition whatsoever of the divine law or of natural law. In reaction to this approach Leo called for the union of church and state as the way rightfully recognizing and protecting the role and function of the church. However, the constitutional understanding of separation of church and state was based, not on a Continental liberalism, but on a notion of a constitutional government which claimed only a limited role for itself in the life of society. The constitutional understanding did not deny a role or a place for religion in society; the role and function of religion existed beyond the pale of the limited scope and function of the state. Murray's historically conscious hermeneutic distinguished the polemical-historical aspect of Leo's teaching from the doctrinal aspect. There has been no change in the doctrinal. The recognition of historical consciousness provided the key to the problem of development and change in the church's teaching.[45] Murray made a remarkable contribution by his historical hermeneutic. In retrospect it is both easy and necessary to criticize Murray's theory as too benevolent. One should admit some error in the church's teaching in the nineteenth century and even some doctrinal discontinuity and evolution in the teaching on religious liberty.

The acceptance of historical consciousness in our understanding of anthropology also has important methodological ramifications in the papal social teaching. The earlier teachings were deductive, stressing immutable eternal principles of natural law. However, a more inductive approach began to appear in the 1960s. The encyclical *Pacem in terris* is divided into four major parts: order among people, relations between individuals and public authority within a single state, relations between states, relations of people in political communities with the world community. Each part concludes with a section on the signs of the times — the distinctive characteristics of the contemporary age.[46] There was much debate about the term "signs of the times" at the Second Vatican Council. Early drafts and versions of the Constitution on the Church in the Modern World gave great importance to the term. In the final version "signs of the times" was used sparingly because some council fathers did not want to use a term whose biblical meaning was quite different — the eschatological signs of the last days.[47] However, in the second part of the Pastoral Constitution which treats five problems of special urgency in the contemporary world, each consideration begins with an empirical description of the contemporary reality even though the terminology "signs of the times" is not employed. Such an approach gives greater emphasis to the contemporary historical situation and does not begin with a universal viewpoint and deduce an understanding applicable to all cultures and times.

Methodological consequences

The anthropology of the papal social teaching by the time of *Octogesima adveniens* in 1971 stresses freedom, equality, participation, and historical mindedness. The methodological consequences of such an anthropology are quite significant and show a remarkable change from the methodology employed in the earlier documents. The earlier approach highlighted the universal, all-embracing character of the teaching. In retrospect, however, the claimed universalism of the earlier encyclicals was really limited to European socioeconomic conditions. In the economic realm there appeared especially with Pius XI in 1931 a plan for the reconstruction of the social order in accord with what was called a theory of moderate solidarism. Pope Pius XI was much more negative about the existing abuses and injustices of the social order than was Leo XIII. Undoubtedly the problem of the depression influenced Pius's negative judgment about the existing social order and the call for a more radical reconstruction of society according to a solidaristic model based in general on the guild system with its intermediary institutions bringing together both workers and owners. The pope continued to condemn laissez-faire capitalism and the opposite extreme of socialism. In place of these two systems Pius XI proposed a third way which would eliminate the bad features of extreme individualism and extreme socialism while giving due importance to the personal and social nature of the individual person. This third way, although somewhat vague in its development and detail, was thought to be a universally applicable plan.[48]

Pius XII continued in the same line as his predecessor with an emphasis on reconstruction and not merely on reform. Professional organizations and labor unions are provisional and transitory forms; the ultimate purpose is the bringing together and cooperation of employees and employers in order to provide together for the general welfare and the needs of the whole community. Pope Pius XII also distinguished his reconstruction plan from mere comanagement, or participation of workers in management. Pope Pius XII originally followed the footsteps of his predecessor in proposing a universally applicable plan of reconstruction deduced from the principles of the natural law and corresponding in significant ways to the guild system of the middle ages. However, after 1952 Pius rarely mentioned such a plan of reconstruction.[49] In *Mater et magistra* Pope John XXIII merely referred to Pius XI's orderly reorganization of society with smaller professional and economic groups existing in their own right and not prescribed by public authority.[50] In John's encyclicals, in the conciliar documents, and in Paul's teaching there was no further development of Pius XI's plan for social reconstruction.

Reasons for the abandonment of a plan of social reconstruction applicable throughout the world can be found in the later documents themselves. These documents recognize the complexity of the social problem and historical and cultural differences which make it difficult for a universal plan to be carried out in all different areas. *Mater et magistra* emphasized the complexity of the present scene, the multiplication of social relationships, and many new developments in the field of science, technology, and economics as well as developments in the social and political fields.[51] The social questions involve more than the rights and duties of labor and capital. In *Populorum progressio* Pope Paul VI early in his encyclical stated that today the principal fact that all must recognize is that the social question has become worldwide.[52] The complexity of the question increases enormously when one brings into consideration the entire world and the relationship between and among countries, especially poor nations and rich nations. The approach of the Pastoral Constitution on the Church in the Modern World by beginning with the signs of the times also called for doing away with a deductive methodology resulting in an eternal, immutable plan of God for the world.

At the same time as Pius XI and Pius XII were talking about a program of reconstruction according to solidaristic principles of organization, the term "social doctrine" was used by these popes to refer to the official body of church teaching consisting of the principles of the economic order derived from the natural law and the plan of reconstruction based on them. Pius XI distinguished this social doctrine from social and economic sciences. The social doctrine contains the immutable truths taught by the popes, whereas social science is the area for research and scholarly enterprise. Precisely the authoritative nature of the doctrine distinguishes it from the empirical social sciences of economics or sociology.[53] Such an approach was called for by some Catholic sociologists who claimed that the major of their argument was supplied by authoritative church teaching, the minor came from their scientific research, and from these one drew the conclusion.[54] Pope Pius XII frequently speaks about Catholic social doctrine. According to Pius XII the earlier papal teaching became the source of Catholic social doctrine by providing the children of the church with directives and means for a social reconstruction rich in fruit.[55] Social doctrine is the authoritative teaching proclaimed by the hierarchical magisterium, deduced from the eternal principles of the natural law, and distinguished from the contribution of the empirical sciences.

Both the term "social doctrine of the church" and the reality expressed by it — namely, a papal plan or ideology of social reconstruction — gradually disappear from official church documents after Pope Pius XII. Later references are to the social teaching of the gospel or the social teaching of the church. Gone is the vision of the universal plan deductively derived from natural law and proposed authoritatively by the church magisterium to be applied in all parts of the world. No longer will there be such a separation between ethically deduced moral principles and the economic and social analysis of the situation. Rather, one now begins with the signs of the times and with an analysis of the contemporary situation and not with some abstract principle divorced from historical reality.[56]

Octogesima adveniens with an anthropology insisting on personal freedom, equality, participation, and historical consciousness employs a methodology quite at variance with that employed in the early papal documents. Early in the document Pope Paul VI recognizes the wide diversity of situations in which Christians live throughout the world. In the face of such diversity it is difficult to utter a unified message or to put forward a solution which has universal validity. The Christian communities themselves must analyze with objectivity their own situation and shed on it the light of the gospel and the principles of the teaching of the church. It is up to the Christian communities with the help of the Spirit in communion with the bishops and in dialogue with other Christians and people of good will to discern the options and commitments necessary to bring about the urgently needed social and political changes.[57] Rather than a universal plan based on natural law, Pope Paul VI recalls the importance and significance of utopias. Utopias appeal to the imagination of responsible people to perceive in the present situation the disregarded possibilities within it and to provide direction toward a fresh future. Such an approach sustains social dynamism by the confidence that it gives to the inventive powers of the human mind and heart. "At the heart of the world there dwells the mystery of man discovering himself to be God's son in the course of a historical and psychological process in which constraint and freedom as well as the weight of sin and the breath of the Spirit alternate and struggle for the upper hand."[58]

The methodological changes are quite significant. There is no universal plan applicable to all situations, but rather Christians discern what to do in the midst of the situation in which they find themselves. What to do is not determined by a deductive reasoning process based on the eternal and immutable natural law. Rather, a careful and objective scrutiny of the present reality in the light of the gospel and of the teaching of the church is central to the discernment process. Commitments and options are discerned in the situation itself. The approach is dynamic rather than static. The appeal to utopias, imagination, and the mystery of the human person at the heart of the world all testify to a less rationalistic discernment process. There is also an admonition for the individual in the church to be self-critical, thereby recognizing the dangers that might come from one's own presuppositions.

Octogesima adveniens concludes with a call to action.[59] All along the church's social teaching has called for action, but the call is now more urgent and more central to the very notion of the social mission of the church. The condition of individual responsibility and the urgent need to change structures require the active involvement of all. Once again emphasis is on the need to take concrete action despite the fact that there can be a plurality of strategic options for Christians.

Both the anthropology and the methodology employed in *Octogesima adveniens* outline a different understanding of the role of persons in the church itself and in the social mission of the church. An older approach, especially associated with the concept of Catholic Action proposed by Pope Pius XI and Pope Pius XII, saw the function of the laity to carry out and put into practice the principles which were taught by the hierarchical magisterium. As is evident in this document, the whole church must discern what options are to be taken in the light of an analysis of the signs of the times and in the light of the gospel even though there remains a distinctive role for hierarchical magisterium. No longer are the laity the people who receive the principles and the instruction from the hierarchy and then put these plans into practice. All in the church have a role in discerning and in executing.[60]

Contemporary Catholic social ethics mirrors and at times even goes beyond the approach and methodology employed in *Octogesima adveniens*. David Hollenbach has recently employed a similar methodology in his attempt to revise and retrieve the Catholic human rights tradition.[61] Political and liberation theologies show some of the same tendencies but even go beyond the methodological approach of *Octogesima adveniens*. Critical reason insists on the importance of action. Praxis becomes primary in many of these approaches, and theology becomes reflection on praxis. For many liberation theologians, true theology can only grow out of praxis.[62] At the very least the methodology of Catholic social ethics is thus greatly changed from the time of Leo XIII, especially in the light of changing anthropological understandings.

II. Social Aspects of Anthropology

Another important aspect of anthropology concerns the social nature of human beings. Catholic social ethics has consistently recognized the social nature of human beings. As a result Catholic social ethics looks upon the state as a natural society, for human beings are called by nature to live in political society. In some Christian ethics the origin of the state is grounded on human sinfulness. The power and coercion of the state are necessary to prevent sinful human beings from destroying one another.[65] Pope Leo XIII follows in the Catholic traditon by his insistence that the state is a natural society. Human beings with their inequality and differences come together to achieve what the individuals as such are not able to accomplish. Leo's understanding of political society as an organism and an organic whole with individuals carrying out different functions shows that the state is based on human nature and does not exist merely on the basis of a contract made by discrete individuals.[64]

The papal social teaching in the last century has recognized both the legitimate rights of the individual and the social nature of human beings. The Catholic approach to the economic problem traditionally has condemned the two extremes of individualistic capitalism and collectivistic socialism. Throughout its history Catholic social ethics has tried to uphold both the personal and the social aspects of anthropology. However, there have been varying nuances in the approach over the years. This section of the chapter will now consider two significant questions in which there has been a development in giving more importance to the social aspects of anthropology — private property and socialism.

Private property

Pope Leo XIII recognized the misery and wretchedness pressing so urgently upon the majority of the working class because of the hard heartedness of employers and the greed of unchecked competition. To remedy these ills the socialists do away with private property. However, Leo's solution is the opposite. Everyone has a right to private property. The dignity of the individual will be protected if one is able to have one's own property and thus make oneself secure against the vicissitudes of the industrial order. Private property protects and promotes the security of the individual and of the family. By investing wages in property and in land the worker has the hope and the possibility of increasing personal resources and of bettering one's condition in life.

However, the most important and fundamental fact for Leo is that private property is a demand of the natural law. The human being is distinguished from animals precisely through rational nature, because of which one has the right to possess things in a permanent and stable way to provide for one's own continued existence. The human individual can only provide for the future through private property. By virtue of labor and work the human being makes one's own that portion of nature's field which she or he cultivates. The principle of private ownership is necessarily in accord with human nature and is conducive in the most unmistakable manner to the peace and tranquility of human existence. The right of the individual to private property is strengthened in the light of human social and domestic obligations, for it provides security for the entire family. The first and most fundamental principle to alleviate the impoverished conditions of the masses is the inviolability of private property.[65]

There are a number of interesting facets about Leo's defense of private property as the solution to the misery of the working masses. First, Leo's solution indicates the rural and preindustrial perspective with which he approached the problem. Private property for Leo is usually the land and one's right to the fruits of the labor which has been expended in cultivating the land. If the individual possesses one's own land, then one can provide food and basic necessities for one's family no matter what the vicissitudes of the industrial order. Human dignity is preserved and human needs will be met if the workers can own and work their own plot of land. This solution obviously fits better in an earlier time and in a more agrarian situation. Its practicality as a reasonable solution in the industrial era of the late nineteenth century is open to serious question.

Second, Leo does not deal realistically with the most significant aspect of private property existing at that time—the abuse of private property by the rich at the expense of the poor. The failure to recognize this fact in the very first part of the encyclical and to deal with it realistically marks a definite lacuna in Leo's approach. The real problem of the day concerned especially the ownership of the goods of production, since abuses on the part of those who own the goods of production contributed greatly to the economic woes of the worker. Leo reminds the rich of their obligation to share with the poor, but such a reminder does not go to the heart of the problem. As mentioned above, Leo supports the rights of workers to organize to secure their rights, but he does not directly address the existing structural abuses of great wealth in the hands of a few at the expense of the vast majority.

Third, and somewhat connected with the two previous observations, Leo justifies private property only on the basis of labor. No other titles are mentioned by Leo in *Rerum novarum* to justify ownership. The single title of labor again shows the rural vision which Leo brought to the question and which does not take into consideration the many problems of abuse through inheritance and other ways of accquiring private property. In *Quod apostolici muneris* Leo held that inheritance was a valid means of aquiring wealth but did not justify this title.[66] Leo's discussion of the titles to private ownership is very incomplete and again fails to deal with the real abuses and problems of the times.

Fourth, Leo's teaching on private property disagrees with that proposed by Thomas Aquinas. Thomas Aquinas discusses the question of private property in two articles.[67] First he responds affirmatively to the question whether the possession of external things is natural to human beings. God created all reality and ordained that the lower creation serve the higher. Dominion over external things is natural to humans because as a rational creature made in the image and likeness of God the human being is called to use external goods to achieve one's end. But then in a second question Thomas discusses the right to possess something as one's own with the power of procuring and disposing of it. Human beings have the right to private ownership which involves the procuring and disposing of external goods. This right is necessary for human life for three reasons: 1) Everyone is more solicitous about procuring things that will belong to the individual alone and not to the community. 2) A more orderly and less confusing existence will result from private property. 3) A more peaceful state of existence ensues when everyone is content with one's own things. However, with regard to the use of private property human beings are to use external goods as though they were common and not proper because these goods should serve the needs of all.

Thomas Aquinas' teaching on private property differs from Leo's on a number of significant points. Thomas clearly distinguishes between a generic dominion that belongs to all human beings to use external things and the specific type of dominion in the system of private property. In Leo's discussion in the beginning of *Rerum novarum* this distinction seems to be almost entirely lacking.[68] In fact, the argument based on rational human nature, which Thomas used to prove the generic dominion of all people over the goods of creation, is employed by Leo to argue for the rights of private property in the strict sense. Thomas' arguments for the right to private property in the strict sense are not really based on human nature as such, but, rather, the three arguments given are all grounded in the existence of human sinfulness. If it were not for human sinfulness, there would be no need for private property in the strict sense. Elsewhere Thomas maintains that in the state of innocence there would be no need for the strict right of private property.[69] Thomas makes the right to private property in the strict sense instrumental and sees it in the light of the more general right of all human beings to the use of external goods.

Later on in his encyclical Leo does recognize the social aspect of property and the fact that the use of private property is to be common in accord with Aquinas' teaching. From this communal use of property he derives the duty of charity, not of justice except in extreme cases, to give one's superfluous goods to the poor. Leo's differences with Aquinas' teaching on private property seem to come primarily from what was introduced into the scholastic tradition by Taparelli d'Azeglio in the nineteenth century.[70]

It is interesting to note that John A. Ryan, the major figure in Catholic social ethics in the United States in the first half of the twentieth century, proposed an instrumental understanding of the right to private property understood in the strict sense. Ryan's argument makes explicit some of Thomas' presuppositions and clarifies the whole meaning of an instrumental understanding of private property. For Ryan, who considers the question primarily in terms of the ownership of land, the first thing to be said about the goods of creation is that they exist to serve the needs of all human beings. Ryan accepts private ownership in the strict sense as what he calls a natural right of the third class. A right of the first class has as its object that which is an intrinsic good, such as the right to life. A right of the second class has as its object that which is directly necessary for the individual, such as the right to marry. A right of the third class has as its object, not what is directly necessary for the individual, but what is indirectly necessary for the individual because it is necessary as a social institution providing for the general welfare. Private ownership in the strict sense provides better for the general social welfare than any other institutional arrangement about the distribution of property. This necessity is proved empirically and inductively. If socialism or some other system would better serve the general welfare, it should be adopted.[71] Ryan's position with its clear and careful relativization of the right to private property in the strict sense would find an echo in the later papal social teaching.

In *Quadragesimo anno* Pius XI gave more stress to the social function of property. He notes the right to private property exists not only so that individuals may provide for themselves and their families but also so that the goods of creation which are destined by the creator for the entire family of humankind may serve their God-given purpose.[72] However, precisely how private property accomplishes this purpose is not developed. In addition, Pope Pius XI neatly covers one of Leo's lacunae in *Rerum novarum* by asserting that ownership is acquired both by labor and by occupancy of something not owned by anyone, as the tradition of all ages as well as the teaching of his predecessor Pope Leo clearly states.[73] No footnote or reference is made to where Leo makes that statement about occupancy.

There was some evolution in the teaching of Pius XII and later in John XXIII. John recognized the realities of the modern industrial society and the importance of professional skill, education, and social insurance and security as ways of protecting the dignity of the individual worker. However, he hastens to add that despite all these modern developments the right of private property including that pertaining to goods devoted to productive enterprises is permanently valid.[74] It appears there is still a tendency to give absolute rather than relative or instrumental value to the right of private property understood in the strict sense.[75]

Gaudium et spes and *Populorum progressio* made more clear the distinction between the generic right of dominion which belongs to all human beings and the right to private property in the strict sense. *Gaudium et spes* begins with the recognition that the goods of creation exist to serve the needs of all. All have a right to a share of earthly goods sufficient for oneself and one's family. Whatever forms of ownership might be, attention must always be paid to the universal purpose for which created goods exist.[76] After affirming the principle of the universal destiny of the goods of creation, *Populorum progressio* maintains that all other rights including that of private prop-

erty and free commerce are to be subordinated to this principle.[77] Here we have the same teaching as that proposed earlier
by John A. Ryan. All must admit that in the course of one
hundred years the official Catholic teaching has relativized
the right to private property in the strict sense and called attention to the need to judge all property institutions in accord with the universal destiny of the goods of creation to
serve the needs of all.

Socialism

There has also been a change in the attitude of the papal
teaching to socialism. Pope Leo XIII in the first year of his
pontificate issued the encyclical *Quod apostolici muneris,* which
pointed out the errors of "that sect of men who, under various and almost barbarous names, are called socialists, com-
munists or nihilists."[78] These people deny the supernatural,
the plan of God, God's law, and the role of the church. They
assert the basic equality of all human beings and deny that
respect is due to majesty and obedience to law. They support
a revolutionary doctrine, oppose the indissolubility of marriage, and deny the natural-law right of private property. In
Rerum novarum in 1891 Pope Leo XIII returned in a somewhat systematic way to a discussion of socialism and considered especially its denial of the right of private property,
a denial which is against the law of God and of human nature. However, Leo overemphasized the strength of socialism and its force as a world-wide conspiracy. Also he failed
to recognize the moderate strands which were then existing
in many parts of the world.[79]

Pope Pius XI in 1931 in *Quadragesimo anno* recognized the
differences existing between a more violent socialism called
communism and a more moderate form of socialism which rejects violence and modifies to some degree, if it does not reject
entirely, the class struggle and the abolition of private ownership. Obviously communism with its unrelenting class warfare and absolute extermination of private ownership stands
condemned. But what about a moderate socialism which has
tempered and modified its positions? Has it ceased to be con-
tradictory to the Christian religion? "Whether considered as

a doctrine, or an historical fact, or a movement, Socialism, if it remains truly Socialism, even after it has yielded to truth and justice on the points which we have mentioned cannot be reconciled with the teaching of the Catholic Church because its concept of society itself is utterly foreign to Christian truth."[80] Socialism like all errors contains some truths, but its theory of human society is irreconcilable with true Christianity.[81] However, in his portrayal of moderate socialism he wrongly seems to characterize such socialism as sacrificing the higher goods of human beings to the most efficient way of producing external goods.[82] In the 1930s Pope Pius XI concentrated most of his attacks on communism as seen in his later encyclical *Divini redemptoris* of March 19, 1937.

In other parts of the Catholic world there was even a greater recognition of the changes in moderate socialism. The British hierarchy made it clear that the Labor Party in Britain was not condemned for Catholics.[83] In the United States John A. Ryan, while acknowledging the teaching and practical conclusion of Pius XI, pointed out there were only two questionable planks in the 1932 political platform of the American Socialist Party, and even these could be interpreted in conformity with Catholic principles.[84]

In the aftermath of the Second World War the rise of communism led to the cold war in which the Roman Catholic Church stood squarely against communism. Roman Catholicism underwent persecution in communist countries in Eastern Europe. However, a thaw began with the pontificate of Pope John XXIII in 1958, under whose reign there emerged what was often called "the opening to the left." In *Pacem in terris*, without directly referring to communism, John pointed out the need to distinguish between false philosophical teachings on the nature, origin, and destiny of human beings in the universe and the historical movements which were originally based on these teachings. The historical movements are subject to change and evolving historical circumstances. In addition these movements contain some elements that are positive and deserving of approval. Work in common might be possible to achieve economic, social, political, and cultural ends. Great prudence, however, is required in these common enterprises. "It can happen, then, that meetings for the attainment of some practical end, which formerly were deemed inopportune or unproductive, might now or in the future be considered opportune and useful."[85]

Pope Paul VI in *Octogesima adveniens* built on, made explicit, and carried further the distinction between philosophical teaching and historical movements proposed by John XXIII. Both a liberal and a socialist ideology exist, but there are also historical movements. There are different kinds of expressions of socialism — a generous aspiration and seeking for a more just society, historical movements with a political organization and aim, and an ideology which claims to give a complete and self-sufficient picture of human beings. Marxism also operates at various levels of expression: 1) Marxism as the practice of class struggle, 2) the collective union of political and economic power under the direction of a single party, 3) a socialist ideology based on an historical materialism, 4) a rigorous scientific method of examining social and political realities. While recognizing all these different levels of expression, it would be illusory to forget the link which binds them together. The document then describes the liberal ideology with its erroneous affirmation of the autonomy of the individual.[86]

In the midst of these encounters with the various ideologies the Christian must discern what is to be done. "Going beyond every system, without however failing to commit himself concretely to serving his brothers, he will assert, in the very midst of his options, the specific character of the Christian contribution for a positive transformation of society."[87] This presentation is remarkable in many ways. Both the liberal and Marxist ideology as complete and self-sufficient positions on human nature and destiny are rejected. However, with due prudence and discretion one could opt for a Marxist analysis of social reality provided that one recognizes the danger of its connection with Marxist ideology. As mentioned in the first part of this chapter, the church's teaching is not proposed as a third approach. There is no mention of the social doctrine of the church but rather only the principles which help one to discern the concrete options that are to be taken. The option of a Marxist sociological tool is open to the Christian provided that one recognizes the danger and does not become imprisoned in an ideology. This marks the greatest openness in a papal statement to the Marxist position.

The development in the understanding of Marxism and socialism in the papal documents did not take place in an historical vacuum. In the 1960s discussions between Christians and Marxists began. Once Christian theology gave greater importance to eschatology and the relationship between the kingdom of God and this world, there was ample room for dialogue with Marxists about improving the lot and condition of human beings in their earthly existence. Christian theologians also recognized that the Marxist's critique of religion as the opiate of the people called for a response. Political theology as a fundamental theology examining the context of revelation called for a deprivatization of theology and a greater emphasis on the political and social dimension of human existence and of theology. Especially in Latin America some Catholics struggling for social change on the practical side found themselves working hand in hand with Marxists for particular social goals. The 1979 meeting of the Latin American Bishops' Conference at Puebla has revealed some of the tensions connected with liberation theology and Marxism in South America. Groups of Christians for Socialism began forming in Latin America in the 1970s. But with the return of more repressive regimes these groups have often been scattered. However, in Europe there are small but apparently significant groups of Christians for Socialism.[88]

Meanwhile changes also occurred in Marxism. The differences between Russian and Chinese Marxism became evident as did differences between Moscow and the Eastern European countries. In theory some Marxists called for a humanistic Marxism which gives more importance to the person and also recognizes the importance of the participation of the person in deciding one's future. Eurocommunism also flourished for a while but now seems to have become less important. In these contexts both in theory and in practice some Christians have been trying to discern how they could cooperate with Marxists and even share some of their approaches, especially in terms of sociological analysis of the ills of society.[89] However, many Catholics still remain opposed to any socialist option.

III. Pope John Paul II

Karol Wojtyla became Pope John Paul II in late 1978 and has continued the papal and Catholic tradition in social teaching. His major contribution in this area has been the encyclical *Laborem exercens*, which was originally scheduled to be issued on May 15, 1981, the ninetieth anniversary of *Rerum novarum* but was delayed a few months because of the attempted assassination of the pope.[90] In addition to the encyclical Pope John Paul II has said much about Catholic social teaching in his many trips abroad, especially in Poland and Latin America.

The basic teaching of *Laborem exercens* is in keeping with the developing tradition. The encyclical is critical of both extremes of Marxism and capitalism, and perhaps the pope's criticism of capitalism is more profound than that given by his predecessors.[91] There have been, however, diverse interpretations of the social teaching of Pope John II. In this context one should note the frequent tendency of Catholics to find support for their own particular approach in the official church teaching. Gregory Baum has argued that *Laborem exercens* embraces a moderate socialism.[92] Donal Dorr finds in the papal teaching a continuing of the recent "radical agenda" with its basis in an option for the poor and an openness to the liberation theology of South America.[93] James V. Schall interprets Pope John Paul II as defending a middle-class, free society and as opposed to a radical, this-worldly, socialistic understanding of the social mission of the church.[94]

A complete evaluation of the social teaching of Pope John Paul II lies beyond the scope of this chapter. The question for the present study is how Pope John Paul II relates to the thesis about the changing anthropological bases of Catholic social ethics. Does he continue these developments or tend to block them? In terms of the social emphasis in anthropology there can be no doubt that John Paul II continues the developing tradition. His teaching on the ownership of the means of production stresses the social character of anthropology and the universal destiny of the goods of creation to serve the needs of all.

They [the means of production] cannot be possessed against labor, they cannot even be possessed for possession's sake, because the only legitimate title to their possession—whether in the form of private ownership or in the form of public or collective ownership—is that they should serve labor and thus by serving labor that they should make possible the achievement of the first principle of this order, namely the universal destiny of goods and the right to common use of them. From this point of view, therefore, in consideration of human labor and of common access to the goods meant for man, one cannot exclude the socialization, in suitable conditions, of certain means of production.[95]

The pope thus recognizes the socialization of the means of production, but such a socializing will not come about merely by converting the means of production into state property. True socialization requires that the subject character of society and the human person be highlighted.[96]

The present pope certainly emphasized the importance of the person. The dignity, freedom, equality, and participation of the person are constantly emphasized in *Laborem exercens* and throughout his writings. The basic thesis and thrust of *Laborem exercens* rest primarily on the importance of the person over the work. The primary basis of the value of work is not what is done or made (the objective sense of work) but the person who is its subject. In this light the pope proposes the following as the basic principle for guiding the system of labor—"the principle of the substantial and real priority of labor, of the subjectivity of human labor and its effective participation in the whole production process, independent of the nature of the services provided by the worker."[97] In accord with this principle *Laborem exercens* condemns an economism that considers human labor solely according to its economic purpose.

There is one changed anthropological emphasis pointed out earlier which might not be as strong in Pope John Paul II as in his immediate predecessor. This possible difference concerns historical consciousness and its resulting substantive and methodological consequences. Historical consciousness looks to a more inductive methodology which in *Octogesima adveniens* recognized that it was neither the pope's ambition nor mission to put forward a solution to social questions which has universal validity. The local Christian communities themselves must analyze their own situations and in the light of the gospel and the social teaching of the church discern what is to be done in their given situation.[98] It is impossible to make a definite judgment at this time, but it appears that the present pope has not given such a great support to historical consciousness and its consequences.

Part of the pope's hesitancy might come from his background as a philosopher and the very topic of his first encyclical on the social question. *Laborem exercens* discusses in a somewhat philosophical and deductive manner the meaning of work and its implications for a just society As a philosopher the pope is explaining a very important reality that is of great importance for all human beings and the whole world. No practical importance is given in the encyclical to the diverse situations existing in the various parts of the world. The encyclical proposes guidelines and directions that should be followed in any just social system which truly appreciates the priority of labor. The methodology is definitely not inductive, but in fairness it should be pointed out that the pontiff does on occasion become quite specific in addition to the more general guidelines that are laid down.

In his trips to Latin America it has become obvious that John Paul II has worried about what he might term extremes in liberation theology.[99] With this background one would not expect him to say what his predecessor had said about the importance of local communities discerning things for themselves. The present pontiff sees the need to criticize some of these local developments. Generally speaking, the Roman Church of the present time seems to be fearful of recognizing too much local diversity and pluralism—something which a more historically conscious approach would try to justify and approve. This fear of decentralization and the emphasis on central control go against the logical consequences of historical consciousness. In the present context there is little or no mention of historical consciousness and the consequences that logically follow from it.

Any discussion about Pope John Paul II and historical consciousness must mention a very fascinating discussion that has gone on about the term Catholic "social doctrine." In the late 1970s the French Dominican Marie-Dominique Chenu published a little book in French and Italian entitled *The "Social Doctrine" of the Church as Ideology*.[100] As it is obvious from the title, Chenu understands the "social doctrine" of the church in a very pejorative sense. This term stands for an approach to the social question which is deductive and abstract and consequently insensitive to historical and geographical variations. Chenu sees such a methodology as especially harmful to the church in the third-world countries. The French Dominican traces the development in official church teaching in a way basically in accord with the analysis given above, indicating a shift to a more inductive methodology developing in the 1960s and reaching its culmination in *Octogesima adveniens*. The French Dominican entitles his chapter on *Octogesima adveniens* "An Inductive Method."

Chenu supports his theory by an analysis of the use of the term "social doctrine." The term regularly appears in the earlier papal documents and indicates a deductive and somewhat abstract approach used in elaborating the principles of Catholic social teaching. This term is frequently employed even in *Mater et magistra* in 1961, but according to Chenu it is absent in *Pacem in terris*. *Gaudium et spes* avoids the term except for one unauthorized later addition to the text. The French Dominican objects to the word doctrine here because of the abstractness and deductive methodology connoted by the term. *Gaudium et spes* tends to use the word teaching rather than doctrine. Pope Paul VI also studiously avoided the use of the term. This analysis of a gradual and purposeful disappearance of the term "social doctrine" supports the thesis that the official church documents have gradually adopted a more inductive methodology that is more open to change and the needs of local churches.

The Chenu thesis generated some controversy and debate especially in Italy. In this context there was some surprise when Pope John Paul II in his opening address to the Latin American Bishops' Conference at Puebla in January 1979 used "social doctrine" of the church four times within one comparatively short section near the end of his speech. Ironically, in the short paragraph which introduces the term there is a reference to paragraph four of *Octogesima adveniens*, [101] the very paragraph used by Chenu to prove his own thesis.

The precise meaning of the pope's usage of "social doctrine" is open to different interpretations. The fact of its use and the citation from *Octogesima adveniens* to support its use argue for a direct contradiction of the Chenu thesis.[102] On the other hand, at Puebla Pope John Paul II used social doctrine synonymously with the more general term of social teaching. His use of the term according to Roger Heckel has been discrete and relatively rare.[103]

For all these reasons there is in my mind some question about the extent to which Pope John Paul II is committed to historical consciousness and the methodological and substantive consequences coming from it. However, in all the areas mentioned earlier there is no doubt that the present pope is continuing in the newer developments traced by his more immediate predecessors.

This study has attempted to trace important developments in the anthropology present in Catholic social ethics. Significant changes have occurred in the personal aspects of anthropology, culminating in an emphasis on freedom, equality, participation, and historical mindedness. At the same time the social aspects of anthropology have been stressed as illustrated in the changing attitudes toward private property and socialism. In a sense the perennial challenge of social ethics is to do justice to both the personal and the social aspects of anthropology. However, this challenge now exists in a new context. Christian social ethics building on the present developments must strive to respond to that demand of recognizing the social aspects of human existence and at the same time highlighting the dignity of the human person within an historically conscious perspective.

NOTES

1. For the best commentary available in English, see Jean-Yves Calvez and Jacques Perrin, *The Church and Social Justice: The Social Teaching of the Popes from Leo XIII to Pius XII, 1878-1958* (Chicago: Henry Regnery Co., 1961); also Jean-Yves Calvez, *The Social Thought of John XXIII* (Chicago: Henry Regnery Co., 1964).

2. John F. Cronin, "Forty Years Later: Reflections and Reminiscences," *American Ecclesiastical Review* 164 (1971), 310-318. For

Cronin's major contribution in the field, see John F. Cronin, *Social Principles and Economic Life,* rev. ed. (Milwaukee: Bruce Publishing Co., 1964).

3. The most significant contribution to an understanding of development in the papal teaching on religious liberty was made by John Courtney Murray. For a summary of his approach, see John Courtney Murray, *The Problem of Religious Freedom* (Westminster, Md.: Newman Press, 1965). This small volume originally appeared as a long article in *Theological Studies* 25 (1964), 503-575. See also chapter three.

4. For the best study of development in the papal teaching on economic questions before the Second Vatican Council, see Richard L. Camp, *The Papal Ideology of Social Reform: A Study in Historical Development, 1878-1967* (Leiden: E.J. Brill, 1969). For other helpful studies showing development in Catholic social ethics, see Marie Dominique Chenu, *La dottrina sociale della Chiesa: origine e sviluppo, 1891-1971* (Brescia: Editrice Queriniana, 1977); David Hollenbach, *Claims in Conflict: Retrieving and Renewing the Catholic Human Rights Tradition* (New York: Paulist Press, 1979).

5. One very significant development in Catholic social teaching concerns the relationship between anthropology and eschatology and Christology. The next chapter will give an in-depth analysis of this development. For an earlier discussion of this most significant development in Catholic social teaching, see my "Dialogue with Social Ethics: Roman Catholic Social Ethics — Past, Present and Future," in *Catholic Moral Theology in Dialogue,* paperback ed. (Notre Dame, Indiana: University of Notre Dame Press, 1976), pp. 111-149.

6. To facilitate a further study of the papal and church documents, references will be given to readily available English translations. For the documents from the time of Pope John, see *The Gospel of Peace and Justice: Catholic Social Teaching Since Pope John,* ed. Joseph Gremillion (Maryknoll, New York: Orbis Books, 1976). References will include the page number in Gremillion as well as the paragraph numbers of the documents, which generally are the official paragraph numbers found in the original and in all authorized translations. Thus the present reference is: *Octogesima adveniens,* n. 22; Gremillion, p. 496. Another readily available compendium of Catholic Church teaching on social ethics is *Renewing the Face of the Earth: Catholic Documents on Peace, Justice, and Liberation,* ed. David J. O'Brien and Thomas A. Shannon (Garden City, New York: Doubleday Image Books, 1977).

7. References to the encyclicals of Pope Leo XIII will be to *The Church Speaks to the Modern World: The Social Teaching of Leo XIII,* ed.

Etienne Gilson (Garden City, New York: Doubleday Image Books, 1954). Thus the present reference is *Libertas praestantissimum*, n. 23; Gilson p. 72.

8. *Libertas praestantissimum*, nn. 19-37; Gilson, pp. 70-79. See also *Immortale Dei*, nn. 31-42; Gilson, pp. 174-180.

9. *Quod apostolici muneris*, especially nn. 5, 6; Gilson, pp. 192, 193.

10. *Humanum genus*, n. 26; Gilson, p. 130.

11. *Rerum novarum*, nn. 18, 19; Gilson, pp. 214, 215.

12. Murray, *The Problem of Religious Freedom*, pp. 55, 56.

13. *Libertas praestantissimum*, n. 23; Gilson, p. 72.

14. *Immortale Dei*, n. 5; Gilson, p. 163.

15. *Immortale Dei*, n. 31; Gilson, pp. 174, 175.

16. Murray, *The Problem of Religious Freedom*, pp. 55-57.

17. *Libertas praestantissimum*, n. 15; Gilson, pp. 66, 67.

18. For a similar judgment on Leo's approach to liberty, see Fr. Refoulé, "L'Église et les libertés de Léon XIII à Jean XXIII," in *Le Supplémente* 125 (mai 1978), 243-259.

19. *Rerum novarum*, n. 7; Gilson, pp. 208, 209.

20. *Rerum novarum*, nn. 6-12; Gilson, pp. 208-211.

21. *Rerum novarum*, n. 36; Gilson, pp. 224, 225.

22. *Rerum novarum*, nn. 49-51; Gilson, pp. 231-233.

23. *Rerum novarum*, n. 17; Gilson, pp. 213, 214.

24. *Rerum novarum*, n. 37; Gilson, pp. 225, 226. Here I disagree with Camp, who on page 32 of *The Papal Ideology of Social Reform* seems to deny in Leo a basic equality of all before the law.

25. Reference to the encyclicals of Pope Pius XI will be to *The Church and the Reconstruction of the Modern World: The Social Encyclicals of Pope Pius XI,* ed. Terence P. McLaughlin (Garden City, New York: Doubleday Image Books, 1957). McLaughlin, "Introduction," pp. 6-15.

26. *Divini redemptoris*, n. 10; McLaughlin, pp. 369, 370.

27. For a further explanation of this change in the light of opposition to totalitarianism especially from the left, see G. B. Guzzetti, "L'impegno politico dei cattolici nel magistero pontificio dell'ultimo secolo con particolare riguardo all'ultimo ventennio," *La Scuola Cattolica* 194 (1976), 192-210.

28. Radio message, December 24, 1944; *Acta apostolicae sedis* 37 (1945), 11-12; 22.

29. Murray, *The Problem of Religious Freedom*, pp. 65-67.

30. Guzzetti, "L'impegno politico dei cattolici," p. 202.

31. Radio message, December 24, 1944; *Acta apostolicae sedis 37* (1945), 14.

32. *Pacem in terris*, nn. 8-34; Gremillion, pp. 203-208. See David

Hollenbach, *Claims in Conflict*, pp. 62-69.

33. *Mater et magistra*, n. 212; Gremillion, p. 188
34. *Pacem in terris*, n. 35; Gremillion, p. 208.
35. *Mater et magistra*, nn. 82-103; Gremillion, pp 161-165.
36. *Dignitatis humanae*, nn. 1,2; Gremillion, pp. 337-339.
37. *Gaudium et spes*, nn. 12-22; Gremillion, pp. 252-261.
38. *Gaudium et spes*, n. 29; Gremillion, p. 266.
39. Ibid.
40. *Gaudium et spes*, n. 31; Gremillion, p. 267.
41. *Gaudium et spes*, n. 68; Gremillion, pp. 304, 305.
42. *Gaudium et spes*, n. 75; Gremillion, pp. 310-312.
43. *Octogesima adveniens*, n. 22; Gremillion, p. 496.
44. Bernard Lonergan, "A Transition from a Classicist World View to Historical Mindedness," in *Law for Liberty: The Role of Law in the Church Today*, ed. James E. Biechler (Baltimore: Helicon Press, 1967), pp. 126-133.
45. John Courtney Murray, " Vers une intelligence du développement de la doctrine de l'Église sur la liberté religieuse," in *Vatican II: la liberté religieuse* (Paris: Les Éditions du Cerf, 1967), pp. 11-147; Murray, "Religious Liberty and the Development of Doctine," *The Catholic World* 204 (February 1967), 277-283.
46. *Pacem in terris*, nn. 39-45, 75-79; 126-129; 142-145; Gremillion, pp. 209-210; 217-218; 227-228; 231-232.
47. Charles Moeller, "Preface and Introductory Statement," in *Commentary on the Documents of Vatican II, V: Pastoral Constitution on the Church in the Modern World*, ed. Herbert Vorgrimler (New York: Herder and Herder, 1969), p. 94.
48. *Quadragesimo anno*, nn. 76-149; McLaughlin, p. 246-274.
49. Camp, *The Papal Ideology of Social Reform*, pp. 128-135.
50. *Mater et magistra*, n. 37; Gremillion, p. 150.
51. *Mater et magistra*, nn. 46-60; Gremillion, pp. 152-156.
52. *Populorum progressio*, n. 3; Gremillion, p. 388.
53. *Quadragesimo anno*, nn. 17-22; McLaughlin, pp. 224, 225.
54. Paul Hanly Furfey, *Fire on the Earth* (New York: Macmillan, 1936), p. 8.
55. Calvez and Perrin, *The Church and Social Justice*, p. 3.
56. Bartolomeo Sorge, "E superato il concetto tradizionale di dottrina sociale della Chiesa?" *La civiltà cattolica* 119 (1968), I, 423-436. However, I disagree with the assignment of roles which Sorge gives to the hierarchical magisterium and the laity. See also Sorge, "L'apporto dottrinale della lettera apostolica 'Octogesima Adveniens'," *La civiltà cattolica* 122 (1971), 417-428.
57. *Octogesima adveniens*, n. 4: Gremillion, p. 487.
58. *Octogesima adveniens*, n. 37; Gremillion, p. 502.

59. *Octogesima adveniens*, nn. 48-52; Gremillion, pp. 509-511.

60. The understanding of eschatology mentioned in footnote 5 which tends to overcome the dichotomy between the supernatural and the natural and the church and the world also influences the position taken here. For a refutation of a distinction of planes approach in the social mission of the church, see Gustavo Gutierrez, *A Theology of Liberation* (Maryknoll, New York: Orbis Press, 1973), pp. 53-58. For an approach which still tends to distinguish too much between the teaching role of the hierarchy and the executing role of the laity, see the articles of Sorge mentioned in footnote 56.

61. David Hollenbach, *Claims in Conflict.*

62. Gutierrez, *A Theology of Liberation*; Juan Luis Segundo, *The Liberation of Theology* (Maryknoll, New York: Orbis Books, 1976).

63. For an authoritative study, see Heinrich A. Rommen, *The State in Catholic Thought* (St. Louis: B. Herder, 1945).

64. Gilson, pp. 11-15.

65. *Rerum novarum*, nn. 5-15; Gilson, pp. 207-213.

66. *Quod apostolici muneris*, n. 1; Gilson, p. 190.

67. Thomas Aquinas, *Summa theologiae, IIa-IIae,* q. 66, a. 1 and 2.

68. For an interpretation which sees Leo in greater continuity with Aquinas, see Calvez and Perrin, *The Church and Social Justice*, pp. 259-268.

69. *Summa theologiae, Ia*, q. 98, a. 1 ad 3.

70. Léon de Sousberghe, "Propriété, 'de droit naturel.' Thèse néoscholastique et tradition scholastique," *Nouvelle revue théologique* 72 (1950), 582-596. See also Camp. *The Papal Ideology of Social Reform,* pp. 55, 56.

71. John A. Ryan, *Distributive Justice* (New York: Macmillan, 1916), pp. 56-60; Reginald G. Bender, "The Doctrine of Private Property in the Writings of Monsignor John A. Ryan," (S.T.D. diss., The Catholic University of America, 1973).

72. *Quadragesimo anno*, n. 45; McLaughlin, p. 234.

73. *Quadragesimo anno*, n. 52; McLaughlin, p. 237.

74. *Mater et magistra*, nn. 104-109; *Pacem in terris*, n. 21; Gremillion, pp. 165, 166; 205.

75. Here and in the following paragraphs I am basically following the analysis of J. Diez-Alegria, "La lettura del magistero pontificio in materia sociale alla luce del suo sviluppo storico," in *Magistero e morale; atti del 3° congresso nazionale dei moralisti* (Bologna: Edizioni Dehoniane, 1970), pp. 211-256. For an analysis which disagrees with some of Diez-Alegria's conclusions, especially his denial of the contemporary validity of an approach based on common use and private possession, but which agrees with the material proposed here, see Angelo Marchesi, "Il pensiero di S. Tommaso

d'Aquino e delle enciclice sociali dei papi sul tema della proprietà privata in una recente analisi di P. Diez-Alegria," *Rivista di filosofia neo-scolastica* 62 (1970), 334-344.

76. *Gaudium et spes*, n. 69; Gremillion, p. 305. For an in-depth analysis of the teaching of *Gaudium et spes* on the distribution of the goods of creation, see E. Lio, *Morale e beni terreni: la destinazione universale dei beni terreni nella Gaudium et spes* (Rome: Città Nuova, 1976).

77. *Populorum progressio*, n. 22; Gremillion, p. 394.

78. *Quod apostolici muneris*, n. 1; Gilson, p. 189.

79. Camp, *The Papal Ideology of Social Reform*, pp. 56, 57.

80. *Quadragesimo anno*, n. 117; McLaughlin, p. 260.

81. *Quadragesimo anno*, n. 120; McLaughlin, p. 261.

82. *Quadragesimo anno*, n. 119; McLaughlin, p. 260.

83. Peter Coman, "English Catholics and the Social Order," *Ampleforth Journal* 81 (1976), 47-57.

84. John A. Ryan, *A Better Economic Order* (New York: Harper and Brothers, 1935), pp. 133, 134.

85. *Pacem in terris*, nn. 159, 160; Gremillion, pp. 235, 236.

86. *Octogesima adveniens*, nn 26-35; Gremillion, pp. 498-501.

87. *Octogesima adveniens*, n. 36; Gremillion, p. 501.

88. Peter Hebblethwaite, *The Christian-Marxist Dialogue: Beginnings, Present Status and Beyond* (New York: Paulist Press, 1977).

89. For an attempt to show that Christianity is compatible with a humanistic socialist option, see Gregory Baum, *The Social Imperative* (New York: Paulist Press, 1979), especially pp. 184-202.

90. There are a number of readily available translations of *Laborem exercens* in English. References will be given to the official paragraph numbers and to the page numbers of the text in the widely used commentary by Gregory Baum, *The Priority of Labor* (New York: Paulist Press, 1982).

91. *Laborem exercens*, nn. 7, 8, 11, 14; Baum, pp. 106-110, 114-116, 122-125.

92. Baum, *The Priority of Labor*.

93. Donal Dorr, *Option for the Poor: A Hundred Years of Vatican Social Teaching* (Maryknoll, N.Y.: Orbis Books, 1983), pp. 207-275.

94. James V. Schall, *The Church, the State and Society in the Thought of John Paul II* (Chicago: Franciscan Herald Press, 1982).

95. *Laborem exercens*, n. 14; Baum, p. 123.

96. *Laborem exercens*, n. 14; Baum, p. 124.

97. *Laborem exercens*, n. 13; Baum, p. 119.

98. *Octogesima adveniens*, n. 4; Gremillion, p. 487.

99. For a one-sided interpretation of Pope John Paul's teaching as being almost totally opposed to liberation theology see Quentin L. Quade, ed., *The Pope and Revolution: John Paul II Confronts Libera-*

tion Theology (Washington: Ethics and Public Policy Center, 1982). For an interpretation of John as more open to some of the positions of liberation theology, especially the option for the poor and the solidarity of the poor in trying to bring about social change, see Dorr, *Option for the Poor*, pp. 207-251.

100. Marie-Dominique Chenu, *La dottrina sociale della Chiesa: origine e sviluppo* (Brescia: Editrice Queriniana, 1977); *La "doctrine sociale" de l'église comme idéologie* (Paris: Cerf, 1979).

101. Pope John Paul II, "Opening Address at the Puebla Conference," in *Third General Conference of Latin American Bishops: Conclusions* (Washington: National Conference of Catholic Bishops, 1979), III, 7, p. 13.

102. For such as analysis see Peter Hebblethwaite, "The Popes and Politics: Shifting Patterns in 'Catholic Social Doctrine'," in *Religion and America: Spirituality in a Secular Age*, ed. Mary Douglas and Steven M. Tipton (Boston: Beacon Press, 1983), pp. 190-204.

103. Roger Heckel, *The Social Teaching of John Paul II:* booklet 1: *General Aspects of the Social Catechesis of John Paul II: The Use of the Expression "Social Doctrine" of the Church* (Vatican City: Pontifical Commission *Justitia et Pax*, 1980).

2. A Significant Methodological Change in Catholic Social Ethics

One of the most significant changes in official Catholic social teaching since the Second Vatican Council concerns the methodological approach to social ethics. This chaper will investigate that change in methodology and will then discuss its ramifications for two important questions concerning the social mission of the church and the uniqueness of Christian social ethics.

I. A Methodological Change

That methodological change involved a shift away from a natural-law approach toward a more gospel- and faith-centered approach. To appreciate the change one must understand what is involved in the whole natural-law question. There are two important aspects to the natural-law question — the theological and the philosophical. The philosophical aspect involves what one means by human reason and human nature — the understanding of the human. Chapter one has already indicated a number of significant changes in the understanding of anthropology, human reason, and human nature. This chapter will concentrate on the theological aspect of the question. Natural law in the Roman Catholic tradition has been the answer to a very significant question: Is there a source of ethical wisdom and knowledge for the Christian which exists apart from the explicit revelation of God in Jesus Christ in the Scripture? Does the Christian share ethical wisdom and knowledge with all humankind because of their common humanity?

The Roman Catholic theological tradition has answered the question in the affirmative that human reason on the basis of human nature can arrive at ethical wisdom and knowledge. The theological basis for the Catholic position rests on the goodness of creation. God has created human beings, and on appraising this creation, human reason as God's created gift can discern how God wants human beings to act.

Many in the Protestant tradition have denied the existence of such a source of ethical wisdom based on human reason and human nature. The emphasis on the Scripture alone in some Protestant ethics meant that there are no other possible sources of ethical knowledge, especially sources based on the human and not found in revelation. Some, particularly in the Lutheran tradition, insisted on the presence and power of sin which has greatly infected and disturbed human nature and human reason. How can a sinful reason examining a sinful humanity arrive at any true ethical wisdom?[1] Others, especially in the Barthian tradition, emphasized the impossibility of beginning with the human and going to the divine. By starting with the human and trying to arrive at an understanding of God and God's will one inevitably commits the great Christian blasphemy of making God into one's own image and likeness. For this reason Barth strongly opposed both natural theology and natural law as well as the analogy of being upon which both were based. For Barth one had to begin with God and God's revealing Word.[2] The traditional Catholic theory did not accept these criticisms and continued to view human nature as the basis on which human reason could arrive at true ethical wisdom and knowledge that the Christian shares with all human beings. Such a theological position in Roman Catholicism logically insisted on the continuing goodness of what God had created. The Catholic tradition saw no opposition between grace and nature and between faith and reason. In the words of well-accepted axioms, grace builds on nature, and faith and reason can never contradict one another.[3]

The Roman Catholic theological understanding thus insisted on two different sources of ethical wisdom and knowledge for the Christian—faith and reason, revelation and natural law. The next logical question is how to relate these two sources. Before Vatican II the accepted approach adopted what H. Richard Niebuhr has called with general accuracy the "Christ above culture" or nature approach.[4] The predominant Catholic theology distinguished between the realm of the supernatural and the realm of the natural. The realm of the supernatural was primarily the area of the church and was governed by grace and the gospel. The realm of the natural was the area of the world and was primarily directed by reason and natural law. Catholic Christians lived with others in the world and here shared a common humanity that was the basis for the natural law applied to all human beings. Above there was the realm of the supernatural that in a true sense was a second story added on top of the natural. In considering life in this world, not only social and political life but even family and personal virtues, rights, and obligations, the Catholic approach before the Second Vatican Council based its entire methodology on natural law. At best a few quotations from Scripture were used in a poor proof-text fashion to support positions that already had been proved by the natural law. Grace, the gospel, and Jesus Christ were not directly related to understanding the moral life in this world but were reserved for a realm existing above the realm of creation and the natural.

Official Catholic social teaching as found in the papal documents followed this same methodology—a fact which should not cause great surprise since the official hierarchical teaching office had consistently supported such an approach. The two famous social encyclicals of John XXIII, *Mater et magistra* (1961) and *Pacem in terris* (1963) will serve as a case study to show that even at this comparatively late date papal social teaching was based almost exclusively on natural law. Pope John XXIII begins *Mater et magistra* by summarizing the earlier teaching of the popes from Leo XIII to his day. Leo "proclaimed a social message based on the requirements of human nature itself and conforming to the precepts of the gospel and reason."[5] *Mater et magistra* describes the "natural law character" of Pius XI's teaching[6] and records the words of Pius XII's radio address of Pentecost 1941 claiming the indisputable com-

petence to "decide whether the bases of a given social system
are in accord with the unchangeable order which God our
Creator and Redeemer has fixed both in the natural law and
revelation."[7] In summarizing the previous teaching Pope John
insists on its natural-law basis but acknowledges both revelation and natural law as sources of ethical wisdom and knowledge for the Christian. Note that the papal description of these
two sources is in terms of "both-and."

In practice, Pope John like his predecessors developed his
social teaching exclusively on a natural-law basis with only
an occasional proof text from the Scripture. The encyclical
Pacem in terris well illustrates this natural-law method. There
is a great contrast between this approach to peace and later
Catholic approaches as found in the pastoral letter of the
American bishops issued in May 1983, whose methodology
will be discussed in chapter seven. These more recent writings
stress the Christological and biblical basis of peace as the gift
of Jesus to his disciples. Peace comes from a living out of the
gospel morality of love with its willingness to love even the
enemy. Shalom is a biblical concept which has direct bearing
on Christians working for peace. But *Pacem in terris*'s methodology is not biblical or based on the redeeming work of Jesus.

The introductory paragraphs of *Pacem in terris* set forth the
methodology and the outline which will be followed in the entire encyclical:

> Peace on earth . . . can be firmly established only if the order
> laid down by God be dutifully observed. . . . But the Creator
> of the world has imprinted in man's heart an order which his
> conscience reveals to him and enjoins him to obey. . . . But
> fickleness of opinion often produces this error that many think
> that the relationship between men and states can be governed
> by the same laws as the forces and irrational elements of the
> universe, whereas the laws governing them are of quite a dif-
> ferent kind and are to be sought elsewhere, namely, where the
> Father of all things wrote them, that is, in the nature of man.[8]

Note how the appeal is exclusively to the Father and the
Creator. Jesus and redemption are never mentioned. The
following paragraph then goes on to outline what will be the
subject matter of the four different parts of the encyclical:

By these laws, men are most admirably taught, first of all, how they should conduct their mutual dealings among themselves; next, how the relationships between the citizens and the public authorities of each state should be regulated; then, how states should deal with one another; finally, how, on the one hand individual men and states, and on the other hand the community of all peoples, should act toward each other, the establishment of such a world community of peoples being urgently demanded today by the requirements of universal common good.[9]

The Pastoral Constitution on the Church in the Modern World (*Gaudium et spes*) issued in 1965 employs a different methodology without ever explicitly alluding to the significant change which this involves for Catholic social teaching. The changed methodology exists above all in the chapters of part one of *Gaudium et spes*. Part one, "The Church and the Human Calling," is divided into four chapters: 1) "The Dignity of the Human Person," 2) "The Community of Humankind," 3) "Human Activity throughout the World," and 4) "The Role of the Church in the Modern World." The first three chapters well illustrate a more integrated theological approach which attempts to understand human existence in the world within the light of a more total Christian understanding. The first chapter begins by discussing human creation in the image of God, then explicitly recognizes the presence of sin, and, after a number of specific questions, finally considers Christ as the new human being. The anthropology is no longer based on reason and nature alone but brings together creation and redemption, while explicitly calling attention to sin and its continuing presence in the world. The chapters following on human community and human activity adhere to this same basic approach with the significant addition in the third chapter of the topic of future eschatology, which will be mentioned later.

This newer methodological approach of insisting on seeing the realities of the gospel, grace, and the supernatural as having a direct relation to and an effect on the daily life of Christians in the world is connected with other emphases found in the council and its documents. Throughout the documents the fathers of Vatican II insisted on the importance of Scripture in Catholic life, theology, and liturgy. Such a stress logically calls for the Scripture to have something to say about the daily life of Christians in the world. *Gaudium et spes* itself maintains that the split between the faith which many profess and their daily lives deserves to be counted among the more serious errors of our age.[10]

Gaudium et spes contains other indications of the change in methodology which has been mentioned. It is significant that the term natural law appears only three times in this the lengthiest document of Vatican II, and the three uses of the term are in rather peripheral comments.[11] An important concept which was incorporated into *Gaudium et spes* when the draft was reworked in Ariccia in 1965 is the notion of the truly or the fully human. The fully or truly human is not simply the natural as distinguished from the supernatural but rather the fully human is identical with the Christian and the perfection which Jesus brings to humanity.[12]

One possible objection could be raised against the assertion of a very significant methodological change in Catholic social ethics being found in *Gaudium et spes*. The second part of *Gaudium et spes* considers five specific questions or areas of concern for Christians living in the world, but the methodological approach of these chapters does not seem to follow totally the methodology described and developed in the first part with its more theoretical concerns. Yes, it is true that the methodology in the second part does not completely follow the approach used in the first part. The difference comes from the fact that the first part went through a number of different drafts and developments over the four years of the council. For a long time the plan was to publish the second part as an appendix without integrating it into the council document itself.[13] This earlier plan explains why the second part did not go through the same developments and changes as the first part and therefore does not show forth the newer methodological approach.

Subsequent documents in the official Catholic social teaching have continued along this same line of development of attempting to relate the gospel and the redeeming work of Jesus to life in the world. One of the best illustrations of this change has been the liberation theology which arose in

Latin America in the light of the conciliar developments and as a response to the distinctive characteristics of Latin American life. Liberation theology strongly insists that not only must the gospel message of redemption and freedom affect souls and the sprriritual aspect of human existence but the gospel also is a call to liberation from oppression and injustice in all the spheres of human existence, including the political, the social, the cultural, and the economic.[14]

Further Analysis and Ramifications

Gaudium et spes and the work of Vatican II have brought about a very important shift in methodology in social ethics. The separation between the natural and the supernatural, between daily life and the gospel, has been overcome in recent documents of Catholic social teaching. In many ways this change responds to the negative criticisms that had been raised especially in the Protestant tradition against the Catholic natural-law approach.

However, in rightly attempting to overcome this separation there is the danger that everything becomes grace and gospel. In striving to relate grace, gospel, and Jesus to daily life one can forget the realities of human finitude, human sinfulness, and the fact that the fullness of the reign of God lies outside history at the end of time. This danger is an obvious one and at times did seem to be present in both Catholic life and thought after Vatican II. Catholic theology and ethics have historically not given enough importance to the reality of sin as affecting and infecting all human life and structures. The Catholic recognition of sin was primarily restricted to understanding sin as a particular act. It is a sin to do this or a sin to do that. However, sin as a power present in and affecting the world was not emphasized.

Pacem in terris well illustrates the failure of Catholic thought to give enough importance to the continuing reality of sin in the world. Pope John XXIII spoke about the order existing in human nature and in human hearts because of which human beings can perceive how they are to live together in peace and harmony. However, there is something else present in the hearts of human beings and in the world—disorder, a seek-

ing for power, a spirit of aggressive self-aggrandizement both
of individuals and of nations. Look at the world in which we
live. There have been wars in almost all parts of the world
during the memory of all of us. One could start with emphasizing the existence of sin in human hearts and in the world and
write a document entitled *Bellum in terris* which could appeal
to much empirical data both contemporary and historical to
support its thesis. Such an approach would go too far and
overemphasize the presence of sin at the expense of creation
and redemption present in the world, but such an approach
is a sober reminder of the danger in Roman Catholicism of
not giving enough importance to the reality and the effects
of sin in the world. Sin is not the most important or the
primary reality present in the world, but it does exist and exercise its power. If an older Catholic natural-law approach
failed to recognize the importance of sin, the emphasis on the
presence of the gospel and of redemption in the newer approach will be even more tempted at times to forget the impact of human sinfulness.

A similar danger in post-Vatican II developments has been
the failure to insist that the fullness of the reign of God will
only come at the end of time. In striving to overcome the
separation between gospel and daily life, grace and nature,
there is an inevitable tendency to see everything as gospel and
grace. In the 1960s there was a widespread presence of what
might be called a chronic case of collapsed eschaton. In Roman
Catholic life and ethos after Vatican II there was great optimism and a sense that the reign of God would become present in our world somewhat readily, quickly, and easily. Secular
city and death of God theologies in Protestantism likewise
stressed the optimistic possibilities of the contemporary world.
Some have pointed out similarities between the theological
era of the 1960s and the era of the Social Gospel in the first
part of the twentieth century.[15] In retrospect both periods were
characterized by an overoptimism about the possibilities of
making God's reign present in our world. However, both
periods ended with the recognition that history taught human
beings a more sober lesson about the existence of the tragic
and the inability of human beings to live out a life of gospel
love in this world. The overly optimistic ethos of the early

1960s in America soon dissipated in the face of urban riots, the continuing discrimination against blacks, minorities, and women, the unequal distribution of wealth, and above all the war in Vietnam. On the broader world scene people became more conscious of the political and economic exploitation of individuals and nations and the existence of oppression and gross violations of human rights in many parts of the world. Within the Catholic Church itself many people became disillusioned with the slow progress that was being made in the church and with the fact that some in authority seemed to be standing in the way of the promise of Vatican II. The historical realities both in the world and the church thus served to remind theologians of the danger of a too-realized eschatology which fails to recognize that the fullness of the reign of God always lies outside history.

Even parts of *Gaudium et spes* so stress the presence of redemption in Christ Jesus that as a result the future aspect of eschatology is not emphasized enough. There is a fascinating difference between chapter three and the first two chapters of part one. Chapter one ends with a section entitled "Christ and the New Human Being," while the final section of chapter two finishes with a section on "The Incarnate Word and Human Solidarity."[16] However, chapter three presents a different picture. After sections on human activity as infected by sin and on human activity as finding its perfection in Jesus and in the paschal mystery, there is a final section dealing with the eschatological future under the title "A New Earth and a New Heaven."[17] The council document itself definitely shows signs of an overly realized eschatology which was corrected in one of its important chapters but not in all.

In summary, I am in total agreement with the thrust of Vatican II to overcome the separation between the gospel and daily life, between the realm of redemption and the realm of creation. However, in overcoming this separation it is important not to go to an opposite extreme with a collapsed eschatology which fails to give enough importance to human finitude, human sinfulness, and the fact that the fullness of the reign of God will only come at the end of time.

In the light of these developments and criticisms, and as the logical first step in the systematic construction of a moral

theology, I have proposed the stance, posture, or perspective
for moral theology of looking at the world and human existence
in the light of the fivefold Christian mysteries of creation, sin,
incarnation, redemption, and resurrection-destiny. Failure to
include one or other of these elements or an overemphasis
on any one of them will result in a distorted picture. Creation insists on the basic goodness of all that God has made
in the world, but creation must be integrated into the fullness
of the Christian understanding, which had not been done in
the older two-level natural-law approach. Sin is present in our
world and affects all existing realities, but sin does not completely destroy the goodness of creation; nor is it the last word,
for the presence of redeeming love is also active in our world
through the work of Jesus and strives to overcome sin. Incarnation recognizes that everything human has been brought
into the plan of God and belongs to the reign of God. Redemption points to the fact that redemption has already occurred
in Christ Jesus and thus affects not only souls but persons
and the world. However, resurrection-destiny has not yet occurred and preserves the tension between the already and the
not-yet aspect of the reign of God, recognizing that redeeming love continues to transform the present realities, but the
fullness of the transformed reality will only come at the end
of time as God's gracious gift.

This stance based on the fivefold Christian mysteries can
thus serve both as guide for Christian ethics and as a source
of criticism of other proposals that have been put forth. The
Catholic natural-law approach as found in the theology manuals before Vatican II rightly emphasized the goodness of creation and to an extent the reality of incarnation, but it failed
to give due weight to the presence of sin and to the effect of
redemption in the world. Protestant Social-Gospel approaches
stressed the significance of redemption but failed to appreciate
the effects of sin and the fact that the fullness of the reign of
God will only come at the end of time. The Lutheran Two-
Realm tradition so emphasized sin that it did not give importance to the goodness of creation and the presence of
incarnation and redemption. Niebuhrian Christian realism
attempted to cover all the bases but tended to downplay creation somewhat, overstressed sin, did not recognize enough

the presence of incarnation and redemption, and made resurrection-destiny too future. In terms of contemporary approaches to social ethics the approach of Michael Novak tends to suffer from the same defects as the earlier Christian realism of Reinhold Niebuhr.[18] On the other hand, Stanley Hauerwas' approach to Christian ethics does not give enough importance to the reality of creation, downplays the effects of incarnation, and too narrowly interprets redemption.[19]

The stance based on the fivefold Christian mysteries rests on an eschatology that recognizes the tension between the already and the not yet. Such a perspective leaves open the possibility of some limited human progress but rejects any utopian or melioristic evolutionary growth as an expected reality. The stance is in basic agreement with the position "Christ transforming Culture" proposed by H. Richard Niebuhr.[20] And especially such an outlook is in continuity with contemporary Catholic approaches which continue to recognize the goodness of creation but want to integrate creation into a fuller Christian perspective.

Recent developments in Catholic social ethics since Vatican II can best be described as attempting to fuse its understanding of human reason and human beings into a total Christian perspective. Traditional Catholic natural-law approaches rightly stressed the role of reason and also, at least in theory, the importance of all the human sciences in arriving at ethical wisdom and knowledge. Contemporary Catholic social ethics must still give great importance to reason and all the human sciences, but these must be seen primarily as mediating the meaning and symbols of faith.

In my judgment Catholic social ethics with its rightful emphasis on the role of reason and the human sciences avoids the danger of what might be called theological actualism. Theological actualism can be understood as the moving from a particular scriptural quotation or from the fact that God is working in the world to a very specific, concrete ethical conclusion and claiming great certitude for that conclusion. One illustration of such a methodology can throw some light on this approach. A few years ago I received a one-page handout from a Catholic justice and peace commission. The first paragraph was a paraphrase of Matthew 25 — when I was hungry, naked, thirsty, imprisoned, you comforted me in doing these things for the least of my sisters and brothers. Then the second paragraph very succinctly concluded that multinational corporations are immoral. The present purpose is not necessarily to disagree with the conclusion but to point out the inadequacy of the method. One cannot go from one Scripture text to a very specific conclusion on a complex matter. At the very minimum in a rational debate with spokespersons for a multinational corporation one would need a wide knowledge of facts and figures from economics and many other sciences to make the point that a multinational corporation is immoral.

In accord with both the stance outlined herein and the traditional Catholic emphasis, a contemporary Catholic social ethics must still give great importance to reason and all the human sciences involved in a particular situation. A truly Catholic ethic can never short-circuit or find a way around the human. The human in all its complexity and specificity must be thoroughly examined and studied. However, human reason and human sciences must be seen as mediations of faith values and meanings. For example, recent Catholic social documents have rightly insisted on the principle that the goods of creation exist to serve the needs of all human beings. But how should this work out in practice? It is necessary to deal with very complex economic questions to determine how best the common destiny of the goods of creation should be incorporated into a concrete economic system. There is no way to solve the problem of distribution without a broad and deep knowledge of all the factors involved.

While emphasizing Scripture and especially Christian understandings, contemporary Catholic social ethics cannot forget the role of reason and the need to mediate the more general values and common understandings to the level of the concrete. Such a mediating approach not only avoids the extreme of theological actualism but also the opposite extreme of saying that Christian ethics and the Christian churches have no competence in these complex human matters. According to this other extreme position economic questions must be solved by economists; military quesitons should be handled by the military; legal questions belong to the province of lawyers.

In a sense there is truth in the recognition that there are economic, military, and legal questions that are purely technical. However, the vast majority of decisions about military policy and deterrence are not merely technical military decisions but truly human moral decisions involving a great amount of data and input from military and political sciences. The size and means of deterrence are more than simply military decisions — a fact which our society has always recognized by making sure that military policies are made by civilians in the executive and legislative branches of government and not by the military themselves. Since these decisions are more than merely technical decisions, they are truly human, moral, and Christian decisions. Christian ethics and the church have something to say about these significant human issues. However, Christian ethics and the church must also recognize the limitations brought about by this mediating role of human reason, the human sciences, and human experience. In order to address these complex issues, one must be schooled in all the necessary data from the appropriate sciences. There is no way to shortcut the need to know all that is involved. The very complexity of the situation and the lack of certitude of the sciences involved means that conclusions in these complex matters will ordinarily not be able to achieve a certitude that excludes the possibility of error. The stance based on the fivefold Christian vision and the mediating role of reason and the sciences are in my judgment two very important approaches to Catholic social ethics and its proper methodology as these have evolved since Vatican II.

II. Social Mission of the Church

The change in methodology in Catholic social ethics has also affected the Catholic understanding of the social mission of the church. To its credit, an earlier Roman Catholicism had developed a body of social teaching and even talked about the social mission of the church, but a changing ethical methodology has now called for a changed understanding of the social mission of the church. In the earlier pre-Vatican II period the life of human beings in the world was not seen as intimately and intrinsically connected with the gospel and the reign of God. Life in the world involved only the natural. The church was primarily interested in the spiritual and supernatural welfare of human beings, but the spiritual welfare was obviously affected by what took place in the natural order. A sufficiency of the goods of this world is ordinarily necessary for human beings to live properly the spiritual life. This was one reason for the involvement of the church in the natural order of human social existence. In addition, the church has the function of teaching its members to live properly in this world, to obey the law of God, and to achieve eternal salvation. The church should thus point out the duties and obligations placed on Christians in their daily human life. These two reasons thus constituted the rationale and the justification of the church's involvement in teaching and trying to bring about a more just society.[21]

The methodological shift at Vatican II overcame the grace-nature, gospel-daily life separation and had enormous repercussions in understanding the social mission of the church. Now the gospel itself calls Christians to work for social justice in the world. If the church is to preach the gospel and work for the presence of the reign of God in this world, then working for social justice becomes a very necessary and essential part of what it means to preach and live the gospel. The application of the change in ethical methodology to a changed understanding of the social mission of the church was explicitly made by the International Synod of Bishops in 1971: "Action on behalf of justice and participation in the transformation of the world fully appear to us as a constitutive dimension of the preaching of the gospel or, in other words, of the church's mission for the redemption of the human race and its liberation from every oppresive situation."[22] The term constitutive has a very strong meaning in Catholic theology. Without a constitutive part the reality itself cannot exist. There is no preaching of the gospel and no mission of the church without a social mission. Such an understanding is a challenge to the church on all levels of its existence, whether in the local congregation, the nation, or the world. One can have the best preaching in the world or the best liturgy, but if there is no social mission, there is no church. There have been some attempts within Catholicism to water down the interpretation of constitutive to mean an integral but not an essential part. Something can still exist but not exist well without an integral part (e.g., a human being can exist with only one arm). However, there is strong support for understanding constitutive as an essential dimension without which there is no church.[23]

This methodological shift in overcoming the separation between gospel and daily life has not only changed the understanding of the importance of the social mission but has also dramatically altered the way in which the social mission of the church is structured and practiced.

Corresponding in a rough way to the separation between the supernatural and the natural, the realm of the gospel and the realm of daily life, was the separation between church and world. The upper layer was the layer of the supernatural, the gospel, and the church. The lower layer was the realm of the natural, daily living, and the world. In the world one lived a natural-law existence, and life in the world in a sense was of secondary importance to life in the church, where grace, gospel, and the supernatural exist. An older Catholic approach often described religious life as a calling to leave the world, to enter the religious life, and to follow the evangelical counsels. Note the very term evangelical counsel. The full gospel was not obligatory for all people living in the world but was only a counsel given to the few who left the world. This brief description is somewhat simplistic but still basically accurate.

The church-world separation served as the basis for understanding the mission of the church as primarily structured to take care of its own members. The church was the end of its own mission, and in a sense the world existed to serve the needs and the work of the church. The mission of the church was primarily to take care of its own. Thus we had Catholic hospitals, Catholic schools, and Catholic cemeteries. In the United States the Catholic educational system stands as a monument to the sacrifices of an immigrant people who were willing to provide an education for their own. In a general sense lay people worked to support the church and its supernatural mission understood as somewhat apart from and above life in the world.

In the light of such a two-layer understanding of human existence the social mission of the church was structured. Recall that in this way the social mission of the church was not core and central to its primary and real mission. Corresponding to the different two layers mentioned above was the distinction between clergy and religious on the one hand and laity on the other. According to the best pre-Vatican II understanding, the role of the laity was in the realm of the world. The laity received from clerics and religious the principles and the grace which they needed to live out their human existence on the natural plane in the world. The role of the laity was in the world, while the role of clerics and religious was withdrawn from the world and for all practical purposes identified with the core aspect of church. Such an understanding was the basis for the theory and practice of Catholic action and the proper role and function of the laity in the church. Sometimes the distinction was made between the function of divinization, which belongs primarily to clerics and exists on the level of the church, the gospel, and grace, and that of humanization, which is the function that the laity bring to the world. Such a distinction of functions did give a definite role to the laity, but it was obviously a subordinate role dealing with the secondary aspect of humanization.

The methodological shift that overcame the separation between the gospel and daily life also affected the understanding of the relationship between church and world. Grace and the gospel were now recognized as present and operating in the world. No longer could the church be looked on as the only place in which grace and gospel were operative. In this newer perspective the ministry of the church is to be present wherever the freeing grace and gospel of Jesus are present and operating, as exemplified in the call for the church to make an option for the poor.[24] The mission of the church cannot be merely to its own but must be present wherever the liberating power of the gospel is trying to free people from all forms of oppression — spititual, social, political, and economic.

The changing role of religious in the church, especially women religious, well illustrates the change in the understanding of the mission of the church. In a true sense the church now exists to serve the world and not the other way around. This changed understanding of the mission of the church has created great tensions in the church. Such an approach does not necessarily rule out a heavy educational involvement by the church. However, by expanding the mission of the church to be present wherever the gospel and God's grace are trying to liberate and redeem human beings from all different types of enslavement, the possibilities for the social mission of the church are almost infinite. Now more than ever there is the need to settle on priorities. Obviously the church has only a limited amount of resources in terms of finances, personnel, and time. It will be important through communal discernment for the whole church and for groups within the church to agree what are the principal ways in which the church should structure its mission.

This shift has caused some tensions not only because many church ministers are abandoning older ministries which primarily served the church in favor of those that are serving the world but also because church ministers and religious are appearing in new and, for some, perhaps upsetting roles. In the 1960s some Catholics were scandalized to see religious or priests on picket lines, involved in civil disobedience, and even going to jail. Often the cry was heard that they should go back to the convent and sacristy where they belonged. But a newer understanding of the mission of the church was developing. The social mission involves the whole church and not simply the laity. Religious and priests should also work for social justice and the transformation of the world.

There have been negative reactions to this changed structuring of the social mission of the church. On the one hand there has been objection to the involvement of priests and especially religious in so-called secular affairs. Some Roman documents still seem to insist too much on a sacred-secular duality.[25] Others maintain that this development has downplayed the role of the laity. The Chicago Declaration of Christian Concern issued in 1977 argued that developments since Vatican II have taken away the proper role and function of the laity as working in the secular sphere and in the world. Unfortunately, much lay involvement has recently seen lay people taking over church-related roles such as religious education, readers in church, and pastoral care of the sick, which have traditionally been assigned to priests and sisters. The document also points a finger at a new clericalism of the left because priests and religious have acted as if the primary responsibility in the church for overcoming injustice, defending human rights, and bringing about peace rests with ordained ministers and religious. The authors regret the passing of many organizations which used to organize lay involvement in many different social areas.[26]

In general I think the Chicago Declaration is itself working out of a two-layer view of reality which thus supports a clear distinction between clerics and religious on the one hand and laity on the other. In a sense there will be and should be a greater confusion between the role of clergy and laity than there was in the past. The church itself involves all the people of God, so that contemporary theology recognizes a role for all God's people in worship and even to an extent in the teaching function of the whole church. Likewise the whole church has a mission in transforming the world, not only the laity. However, there are still some distinctive roles for different individuals in the church.

In this light I would strongly defend the involvement of the American Catholic bishops in social issues over the last few years. The book *Quest for Justice* is a compendium of statements made by the American bishops on the political and social order from 1966 to 1980.[27] The American bishops have addressed many different questions, including peace and war especially in Vietnam, world development, human rights, specific treaties such as SALT II and the Panama Canal agreement, abortion policy, capital punishment, prisons, poverty, welfare legislation, the economy, housing, the family, immigration, labor, race, minorities, the role of farmers. In speaking out on these issues the American bishops have generally recognized and followed the approach mentioned in the first section of this paper. The gospel message and vision must be mediated through human reason, human sciences, and concrete human experience. (The Chicago Declaration has also insisted on the need for mediation and rejects direct appeal to the gospel to justify specific solutions to social problems.) In the midst of such complex problems the bishops have usually recognized the fact that on specific issues one cannot achieve a certitude that excludes the possibility of error. In practical applications there is room for disagreement within the church.

Thus, as an example, we find that J. Brian Benestad has disagreed with the approach of the American bishops to political and social issues. Benestad insists that the bishops have overstressed the political aspects of situations and not given enough importance to evangelization, conversion, and education. Benestad sees a difference between the approach of John Paul II and that of the American bishops.[28] I agree that the social mission of the church should work for both a change of hearts and a change of structures, but Benestad places too great a separation between evangelization and political involvement, so that the work for social justice and the transformation of the world would not appear to be a constitutive dimension of the gospel. The spiritual on the one hand and the political and the social on the other are too far separated in this criticism. The involvement of the bishops working for a change of concrete structures in this area is a legitimate and important part in the mission of the church for social justice, provided such an approach follows the methodology described above. The word "political" is used here in the Aristotelian sense of the just structures and institutions of civic life and does not mean partisan politics.

Although I generally applaud the efforts of the American bishops in their statements on political and social justice and argue that they usually follow a sound methodology, there has been a problem with the process used by the bishops in the past in preparing these statements. Usually the statements were drafted by an individual or a small group of people and then approved in a general meeting with little or no real debate or discussion. As a result of this process the political statements of the American bishops made before 1980 have had very little impact on the life of the church in the United States, to say nothing of the life of society itself.

In preparing such statements the bishops should recognize that they are trying to speak for the whole church and consequently should involve as many people as possible in a consultation process. The bishops themselves must enter into a true study and debate about all the pertinent issues so that they clearly understand and ultimately own what is passed at a meeting. In this way the whole church will be involved in the elaboration of the document, and the whole church will be more open to accept, understand, and put into practice what is contained in the document. Fortunately in the past few years the American bishops have adopted just such a wide-ranging process and dialogue in their pastoral letters on peace and the economy. Hopefully this process will continue to be followed in further statements. Such a process also means that the bishops and the whole church must be more selective in the questions addressed in order that the whole church as such might be truly involved in the issue.

Although I disagree with the theoretical grounding of the Chicago Declaration with its presupposition of a rather strict separation between the sacred and the secular, between the role of priests and religious on the one hand and the role of laity on the other, in my judgment there is some truth to the charge that not enough emphasis is given to the role of the laity in the social mission of the church in recent Catholic writing and thinking. Here it is important to identify the problem as clearly as possible. One of the dangers in the present development has been a reduction of the social mission to the political order. The political realm is very important, but it is not the total realm of the social mission of the church. In the political order it is important to work for structural change, and here the whole church through bishops and others can and should speak to and work for legislation and public policies that bring about a greater justice and peace. There are many other aspects of social existence such as the cultural, the educational, the world of work, and even the world of recreation. In addition, it is important to recognize that, especially as viewed in the Catholic tradition, human life should exist in and through many other voluntary organizations and societies. In fact, most people live out their daily lives in and through these intermediary institutions of many different types — schools and universities, labor unions, cultural associations, organizations involving different groups of people working for a variety of social and civil endeavors. Above all, in one's own job and vocation there is the need to work for true justice.

The tendency in recent church life has been to neglect one's involvement in family, neighborhood, work place, and many other voluntary associations that play an important role in the forming of society.

The emphasis on relating the gospel to life in the world with its changed understanding of the mission of the church to the world has another important consequence for the social mission of the church. There exists a significant connection between the internal life of the church and its social mission. Justice in the World, the document of the 1971 International Synod of Bishops, emphasized this connection. "While the church is bound to give witness to justice, she recognizes that anyone who ventures to speak to people about justice must first be just in their eyes. Hence we must undertake an examination of the modes of acting and of the possessions and life style found within the church itself."[29] Internal church reform is intimately associated with the social mission of the church, for the church is called to be a sign of what should take place in the wider world. In this connection there are three very important issues that have not been adequately dealt with — poverty in the life-style of the church, human rights, and especially the rights and role of women in the church. In my estimation the question of the role of women in the church is and will be the most crucial "internal" issue facing the Catholic Church in the immediate future, for this internal issue will have a great impact on the credibility of the social mission of the church.

Thus, the shift which tries to overcome the false separation between the gospel and daily life by relating the gospel and the reign of God to human existence has important ramifications in understanding and structuring the social mission of the church.

III. The Relationship between the Human and the Christian

The shift we are discussing also raises in a new way the question of the precise relationship between the Christian and the human. The older two-tiered approach, dubbed correctly by H. Richard Niebuhr as the Christ-above-culture model, had a sharpness and a simplicity about it. Life in the world was based on the natural law which the Christian shared with all human beings. Since Christian social ethics was based on this natural law, it did not claim anything distinctively or uniquely Christian. *Pacem in terris* again serves as an excellent illustration of such an approach.

Two important considerations followed from this basic insistence on a natural-law ethic. There is no distinction between the way Christians are to live in this world and what is required of others. Christians and all others are called to do the same thing based on the common humanity they share. Second, such an ethic and the church teaching based on it use the same language to address the Christian community of the church and the wider human community of the world. The reception given to *Pacem in terris* testifies to the strength of this approach. The secular world has taken this document very seriously and entered into dialogue with it, for Pope John XXIII makes no appeal to distinctive or unique Christian concepts, understandings, meanings, and symbols.

The newer methodological development involving the direct relationship of the gospel and the reign of God to human social existence now raises questions about the proper understanding of the relationships between the human and the Christian. The older approach did not look for or stress the distinctively Christian in the human social sphere, but the contemporary approach insists on relating the gospel to daily life. The emphasis on the distinctively Christian raises more acutely than before the relationship between Christian morality and human morality and its ramification for Christian social ethics and the social mission of the church.

In its older understanding the gospel and grace definitely added something new and different as a second layer on top of the realm of the natural and daily life in this world. At first sight it would now seem that the distinctively Christian is different from the human and again adds something to it. However, I have proposed there is no unique Christian content to morality in the sense that non-Christians can and do share and prize the same general attitudes, virtues, and goals such as love, hope, self-sacrifice, and care for the neighbor in need, which Christians sometimes have erroneously claimed as uniquely their own.[30] Likewise, non-Christians can and do accept the same principles and come to the same concrete decisions as Christians. There might be many of these moral content aspects which are distinctively Christian, but none of them can claim to be uniquely Christian in the sense that no other people can acknowledge and prize these moral realities. Briefly a number of reasons support such a thesis.

At first sight it might seem that Christians are quite different from non-Christians, and a different anthropology obviously should ground a different morality. But the Catholic tradition has always insisted on the universal salvific will of God—God calls all people to share in the fullness of God's love and life. Christians are not necessarily that different from all these others, because salvation somehow or other is offered to all human beings.

Within this theological perspective many contemporary Catholic theologians follow Karl Rahner in maintaining that grace is not something added to an already-existing order of nature. God historically calls all existing human beings to share in the fullness of God's love and self-communication. The natural order has never existed as such. It is only an abstraction and a remainder concept necessary to safeguard the gratuitousness of God's saving gift to human beings. There is only one historical order; there is not a natural order and a supernatural one, or a salvation history and a human history. Karl Rahner even affirms that one who categorically professes atheism can even be a true believer because the saving relationship with the mystery of God transpires on the transcendental level and not on the categorical.[31]

In addition, the Christian cannot be opposed to the human, because we are human beings who are saved by Jesus Christ. Salvation does not deny our humanity but rather brings it to the fullness of the human. The Christian and the fully human are the same.

These are the principal reasons for my contention that Christians do not have a unique morality in the sense that non-Christians cannot arrive at the same dispositions, values, virtues, goals, norms, and decisions as Christians do. Three clarifications are in order. First note that the thesis deals with morality as such and not ethics. Christian ethics reflects in a systematic, reflexive, and coherent manner on Christian life and existence. By its very nature Christian ethics or moral theology must appeal to distinctive and even unique Christian concepts (e.g., the reign of God in Jesus), symbols (the cross), and sources of ethical wisdom (Scripture). In accord with the understanding developed earlier, my approach to Christian ethics gives a great place to human reason, the sciences, and human experiences as mediating the gospel values and symbols. The morality proposed in Christian ethics, however, cannot claim to have a unique content but is available to all human beings. Christian belief will affect our motivation, intentionalities, and reasons, but not the material content as such. Christians will try to love one another as Jesus has first loved us, but the non-Christian can arrive at the same conclusions about the meaning of love.

The thesis denying a unique content to Christian morality unavailable to all others is an "in-principled" statement. There is no contention that all others do arrive at and practice the same morality. For that matter, not all Christians acknowledge and live the tenets of Christian morality. Despite the fact that my contemporary Christian ethical methodology is insisting on distinctive Christian aspects to ethics, still it does not claim a unique moral content that is unavailable in principle to all others.

This understanding of the relationship between Christian morality and human morality means that there are not two different moralities for life in this world — that we Christians are called to do one thing, whereas non-Christians are called to do other things. There is only one history and one moral order. In principle there is no necessary opposition or difference between Christians and others in terms of social morality or life together in the world. Christians are called to work with all others to bring about a more just world — more in conformity with the one moral order. The Christian church in this view cannot be a sect which withdraws from the world and from others, living in isolation lest it be contaminated by the world. However, it is important to remember, especially in the light of the proposed stance, that sin will always affect the world and all people. Christians must prophetically point out the existence of sin and try to overcome the sin that exists in the world, although recognizing that they themselves both individually and corporately are also subject to the presence of sin.

Since there are not Christian and non-Christian moralities for life in the world but only one, then Christians can and should work together with all others for a more just and equitable society. But the pluralistic reality of American society raises a question about how Christians individually and collectively are to speak about justice and human rights in our society. The question is of paramount importance for those who would speak and teach in the name of the church in striving for a more just social order. There are two different audiences that are addressed.—the community of believers in the church and the broader human political community. When addressing the community of the church itself, spokespersons and teachers should generally use distinctive Christian symbols, meanings, and sources. In the Christian community we live our lives in and through these realities as celebrated in our liturgy and communicated to the members, so that our moral relationships should be based on them. However, this moral content involved in such teaching is per se communicable to and available to all other human beings. In speaking to the broader and pluralistic community, bishops and other Christian spokespersons and leaders might find it more effective to prescind from the specifically Christian. However, at times even in pluralistic societies it should not always be necessary for Christians and others to prescind from their own unique approaches in addressing questions affecting the whole society. Thus, the insistence on emphasizing in social ethics the explicitly Christian concepts, meanings, and symbols has raised in a different context the important question of the relationship between human morality and Christian morality and its consequences for a just social life in a pluralistic society.

This chapter has pointed out an important development that occurred in official Catholic social teaching at Vatican II, in which an attempt was made to relate the gospel and specifically Christian content and meanings to social justice in our world. This methodological development not only involved a significant change for Catholic social ethics as such but also for an understanding and structuring of the social mission of the church.

NOTES

1. Helmut Thielicke, *Theological Ethics,* vol. 1: *Foundations* (Philadelphia: Fortress Press, 1966).

2. Robert E. Willis, *The Ethics of Karl Barth* (Leiden: E. J. Brill, 1971).

3. Josef Fuchs, *Natural Law: A Theological Investigation* (New York: Sheed and Ward, 1965).

4. H. Richard Niebuhr, *Christ and Culture* (New York: Harper Torchbook, 1956), pp. 116-148.

5. *Mater et magistra,* n. 15. Throughout this chapter references to official church documents will also include the page references from Joseph Gremillion, ed., *The Gospel of Peace and Justice: Catholic Social Teaching Since Pope John* (Maryknoll, NY: Orbis Books, 1976). This reference is found on p. 147.

6. *Mater et magistra,* n. 30; Gremillion, p. 149.

7. *Mater et magistra,* n. 42; Gremillion, p. 151.

8. *Pacem in terris,* nn. 1-6; Gremillion, pp. 201-203.

9. *Pacem in terris,* n. 7; Gremillion, p. 203.

10. *Gaudium et spes,* n. 43; Gremillion, p. 278.

11. *Gaudium et spes,* nn. 74, 79, 89; Gremillion, pp. 310, 315, 325.

12. William J. Bergen, "The Evolution of the Pastoral Constitution on the Church in the Modern World: A Study in Moral Methodology" (S.T.D. diss., The Catholic University of America, 1971), pp. 241-291.

13. Mark G. McGrath, "Note storiche sulla Costituzione," in *La Chiesa nel mondo di oggi,* ed. Guilherme Baraúna (Florence: Vallechi, 1966), pp. 141-156; Charles Moeller, "History of the Constitution," in *Commentary on the Documents of Vatican II,* vol. 5: *Pastoral Constitution on the Church in the Modern World,* ed. Herbert Vorgrimler (New York: Herder and Herder, 1969), pp. 1-70.

14. Second General Conference of Latin American Bishops, *The Church in the Present-Day Transformation of Latin America in the Light of the Council,* vol. 2: *Conclusions* (Washington, D.C.: United States Catholic Conference, 1973).

15. David Little, "The Social Gospel Revisted," in *The Secular City Debate,* ed. Daniel Callahan (New York: Macmillan, 1966), pp. 69-74.

16. *Gaudium et spes,* nn. 22, 32; Gremillion, pp. 260-261, 268.

17. Chapter three of part one was almost completely rewritten at the last session of the council in the light of different criticisms,

including an overoptimism, a failure to appreciate the presence of sin, and a too-realized eschatology. See Moeller, "History of the Constitution," pp. 59ff.

18. Michael Novak, *The Spirit of Democratic Capitalism* (New York: Simon and Schuster, 1982), especially as found on pp. 337-358.

19. Stanley Hauerwas, *The Peaceable Kingdom* (Notre Dame, IN: University of Notre Dame Press, 1983).

20. Niebuhr, *Christ and Culture*, pp. 190-229.

21. John F. Cronin, *Social Principles and Economic Life*, rev. ed. (Milwaukee: Bruce Publishing Co., 1964), pp. 30-32.

22. *Justice in the World*, n. 6; Gremillion, p. 514.

23. Charles M. Murphy, "Action for Justice as Constitutive of the Preaching of the Gospel: What Did the 1971 Synod Mean?" *Theological Studies* 44 (1983): 298-311.

24. Donal Dorr, *Option for the Poor: A Hundred Years of Vatican Social Teaching* (Maryknoll, NY: Orbis Books, 1983).

25. For a discussion of the case of Sister Agnes Mary Mansour, see Richard A. McCormick, "Notes on Moral Theology," *Theological Studies* 45 (1984): 119-122.

26. "The Chicago Declaration of Christian Concern," in *Challenge to the Laity,* ed. Russell Barta (Huntington, IN: Our Sunday Visitor Press, 1980), pp. 19-25. This small book contains five essays commenting on this declaration.

27. J. Brian Benestad and Francis J. Butler, eds., *Quest for Justice: A Compendium of Statements of the United States Catholic Bishops on the Political and Social Order 1966-1980* (Washington, D.C.: United States Catholic Conference, 1981).

28. J. Brian Benestad, *The Pursuit of a Just Social Order: Policy Statements of the U.S. Catholic Bishops, 1966-1980.* (Washington, D.C.: Ethics and Public Policy Center, 1982).

29. *Justice in the World*, n. 40; Gremillion, p. 522.

30. For a fuller development of my position and for an overview of the contemporary debate see Charles E. Curran and Richard A. McCormick, eds., *Readings in Moral Theology No. 2: The Distinctiveness of Christian Ethics* (New York: Paulist Press, 1980).

31. Karl Rahner, *Foundations of Christian Faith: An Introduction to the Idea of Christianity* (New York: Crossroad Books, 1978).

3. American Catholic Social Ethics, 1880-1965

Catholic ethics in the United States has seldom reflected on its own historical development. Nevertheless, a Catholic social ethics did develop in this country and played a very significant role in the life of the church. Church historians have devoted time and energy to studying this movement, but unfortunately Catholic ethicists have not reflected on it. This chapter will not reduplicate the historical work that has already been done; nor will it consist primarily in explaining the substantive positions of different authors. Rather, the scope of this study is to analyze American Catholic social ethics from the perspective of the relationship between "American" and "Catholic" with special emphasis on the theological and ethical methodologies employed.

I. Historical Background

After 1880 there emerged what Aaron Abell, the foremost historian of American Catholic social thought, has described as Catholic social liberalism, which was to become the mainstream of Catholic social thought in the United States down to contemporary times. According to Abell three factors characterize Catholic social liberalism: a crusade for social justice, cooperation with non-Catholics and the rapid Americanization of the immigrants.[1]

In the nineteenth century the primary problem facing the

Catholic Church in the United States was its relationship to the American ethos. Could one be both Catholic and American at one and the same time?[2] This question has remained central down to the present day. Native and Protestant Americans tended to be suspicious of Roman Catholics who, as mostly an immigrant people, spoke often in a foreign language, constituted a distinct minority and owed allegiance to a foreign ruler. Prejudice, bias and even violence against these immigrants often existed in all parts of the United States. But there was another side to the dilemma. Rome tended to be suspicious of American Catholics. America was the land of freedom, but in the nineteenth century Roman Catholicism strongly attacked the concept of freedom that was then present in Europe. The problem of freedom, seen especially in terms of religious freedom, was to remain a source of tension until the 1960s.

In the earlier part of the nineteenth century the practical aspect of this question centered on the Americanization of the Catholic immigrants. Is the American ethos compatible with the Catholic faith? One side argued that the immigrant Catholics should maintain their language, their culture and their differences from other Americans. Any loss of distinctiveness would result in a loss of faith. Such a position was frequently taken by German-American Catholics.[3] The other side saw no incompatibility between the Catholic faith and the American ethos. In fact, Orestes Brownson and Isaac Hecker, the founder of the Paulists, saw American people in their environment and mentality as ripe for Catholic teaching and conversion provided only the teaching was properly understood and that some of the authoritarian rigidities that had arisen in reaction to the Protestant reform were rightly discarded. The hierarchical leadership of the American Catholic Church generally solved the problem in favor of the Americanization of the immigrants.[4]

In the last two decades of the nineteenth century the position asserting no basic incompatibility between American and Catholic was solidified and applied to questions of social ethics under the leadership of Bishops Ireland, Spalding, Keane and especially Cardinal Gibbons, the head of the

American hierarchy.[5] Four historical events of that period deserve mention here in this context. Most significant was the support given by Cardinal Gibbons and the American Catholic Church to the Knights of Labor. In July 1886 Rome reaffirmed its earlier condemnation of the Knights of Labor in the province of Quebec, Canada. Despite opposition from two of the eleven American archbishops, Gibbons, with prodding and support from Ireland and Keane, strongly defended the Knights of Labor in a memorandum submitted to the Congregation for the Propagation of the Faith, which in 1888 decreed that the Knights of Labor could be permitted and tolerated.[6]

Gibbons in his brief to the congregation responded to the charges of indifferentism and of dangers to the faith because the Knights of Labor were a nondenominational organization and Catholics would be mixed with Protestants, secularists and even atheists. Gibbons saw no ultimate harm coming from this, and he pointed out that only through organized effort could labor obtain justice. A condemnation of the Knights of Labor by the church would make the church appear to be against the poor and the worker, and also the church would be out of tune with the political powers in this country. The accusation of being un-American—that is to say, alien to our national spirit—is the most powerful weapon which the enemies of the church can employ against her. Supporting progressive reform and labor was both the American and the Catholic thing to do. Separate Catholic labor unions would be neither appropriate nor effective in this country.[7]

A second significant event concerned Fr. Edward McGlynn, a New York priest who was excommunicated by Archbishop Corrigan of New York for his support of Henry George. George, running for the office of mayor of New York in 1886, advocated a single tax theory according to which all the increased value of land should be taxed. Since increased land value was not attributed to the owner, it should be given back to the people in the form of taxes. Corrigan also attempted to place George's book *Progress and Poverty* on the index. The more liberal bishops were upset with the excommunication of McGlynn because it played into the hands of those who would condemn the church as being against the poor and as not allowing freedom of political thought within the church. Here again the liberals ultimately won. The McGlynn case was reopened in 1892, and he was ultimately reconciled with the church. The Holy Office decreed that Henry George's doctrines were deserving of condemnation but refrained from promulgating and officially making public the decree.[8]

Circumstances surrounding two national, lay Catholic congresses in Baltimore in 1889 and in Chicago in 1893 showed the same approach. The speakers, especially in the Chicago congress, definitely favored social reform, opposed the abuses of excessive wealth and defended the rights of the worker. The bishops took care to make sure that the congresses adopted a more liberal, reform-minded tone and avoided controversial issues such as the temporal power of the papacy. In his address to the 1893 Columbian Catholic Congress in Chicago, Archbishop Satolli, the papal delegate to the United States, urged the delegates to go forward with one hand bearing the book of Christian truth and the other the Constitution of the United States.[9]

In the last decade of the nineteenth century American Catholic liberals (to use the term of Professor Robert Cross) had to yield some ground, especially in terms of Roman approval. There were different causes: exaggerations and misunderstandings of what liberals such as Ireland, Keane and Hecker stood for; hyperbolic and flamboyant statements by American liberals; political pressure from conservatives in Europe and in the United States. In 1899 Pope Leo XIII sent a letter to Cardinal Gibbons (*Testem benevolentiae*) condemning ideas associated with Americanism—the need to modify doctrines in accord with the times in order to attract converts; a deemphasizing of external guidance, of the supernatural, of passive virtues and of religious vows; discussions with heretics.[10]

The liberals responded that these positions were not really held in the United States but were misunderstandings based on defective translations of Hecker's writings. Conservatives replied that the letter was badly needed to correct abuses in

America. At the very minimum the condemnation showed how American Catholics continually had to struggle to overcome the suspicions of Americanism on the part of Roman authorities and European Catholics.[11] Undoubtedly Leo's letter had an effect in dampening the cause of the American liberals, especially in the area of doctrine, but it does not seem to have seriously affected the more practical question of social ethics and the working with non-Catholics on common societal concerns. Thus history shows the problematic that faced the American Catholic Church in general and social ethics in particular—the compatibility or incompatibility between Catholic and American.

II. Catholic Ethical Methodology

Catholic theology itself provided an impetus to the approach which saw basic compatibility between the American ethos and environment and the Catholic understanding. Especially from the time of Leo XIII Catholic social ethics had been developed methodologically in terms of natural law theory. In theological ethics the first methodological question concerns the source of ethical wisdom and knowledge for the Christian. Catholic theology has traditionally accepted that ethics is based on faith and reason, on revelation and on natural law; but the primary, and at times almost the sole, emphasis has been on natural law.[12] Chapter Two showed that the acceptance of reason, the human, and natural law in the Catholic tradition is grounded in the importance of mediation.

Perhaps the best example of the Catholic approach is seen in the introduction of Pope John XXIII's encyclical *Pacem in terris* issued in 1963. The laws governing human existence are to be found in the nature of man where the father of all things wrote them. The creator has imprinted in man's heart an order which conscience reveals to him and enjoins him to obey. By these innate laws human beings are taught how to live in peace and harmony with other human beings in human society. Such an approach is not based on scripture, revelation and redemption but primarily on reason, nature and creation. If anything, nature and supernature are clearly separate and almost dichotomized, so that the social life of the Christian is seen almost exclusively in terms of nature.[13]

Such an approach stresses what the Catholic or Christian shares with all others — human nature and human reason. The distinctively Christian aspect of the supernatural, grace and redemption does not enter decisively into the picture. Consequently such a methodology opens the door to recognize that in theory one shares much ethical wisdom and knowledge with all human beings and in practice Catholics could collaborate and cooperate with all people of goodwill to work for justice and peace. Pope Leo XIII in his famous encyclical *Rerum novarum* of 1891 on the condition of the workers appeals to this "common opinion of mankind . . . found in the careful study of nature and in the laws of nature."[14] The natural law thus provides a bridge by which American Catholics can find agreement in theory and collaboration in practice with other Americans in working for the betterment of society.

Rerum novarum also provided the basic substantive positions for much of what characterized the mainstream of American Catholic social ethics in the twentieth century. Such an ethic proposes a middle course between the evils of laissez faire capitalism, which so exalts the freedom of individuals that it forgets about justice and obligations to others, and the opposite evil of socialism, which so stresses the collective that the rights of the individual are trampled on. The pope supported nonrevolutionary labor unionism as a means for obtaining justice for the worker. The state has a positive role to intervene and make sure that justice is protected through social legislation, although the state cannot take over functions belonging to others. Thus both the unique situation of the Catholic Church in the United States and the theological methodology employed in Catholic social ethics set the stage for the mainstream approach of American Catholic social ethics which can properly be described as reformist and gradualist. Yes, there were some problems and difficulties in the American economic and political system, but the American system was not radically out of tune with Catholic ethics. Catholics collaborating with others in society could bring about the necessary reforms of the existing structures.

III. John A. Ryan

The best illustration of the mainstream of reforming or liberal Catholic social thought can be found in the Bishops' Program of Social Reconstruction issued by the Administrative Committee of the National Catholic War Council on February 11, 1919. This forward-looking document was very much in tune with the progressive reforming element in American society in the first two decades of the twentieth century.

Rather than proposing a comprehensive scheme of reconstruction, the bishops focused on those reforms that seemed desirable and obtainable within a reasonable period of time. The short-term aspects of the program called for: continuation of the United States Employment Service to deal with unemployment after the war; continuation 'of the National War Labor Board with its emphasis on a living wage and labor's right to organize; sustaining the present wage scales; housing for the working class; reduction of the cost of living with government checks on monopolies and perhaps even government competition for monopolies; an enactment of a legal minimum wage; provision by the state for insurance against illness, unemployment, old age and other disabilities; labor participation in industrial management; vocational training; state laws against child labor. In the light of the defects of the present system fundamental and long-term reforms were mentioned—cooperation, copartnership and the call for the majority of workers to become owners, at least in part, of the instruments of production. However, the primary emphasis was on the gradualist approach. Some even condemned the approach as being socialistic, but this is not an accurate description of what is primarily a progressive and reform-minded document. Notice, too, how its appeal based on reason alone was to all people and contained little that was distinctively Christian except for a closing paragraph calling for a reform in spirit and a return to Christian life and Christian institutions.[15]

The author of the document was John A. Ryan, who for almost half a century was a leader and symbol of liberal, reforming social Catholicism. As author of important theoretical works such as *A Living Wage* (1906) and *Distributive Justice* (1916) and as a professor at The Catholic University of America, he was a leader in Catholic social theory.[16] As director of the Social Action Department of the National Catholic Welfare Conference from 1920 until his death in 1945, he educated Catholics, directed programs and actively collaborated with many people on a practical level in pursuing his goals of social reform. There were occasional problems with some more conservative members of the American hierarchy, but Ryan remained a firm spokesperson in the cause of social reform and justice—one whose views were appreciated by Catholics and non-Catholics alike.[17]

A more detailed evaluation of Ryan's ethical methodology will show how such an approach was appropriate for the substantive ethics of a reformer or liberal who accepted the fundamental goodness of the American system, pointed out deficiencies and believed that people of goodwill could work together to bring about the required changes toward a greater social justice.[18]

First, Ryan employed a natural law theory which from the theological perspective meant an emphasis on human nature and human reason. At best one finds in *A Living Wage*, Ryan's doctoral thesis first published in 1906, a very occasional reference to or citation from scripture, but there is no sustained development of a biblical theology. Such a methodological approach is completely different from that of his contemporary, the Protestant social gospel theoretist Walter Rauschenbusch, whose first significant work on social ethics, *Christianity and the Social Crisis*, was published by Macmillan, Ryan's publisher, in 1907.[19] Rauschenbusch based his ethics primarily on the concept of the kingdom of God and making that kingdom present in this world, and he moved from the biblical teaching to moral conclusions. A little later Ryan wrote that he disagreed with the Protestant approach which too often identified religion with humanitarianism. The kingdom of God is in heaven, and the church is primarily interested in the salvation of souls in comparison with which temporal goods are utterly insignificant. The church must teach us how we are to live in this present world, and this explains the social mission of the church and its function in teaching social ethics.[20] Ryan's own works were generally well received and well reviewed in the secular press, especially by progressives who agreed wholeheartedly with his reforming proposals and the reasons on which they were based.[21]

Second, Catholic natural law theory emphasizes order and harmony. The divine plan, or law, is itself an ordering. The vision shaped by natural law theory does not see relationships in terms of hostility, opposition and conflict but rather understands that all are called to work together harmoniously for the common good, which then redounds to the good of the individual. In Catholic natural law theory there is no opposition between the common good and one's individual good. Ryan's major work on *Distributive Justice,* first published in 1916, follows this basic approach by considering the proper distribution of the products of industry among the four classes that contribute to these products—landowners, capitalists, businessmen and laborers.[22]

Ryan added his own distinctive developments to the basic natural law emphasis on harmony and balance—the principle of expediency. The ultimate test of the morality of any social system is its bearing on human welfare. In the matter of social institutions moral values and genuine expediency are in the long run identical.[23] Ryan the economist and Ryan the ethicist collaborated to work out this theory of harmony and expediency. Influenced by John A. Hobson, an economist from The Johns Hopkins University, and others, Ryan proposed an economic theory of underconsumption according to which prosperity exists in our society only if the wage earners have the money to buy goods.[24] The payment of a living wage is a moral obligation based on the rights of the individual laborer to the goods of creation, but industry by paying such a living wage to all its workers will thereby secure its own continued prosperity. Good morality and good economics are in harmony. Ryan in 1932 declared it a fundamental task for Catholic Action "to bring about the identification of morality and expediency in our industrial system, by persuading all classes that prosperity cannot be maintained unless the receivers of wages and salaries obtain a considerable increase in purchasing power."[25]

Third, Catholic natural law theory sees the state as a natural society based on the social nature of human beings who are called to band together with others to accomplish what as individuals they cannot do. Again there is a basic harmony between the individual and the state, not an opposition as if the state had the primarily negative function of preventing sinful human beings from harming one another. Ryan maintains that the end of the state is to promote the welfare of its citizens, as a whole, as members of families and as members of social classes. Thus Ryan readily calls upon the state to bring about a greater justice in industrial relations by legislating a minimum wage, prohibiting child labor, and providing for insurance against unemployment and disabilities. This dependence and reliance on the state as the primary factor in social reform is characteristic of Ryan's thought, especially before 1931.

Fourth, Ryan insisted on distributive justice as the primary category, not commutative justice, which views the problem too narrowly in terms of the rights of one individual vis-à-vis another. In accord with this position Ryan maintained that the primary ethical consideration rests on the fact that the goods of creation exist for all human beings. This primary consideration governs everything else. As a result Ryan stressed more the limits of private property than did the early papal encyclicals. The natural right of ownership is always qualified by the higher common right of use which is based on the universal destiny of the goods of creation for all human beings. In Ryan's understanding of property the emphasis is on the human person's needs as the primary title to property.[26]

Private ownership (he considered private ownership

primarily in terms of land ownership) is a natural right, but of the third kind or class. Private ownership is not an intrinsic good (a right of the first class such as life); nor is it directly necessary for any individual (like marriage as a natural right of the second class). Private land ownership is necessary as a social institution providing for the general welfare and hence is indirectly necessary for the welfare of the individual. This is what Ryan meant by calling it a natural right of the third class. The utlimate justification for private property in Ryan's thought lay in its ability to obtain the end, or objective, of property better than any other system.[27] Some have disagreed and pointed out that Ryan should have based his argument for private property more on metaphysical considerations and the inherent rights of the human person.[28]

Fifth, John Ryan's natural law methodology was much more inductive and empirical than the natural law of the manuals of Catholic theology—a fact that was heavily influenced by his teachers Thomas Bouquillon in moral theology and William Kerby in sociology.[29] Some of the features already alluded to fit in with a more inductive methodology. Ryan was an economist and acknowledged the limits of dealing with ethical problems merely in the light of philosophy and theology. The acceptance of the public welfare as the determining criterion, the principle of expediency, and the use of economics to determine what was expedient in practice all characterized his more inductive understanding of natural law. A more inductive methodology will always be more in tune with the existing situation even though reforms are called for.

On the basis of his ethical methodology one can see how Ryan was a liberal, a reformer and the leading figure in American Catholic social liberalism in the first half of the twentieth century. There is no doubt that Ryan and his followers were far out in front of the majority of Catholics, and often their thoughts were not translated into either teaching or action at the grass-roots level. At the same time Ryan was frequently under attack from conservative groups and individuals both inside and outside the church.

Ryan was not a radical but a reformer who tried to change

and modify the system with the help of much broad-based support. Unlike many reformers, however, he was apparently never satisfied with the changes and reforms that were made. In my judgment his methodology kept him always open to demanding new and further reforms. Although his basic theory did not change much after his more theoretical writings in the first two decades of the twentieth century, there was a development in his understanding of the reforms necessary in keeping with what was required by the public welfare. Patrick Gearty points up four different phases in the development of Ryan's thought on the economic order. The first stage extending to 1913 emphasized legislative reform to combat social problems. Beginning with his debate with the socialist Hillquit, Ryan advocated a more widespread ownership of property so that workers would become part owners of the tools they used. After World War I he developed a third stage called industrial democracy and advocated labor's sharing in management, profits and ownership. The fourth phase after Pope Pius XI's encyclical *Quadragesimo anno* of 1931 advocated the occupational group system.[30]

However, many of the criticisms and defects of a reforming position and of natural law theory apply to Ryan's theory. From the theological perspective he obviously did not integrate the supernatural and the natural orders as well as subsequent theology is trying to do. Likewise, Ryan's theory tends to forget the reality of sin and its many ramifications in human lives and relationships. His emphasis on social and institutional reform seems to imply that there is no great need for change on the part of individuals. Personalists contend that the primary center for change is the heart of the individual person and that it is not enough just to talk about changing the structures of society. In addition, his perspective did not allow him to see the deeper incompatibilities that might be existing between the American economic system and the gospel message, or in his case the natural law. The other approaches to be explained later involve further criticisms of Ryan's approach.

One final point of historical importance deserves mention in this context. The election of 1928 with the defeat of Al Smith brought out many anti-Catholic prejudices and saddened Ryan immensely because he thought these attacks against Catholics were totally unfair and uncalled for.[31] Ryan himself became a part of the controversy as opponents of Smith cited Ryan's book on *The State and the Church,* which upheld in theory the obligation of the state to support the one, true church, although it pointed out that in practice this had application only to the completely Catholic state. Ryan himself doubted that such a state still existed in the world, and certainly not in the United States today. Most probably such an obligation would never apply in the American future, but one cannot yield on principles of unchanging and eternal truth. Logically it could happen even in the United States that non-Catholic sects may so dissolve to such a point that the political proscription of these may become feasible and expedient.[32] Ryan who had done so much to advance the cause of Roman Catholicism in the eyes of many non-Catholics in the United States because of his efforts at reform of the social economic order was not able to bridge this gap between Catholicism and Americanism with regard to the political order and the question of religious liberty. Religious liberty would still remain a problem for Roman Catholics in the United States for a few more years.

IV. German-American Catholics

In addition to the mainstream approach exemplified by the reformist and gradualist approach of Ryan there were two other significant approaches in the first half of the twentieth century that deserve mention—the German-American Catholics and the Catholic Worker Movement. German-American Catholics formed a Central Verein in 1855 as a national federation of all the German Catholic benevolent societies existing throughout the country especially on the parish level. The group took an interest in social reform in the light of the injustices of the industrial order and established the Central Bureau in 1909 to carry out this work. A journal *Central-Blatt and Social Justice* was started to publish articles in both German and English to educate the members about social justice. The leading individual in the movement was Frederick P. Kenkel, who was the key figure in the formation of the Central Bureau and remained its active director until his death in 1952 at the age of 88. Kenkel and the Central Bureau have been described as conservative reformers—but their general conservativism in all matters made them much more discontent with the existing industrial society in the United States and therefore more radical in their reform proposals than the liberal or meliorist reformers in the mainstream.[33]

In opposition to both capitalism and socialism they advocated a fundamental reorganization of society based on a corporate, or organic, society which called for a hierarchical ordering of all elements in society in which the state respected the lesser social groupings and did not usurp their functions. The economic order was to be run by vocational groups in which labor and capital were not opposed to one another as in the more liberal approach but in which labor, capital and management working together in a particular industry were united in running that industry for the common good of all.[34]

Again, both their understanding of the relationship between Catholicism and the American ethos and their theological methodology influenced the conclusions to which they came. In the basic question of the relationship between Catholic and American the German-American Catholics stressed much more the differences and incompatibilities. They had generally opposed the rapid Americanization of the immigrants, and they held onto their language, customs, social groupings and their faith. In fact the Central Verein as an organization fostered this German consciousness. They were not readily disposed to accept Americanization, and their journal often pointed out the problems with the idea of freedom behind the political and economic orders in American society. German-American Catholics feared liberalizing Catholics went too far in their acceptance of things American. They also brought with them from Germany their traditional suspicions of and even hostility toward Protestantism, so that they were not willing to work together with Protestant groups, even with German Protestant groups.

From their German origins many learned opposition to the entire nineteenth-century liberalism and its ramifications in political, social and economic life. In reacting against the nineteenth-century political, social and economic development, German-American Catholics often embraced a romanticism which glorified the Middle Ages and the past. There was a heavy emphasis on agrarianism and the evils of the city and the industrial world.[35] Kenkel himself has been described as a romantic and utopian who gradually became even more alienated from American culture and industrial society. Kenkel was heavily influenced by some German-Catholic thinkers, especially by Karl von Vogelsang, a romantic visionary who proposed an extreme corporatism in Germany in the nineteenth century.[36] Von Vogelsang's solidaristic opinions in Germany in the nineteenth century differed from the more realistic and reforming approach of Hitz and of the later von Kettler.[37]

Although *Central-Blatt and Social Justice* was not a theological journal as such, theological methodology definitely influenced the position of the Central Verein. They too employed the natural law method which appealed to reason and human nature and not to the supernatural and revelation. However, their approach to natural law was more deductive and abstract in comparison with Ryan's more inductive and concrete methodology. Beginning with the concept of human nature, the human person and society, the solidarists deduced the way in which such a society should be structured. The traditional emphasis of Catholic theology on hierarchical ordering and harmony in this theory resulted in the call for an organic society in which all the parts work together for the good of the whole.[38]

Ever fearful of socialism, they insisted on what was later called the principle of subsidiarity, which limited intervention by the state and left many things in the hands of intermediate bodies. Kenkel, for example, opposed Ryan's call for a constitutional amendment to prevent child labor because he saw it as undue exercise of the power of the federal government in a matter that should be handled on the local level, even though he himself was opposed to child labor.[39]

Such a deductive, abstract approach also influenced their stance concerning how change is to be brought about. The ideal proposed is quite critical of the existing structures, but little or nothing is said about how to effectuate their program in practice. Kenkel and the Central Verein were opposed to the gradualist approach of the mainstream liberals as exemplified in the latter's calling upon the state to legislate reform and in their strong backing for labor unions. Not only were these reforms not radical enough for Kenkel but they actually hindered the ultimate achievement of the corporate society. Unfortunately, the Verein never did address the question of how this ultimate reform was to be brought about.

Another weakness of such a method concerns its abstract, universalist and ahistorical approach. No one can ever approach reality from such an impartial and universal perspective. We are all the creatures of our own historical and cultural times and places, so that we should never be deceived into thinking that ours is a perfectly neutral, universal and abstract perspective. In fact, it seems the romantic vision of the medieval world actually influenced and colored the method and conclusions of the Verein. The idea of society which they deduced from their understanding of the nature of the human person and of human society was that medieval ordering to which they were so attracted.

The approach and the conclusions of Kenkel and the Central Bureau stand in contrast and even in opposition to the mainstream liberal approach. Their influence unfortunately was limited to the German community, and in the last few years the *Social Justice Review* (this new name was given in 1940) seems to have lost its social vision and concentrated on decrying the abuses of the contemporary church and world.

V. The Catholic Worker

A second significant position differing from the mainstream liberal reformers is associated with the Catholic Worker Movement, which is truly a movement inspired by Peter

Maurin and Dorothy Day and not an organization. This movement, which began in 1933, is often characterized as radical because of its opposition to the existing social and economic order. In place of the structures of the contemporary industrial society they proposed to establish farming communes which would put into practice the axiom from each according to abilities and to each according to need and also to found houses of hospitality in which committed Catholics, voluntarily sharing the lot of the poor, offer food and shelter to the victims of industrial society. They propagated their ideas through discussions and through their paper *The Catholic Worker* started by Dorothy Day in 1933 and still published today.[40]

In terms of cultural influences there were not the dramatic and well-defined characteristics which colored the approach of Kenkel and the Central Verein. Perhaps the most significant factor that influenced the movement and others similar to it was the depression. The depression beginning in 1929 showed up the inequities of the economic system and the need for change. To Dorothy Day and her followers problems caused by the depression merely highlighted the radical incompatibility between the gospel and the existing industrial order.[41]

Dorothy Day and Peter Maurin were convinced of the need continually to clarify their ideas and communicate them with others, but neither of them pretended to be a theologian or an ethician. Perhaps the most systematic statement of their approach is found in the writings of Paul Hanly Furfey, a sociologist from The Catholic University of America who wrote a number of books explaining the approach of Catholic personalism or radicalism from the 1930s to the present.[42] Although Dorothy Day and Peter Maurin never developed their approach in any systematic or theological way, the general outlines of their understanding are quite clear.

The Catholic radicals did not employ a natural law approach but instead adopted a method based entirely on the scriptures and the supernatural. Furfey himself called for a supernatural sociology and a pistic society emphasizing the unique importance of grace, redemption and the supernatural.[43] Their

approach was distinctively Christian and Catholic, highlighting the differences with all other approaches and eschewing
cooperation with others that would merely result in watering
down the gospel message. Not reform but radical change was
necessary because the existing social and economic orders
were basically incompatible with the gospel message.

The inequities of the system stand out starkly in the light of
the eschatological ethics based on the gospel teaching of Jesus.
The Catholic Worker constantly stresses the horrible condition of
the poor and the unequal distribution of wealth in our society.
From the very beginning they pointed out the horrendous
injustices based on racism in American culture. They were
strong pacifists and even lost leadership and followers because
of Dorothy Day's continued support of pacifism during World
War II.[44]

Christian personalism characterized the Catholic Worker
approach. First, the heart of the individual had to be changed.
The basic problems were much deeper than mere structural
reform, for all first had to be willing to accept the gospel and
practice a harsh and dreadful love. By voluntary poverty one
shows one's love and solidarity with the poor. In accord with
personalism one must respect the freedom of others, for too
often the objective world impinges itself on the individual and
turns the individual into an object. They were very much
opposed to structure in any form even in their own movement,
since they looked upon structure as a source of objectivization
and the denial of the personal. For this reason they, unlike the
liberals, were very much opposed to state intervention and
even gloried at times in the name of anarchist. A true com-
munitarism could be built only on a true personalism.

The approach of the Catholic Worker stressed the notion of
gospel witness and was based on a deontological understanding that the Christian must bear witness to the gospel no matter
what happens. As a result, they were not primarily interested
in the effectiveness of the approach which they adopted. Some
Christian radicals in the contemporary environment have
tended to stress more the gospel as an effective means of social
change. The Catholic Workers did not deny the effectiveness

of the gospel, but they saw their role primarily as one of bearing witness to the gospel and letting God bring about whatever God would want in his own good time. As an effective means of social change to be embraced by many, it seems that the Catholic Worker Movement will never receive high grades. However, as a witness to a belief which involves a strong, personal commitment, the Catholic Worker Movement evokes the admiration of most people.

Their insistence on a social ethic based on eschatology and on the scriptures tends to result in fundamentalistic and overly simplistic solutions. They make no effort at any kind of reform of the people who come to them because they think this would be against their tenets of personalism. For fear of coercing and taking away the freedom of the individual does the Catholic Worker Movement really fail to engage the person in the depths of one's own being? Christian love seems much more complex than the Catholic Worker recognizes. Also one can question if such an eschatological ethic really appreciates the imperfections and the conflicts which will continue to exist in the present world in which we live. To her credit Dorothy Day herself acknowledged inconsistencies in her own approach because it is ultimately impossible to live out the full eschatological gospel message at all times. However, there are other Christians who wonder if one does not have to take a more realistic approach to the world in which we live.

VI. The Mainstream after World War II

In the first half of the twentieth century John A. Ryan symbolized and led the mainstream position of American Catholic social liberalism with its willingness to accept a compatibility between the American system and Catholic ethics, although it constantly called for continuing reform in the economic area in order to improve the system. After Ryan's death and after World War II this approach continued but seems to have lost some of its reforming zeal and to have accepted even more the basic compatibility between being

American and being Catholic. Historical circumstances again influenced this changing emphasis.

The economic inequalities and inadequacies which the depression pointed up were never structurally solved. Increased productivity and consumption connected with World War II brought a new and greater prosperity to Americans in general, so that the problem of structural change did not seem acute. The general prosperity affected Roman Catholics, who after the war truly moved into the middle class of American society with many able to buy a house in the suburbs, to own a car perhaps for the first time, and to send their children to college. The American dream was apparently becoming true for many Catholics who were no longer on the bottom of the economic and social ladder in this country.

After the war American and Catholic interests merged even more in the common fight against communism. Catholics had long before pointed out the danger of communism and were accused by many in the 1930s of siding with fascist and totalitarian regimes because of their fear of the communist menace. In the late 1940s and 1950s the United States and the Roman Catholic Church were identified as the two bastions of the free world standing up to the communist menace. All these factors influenced the approach of Catholic social ethics at this time.

John F. Cronin, a Sulpician priest with a doctorate in economics, continued the Ryan tradition as the best-known American Catholic author dealing with problems of economic and social justice. Cronin was also assistant director of the Social Action Department of the National Catholic Welfare Conference. He wrote textbooks on economic problems and books on Catholic social principles and Catholic social action. His best known work which was often used as a textbook in Catholic colleges and seminaries in his *Social Principles and Economic Life* published in 1959, after having been published in a slightly different form in 1950, and later revised in 1964 to include the social thought of Pope John XXIII as expressed in his two encyclicals *Mater et magistra* and *Pacem in terris*.

Cronin continued the methodology and approach of John

A. Ryan, but there were significant differences in part attrib-
utable to the changing circumstances mentioned above. Cronin placed much greater weight on authoritative church
teaching than did Ryan—although this significant methodological development of giving more importance to authoritative church teaching had gradually been developed
over the years in Roman Catholic social thought, including
Ryan's. Cronin began each chapter with excerpts of authoritative papal and episcopal statements on the particular topic, and
after having set out this teaching, he then followed with his
own development of the issues. Looking back at Ryan, it is
amazing how few references he has in his major theoretical
writings to the papal documents, and how they in no way
occupy the central place in the development of his thought.
One can understand how even Ryan as the years went on
appealed more and more to papal teaching to give his own
thought more of an authoritative weight and acceptance in the
Catholic Church.

Although continuing to call for reform, Cronin is also more
apologetic and defensive about the American system than
Ryan was. In speaking about social problems today, Cronin
pointed out that the competitive individualism of the post-
medieval period is no longer the dominant form in our society
and that great changes have occurred in our economic structure. However, three points have become particularly clear in
the mid-1960s—the persistence of poverty in certain areas, the
increasing challenge of automation and the stubborn fact of
unemployment. These points should not belittle the achieve-
ments of the American economic system, but they indicate that
social reform is an ongoing challenge. Our living standards are
unquestionably high. The problem of income distribution has
been greatly improved, and more Americans have moved into
the middle class. But we cannot be complacent because material prosperity can never be the ultimate goal of society. The
objectives of Pope Pius XI still remain true—the need for an
organized effort to serve the common good and greater
cooperation in economic life.[45]

Cronin's methodological approach is less dynamic and more

static than Ryan's, so that the reforms he indicates are not as great. In the 1950 version of his work Cronin strongly defends Pope Pius XI's program of the organic or corporate society as the ideal type to be brought about in practice here in the United States.[46] But by 1964 Cronin changed views and agreed with Pope John XXIII's giving in his encyclicals only a passing mention to Pope Pius XI's program for organized economic life. According to Cronin Pope John's approach is more practical, pastoral and evolutionary.[47] However, both Pope John and Cronin are much more optimistic about the entire economic structure and order than was Pius XI. In contrast to Ryan, Cronin in his day is very suspicious of the dangers of overcentralized power in the state and often warns against giving too much of a role to the state, even though Pope John called for more state intervention than had his predecessors.[48]

Cronin was still a reformer in the order of social justice, but he was less a reformer than John A. Ryan. The practical involvements of the two individuals well illustrate this point. John Ryan was labeled by some as a socialist. He anticipated the reforms of the New Deal and later cooperated with many of the New Deal programs. His biographer used as the title of the life of Ryan an accurate and, in this author's view, obviously laudatory description of Ryan—the Right Reverend New Dealer—first used in derision by Father Charles Coughlin. On the other hand, John Cronin was acknowledged as their expert on communism by the American Catholic bishops, with whom he worked to fight communism. He became friendly with Congressman Richard Nixon in his crusade against communism and helped him in the Hiss case. Cronin later became the primary speech writer for Nixon when he was vice-president, although this working relationship did not continue after 1960.[49]

It should also be pointed out that the changing times should also have brought a greater awareness of changing issues and problems. The central problem was no longer the plight of the worker. On the national scene there was the growing recognition of the tremendous problem of racism and the continuing poverty of many people in the midst of the American plenty.

Cronin to his credit recognized these problems but really did not emphasize them, and they received a comparatively cursory treatment from him. In addition, as was becoming clear in some of the papal statements at the time, it was now necessary to consider problems in a worldwide perspective and not just on the basis of a local or national outlook. What effect does the American economic system have on the rest of the world? These problems were certainly present in the 1950s and early 1960s and were being raised by some people, but again one must recognize that they only became conscious problems to many in the subsequent years.

VII. John Courtney Murray

The theologian who contributed the most to solving the problematic of the compatibility of Catholic and American was the Jesuit John Courtney Murray. Murray was more of a systematic and academic theologian than any of the others considered so far. He concentrated more on the political aspect of the question than on the economic aspect. In his own mind Murray proved there was a total compatibility between being American and being Catholic. To the Roman ecclesiastics he showed that religious liberty as practiced in the United States is compatible with Catholic thought. To non-Catholic Americans he argued that Catholics have no difficulty accepting the American political system because it is based on natural law.

Murray's work in religious liberty was preceded by an interesting debate between himself and Paul Hanly Furfey on the question of intercredal cooperation. Murray understood intercredal cooperation, as he was discussing it in the early 1940s, as the working together of people of different creeds in the interest of social justice and reconstruction. It is precisely the natural law which Catholics hold in common with all others which is the basis of a cooperation animated by the common religious tenets and beliefs that are held. Mixed or intercredal cooperation is based, not on the supernatural, divine unity of the hierarchical church, but rather on the natural, spiritual unity of the human race which recognizes belief in God as the fundamental principle of the social order and upholds obedience to that moral order. To be effective such work needs to be organized, and the organization itself can be interconfessional without any danger of indifferentism or of *communicatio in sacris*.[50]

As it might be expected, Furfey held the opposite position. We have been ineffective in changing society precisely because we have been too uncritically cooperative with others. In being overanxious to cooperate with liberals and others we have kept our distinctively Catholic social doctrine in the background. We need to become more aggressively Catholic, not less.[51] Note how the different methodological approaches have influenced the substantative question.

The Murray-Furfey debate actually centered quite heavily on the interpretation of papal documents, especially *Singulari quadam* of Pope Pius X issued in 1912 in response to a question in Germany of whether Catholics could participate in non-Catholic (mixed or neutral) trade unions.[52] Murray interprets the document's conclusion that such participation can be tolerated and permitted as acknowledging the legitimacy of such organized interconfessional activity. Furfey interprets the document not as acceptance and encouragement of such organized cooperation but as a reluctant toleration much like the toleration of mixed marriages. Murray brings to his interpretation of the document an historical, critical hermeneutic—the need to sort out the doctrinal principles from the contingent historical aspects of the question. The pope according to Murray balances off the two poles of the unity of the church and of a concern for the common good to accept ultimately a social peace (not a unity of faith) based on a practical agreement on fundamental religious and ethical principles.

In addition to illustrating how different methodologies approach the practical ramifications of the question of being Catholic and American, this controversy has an importance beyond itself because it indicates the methodological approach which Murray himself would ultimately develop in dealing with the question of religious liberty. The four important elements present in this debate which were further developed by Murray are: natural law, an historical understanding of natural law, recognition that a social peace in the political order does not imply a unity of faith but can coexist with different faiths, and an historical, critical hermeneutic as applied to authoritative papal statements.

According to Murray the church-state and religious liberty questions must be seen in the light of the Catholic tradition which asserts both the distinction between the church and state and the harmony (*concordia*) between the two. The concept of natural law with its recognition of the distinction between the order of grace and the order of nature strongly calls for a distinction between the secular order and the sacred order. One can and should distinguish between the two societies—the church and the state.[53] But what about the harmony between them? In 1945 Murray approached the problem of religious liberty under its ethical aspect and saw the following as important factors in the solution of the problem: God, the moral law, human conscience, and the state (civil authority and its function of effectively directing citizens to the common good of the organized community).[54] However, in his consideration of the state Murray accepts the fact that the state as such has an obligation toward God—to acknowledge God as its author, to worship Him as He wills to be worshipped and to subject its official life and action to His law. The state has the obligation directly to promote public religion and morality as central elements of the common good. From such a perspective Murray could only affirm the basic outline of the older Catholic approach to religious liberty.[55]

As he himself mentions later, his final position rests on acknowledging the distinction between society and the state. The state plays only a limited role within society, for it is only one order within society—the order of public law and public administration. There follows from this the important distinction between the common good which is the care of society as a whole and the more limited concept of public order whose care devolves on the state and which consists in an order of justice, an order of public peace and an order of public morality. Murray is here describing the limited constitutional state.[56]

Natural law theory without further modification was not enough to prove religious liberty, especially if one wants to acknowledge that the state as such has obligations toward God. What was needed was a more historically conscious understanding of natural law. A more historically conscious methodology begins not with an abstract notion of the state from which it deduces certain obligations but with the existing concrete reality, in this case the limited constitutional state. Here was the key methodological and substantive point in solving the problem of religious liberty.[57] The function of the state is limited and does not extend into areas beyond its competency, which is the peace of the earthly city. Yes, there is a harmony between the two societies (the church and the state), and the state does have the obligation of the care of religion; but this is fulfilled when the order of constitutional law recognizes, guarantees and protects the freedom of the church.[58]

Religious freedom understood in this perspective differs completely from the religious freedom often proposed in Europe by Continental liberalism and condemned by the popes. The first amendment of the American constitution with its nonestablishment clause is neither an article of faith nor of theology but rather an article of peace. The first amendment thus corresponds to the need for the public peace and consequently is good law based on the limited function of constitutional government. Continental liberalism upheld the juridical omnipotence and omnicompetence of the state and left no room at all for the church and the order of the sacred. The Continental theory of the omnicompetent state derived from a philosophy that extolled the autonomy of reason and had no room for religion or the church. In the American system of a limited constitutional government the separation of church and state was based on articles of peace and not on faith in the autonomy of reason.[59]

A large portion of Murray's writings on church and state

concentrated on interpreting through an historical, critical method the authoritative teaching of the church especially as it was expressed in the encyclicals and documents of Pope Leo XIII. According to Murray one must recognize the historical-polemical aspect of Leo's writing based on his attack on Continental liberalism with its omnicompetent state. The doctrinal aspect in Leo's writings includes the concept of the two societies, the freedom of the church, the state as based on human nature, the need for harmony between the two societies and the orderly cooperation between the two societies.[60]

Murray contends that Leo's defense of the confessional state belongs to the polemical-historical aspect rather than the doctrinal aspect of his teaching and that Leo XIII himself recognized this fact.[61] The condemnation of the separation of church and state likewise belongs to the polemical-historical part of his writings, since it is based on the particular realities of Continental liberalism.[62] Murray's historical, critical approach and his acceptance of the development of doctrine definitely paved the way for the fathers of Vatican II, who ultimately were able to adopt a new approach to religious liberty.[63] From a contemporary perspective Murray's brilliant theory of development solved the problem of change in Catholic teaching too easily. It is necessary to acknowledge some error in the teaching of Leo XIII.

In theory, John Courtney Murray was able to remove one of the most significant obstacles in the way of reconciling the Catholic understanding and the American political order and ethos. John Ryan had been unable to do this, but Murray by employing a more historically conscious natural law approach (Ryan had worked in the economic area with a more inductive and historically minded approach) was able to solve the dilemma and recognize that religious freedom could be totally reconciled with the Catholic self-understanding.

But the final victory was not yet achieved merely on the basis of Murray's writings. In the middle 1950s Murray was forbidden by Roman authorities to write any more on this particular topic. It was only after many struggles at the Second Vatican

Council that the church officially accepted the teaching on religious liberty, even though the drafts originally proposed to the council went against such a teaching. Religious liberty was *the* American issue at the council both in terms of the American public and press and the concern of the American bishops. Murray himself had no part in the preconciliar debates, nor was he invited to the first session of the council. However, Cardinal Spellman invited him to the second session, and Murray through his own speeches and those he wrote for many American bishops and especially through his active work on the drafts had a great influence on the final document.[64]

Murray in his writings also solved the other half of the American and Catholic compatibility question—the suspicion on the part of Americans that Catholics did not really accept the American political system and ethos. In 1960 Murray published a collection of his essays under the title *We Hold These Truths: Catholic Reflections on the American Proposition.* Murray's basic thesis was simple and audacious. Not only is there no incompatibility between the American proposition and the Catholic understanding, but it is precisely the natural law, which has been accepted and preserved in the Catholic Church, which is the basis for the American proposition. The public philosophy of America is based on the proposition of the Declaration of Independence that we hold these truths to be self-evident that all men are created equal and have certain inalienable rights. "The point here is that Catholic participation in the American consensus has been full and free, unreserved and unembarrassed, because the contents of this consensus—the ethical and political principles drawn from the tradition of natural law—approve themselves to the Catholic intelligence and conscience."[65]

What is the meaning of the natural law on which the American proposition and consensus are based? Murray affirms that there are four metaphysical premises of natural law: 1) a realistic epistemology that asserts the real to be the measure of knowledge; 2) a metaphysic of nature with nature as a teleological concept, so that the form of a thing is its final cause; 3) a natural theology; 4) a morality based on the order of nature which is not an order of necessity but rather an order of reason and therefore of freedom.[66]

Murray pushes the point even further. He recognized that the American university with its acceptance of pragmatism had long since rejected the whole notion of the American consensus about the truths we hold in common and the natural law basis upon which they rest. It is paradoxical that a nation which had thought of its own genius in Protestant terms actually owes its origins and its continued stability to the natural law tradition accepted by Roman Catholicism. If we are to continue as a nation, we must renew the tradition which is no longer accepted by the university in general or by contemporary Protestant thought.[67]

Our proponent of compatibility between American and Catholic was not an uncritical observer of the American political scene, as is exemplified in his criticism of pragmatism and the lack of rational analysis in some Protestant thought. Contemporary American thought is troubled by a vacuum of any overall political moral doctrine with regard to war and the use of force.[68] In general there is a moral vacuum because the doctrine of natural law is dead. But in his last chapter Murray proposes that the doctrine still lives and the resources in the natural law tradition could make it the dynamic of a new age of order and of rational progress.[69]

Murray thus makes a bold case for the proposition that Catholics not only can accept the American proposition, but the proposition itself is based on Catholic natural law theory. Personally I do not think he has proved his point. At best there is a common ground morality behind the consensus proposition, but there is not and need not be agreement on ultimate metaphysical and philosophical premises. Murray's thought, however, represents the culmination of that long struggle to prove that Catholicism, an immigrant and minority religion, is at home in the American ethos.

No sooner had Murray achieved this final goal of proving the compatibility between American and Catholic when the synthesis was strongly questioned. Dissatisfaction with the problems of the poor, of race and of an unpopular war in

Southeast Asia all occasioned the phenomenon of dissent
within the American culture in general and especially within
American Catholic culture. Likewise, from the methodological
viewpoint the theories proposed at the Second Vatican Council
presupposed a methodology no longer based solely or primarily on the natural law. The council documents recognized the
need to overcome the dichotomy between the supernatural
and the natural, to place scriptures at the heart of all theology,
and to make belief in the kingdom of God more relevant to
daily life. But to develop this any further would go beyond the
scope of this present chapter which intends to cover only the
period up to 1965. The purpose here has been to analyze the
story of American Catholic social ethics in terms of its most
central problematic—the relationship between Catholic and
American and the underlying theological methodologies with
which this problem was approached. Other American
Catholics, such as Charles Coughlin and Joseph McCarthy,
undoubtedly exercised great influence in American political
life, but this chapter has been primarily interested in social
ethical methodology and the various theories developed in
American Catholicism.

NOTES

1. Aaron I. Abell, ed., *American Catholic Thought on Social Questions*
(Indianapolis and New York: Bobbs-Merrill Co., 1968), pp. xxiii–
xxvi; 141–262.

2. For an historical study of the question especially in the later part
of the nineteenth century see Robert D. Cross, *The Emergence of Liberal
Catholicism in America* (Cambridge: Harvard University Press, 1958).
The relationship between Catholicism and Americanism obviously
has frequently been discussed. For an overview showing many facets
of the relationship see Thomas T. McAvoy, ed., *Roman Catholicism and
the American Way of Life* (Notre Dame, Indiana: University of Notre
Dame Press, 1960).

3. Emmet H. Rothan, *The German Catholic Immigrant in the United
States (1830–1860)* (Washington, D.C.: Catholic University of
America Press, 1946).

4. Abell, *American Catholic Thought*, pp. 3-51. In this particular book Abell includes selections from significant authors and documents and supplies his own introductions and commentaries. For his own historical study see Aaron I. Abell, *American Catholicism and Social Action: A Search for Social Justice 1865-1950* (Notre Dame, Indiana: University of Notre Dame Press, 1963). The first chapter treats the development of the Catholic minority.

5. Cross (p. vii) describes the tendency to promote a friendly interaction between Catholicism and American life as Catholic liberalism.

6. Henry J. Browne, *The Catholic Church and the Knights of Labor* (Washington, D.C.: Catholic University of America Press, 1949).

7. The text of Gibbons' brief, including differences between the French and the English versions of it, can be found in Browne, *The Catholic Church*, appendix III, pp. 365-378.

8. For a favorable account of McGlynn's life and thought see Stephen Bell, *Rebel, Priest and Prophet: A Biography of Dr. Edward McGlynn* (New York: Devin-Adair Co., 1937).

9. Abell, *American Catholicism and Social Action*, pp. 100-122. The Satolli speech is cited on p. 112.

10. Thomas T. McAvoy, *The Great Crisis in American Catholic History, 1895-1900* (Chicago: Henry Regnery Co., 1957).

11. McAvoy; summarized in Cross, *The Emergence of Liberal Catholicism*, pp. 199-203.

12. Jean-Yves Calvez and Jacques Perrin, *The Church and Social Justice* (Chicago: Henry Regnery Co., 1961), pp. 36-53.

13. Pope John XXIII, *Pacem in Terris*, ed. William J. Gibbons (New York: Paulist Press, 1963), n. 1-7; the original text is found in *Acta Apostolicae Sedis* 55 (1963): 258-259.

14. Pope Leo XIII, *Rerum Novarum* in *The Church Speaks to the Modern World: The Social Teaching of Leo XIII*, ed. Etienne Gilson (Garden City, New York: Doubleday Image Books, 1954), p. 200. no. 11; original text: *Acta Sanctae Sedis* 23 (1890-91): 645.

15. "The Bishops' Program of Social Reconstruction," in Abell, *American Catholic Thought*, pp. 325-348.

16. John A. Ryan, *A Living Wage* (New York: Macmillan, 1906); idem, *Distributive Justice* (New York: Macmillan, 1916).

17. For biographical information see Ryan's autobiography, John A. Ryan, *Social Doctrine in Action: A Personal History* (New York: Harper and Brothers, 1941), and especially Francis L. Broderick, *Right Reverend New Dealer John A. Ryan* (New York: Macmillan, 1963).

18. For a detailed description of Ryan as a liberal and reformer as contrasted with radicals and conservatives see David J. O'Brien, *American Catholics and Social Reform* (New York: Oxford University Press, 1968), pp. 120-149. O'Brien's valuable study contains a very informative short section on how the papal encyclicals were suscepti-

ble to different interpretations (pp. 22–28) as well as a concluding
chapter on "Catholicism and Americanism" (pp. 212–227).

19. Ryan had sent the manuscript to Richard T. Ely, an economist
and Protestant proponent of the Social Gospel, who talked Macmillan
into publishing the book if Ryan would pay for the printing plates.
Ryan, *Social Doctrine in Action*, pp. 80–81.

20. John A. Ryan, "The Church and the Working Man," *Catholic
World* 89 (1908–09): 776–778.

21. Broderick, *Right Reverend New Dealer*, pp. 46–47.

22. Ryan, *Distributive Justice*, p. xiii.

23. Morris Hillquit and John A. Ryan, *Socialism: Promise or Menace?*
(New York: Macmillan, 1914), p. 58.

24. George C. Higgins, "The Underconsumption Theory in the
Writings of Monsignor John A. Ryan" (M.A. dissertation, Catholic
University of America, 1942).

25. John A. Ryan, *Seven Troubled Years* (Ann Arbor, Michigan:
Edwards Brothers, Inc., 1937), p. 59.

26. Ryan, *Distributive Justice*, pp. 356ff.

27. Ibid., pp. 56–60.

28. Patrick W. Gearty, *The Economic Thought of Monsignor John A.
Ryan* (Washington, D.C.: Catholic University of America Press, 1953),
pp. 130ff.; Reginald G. Bender, "The Doctrine of Private Property in
the Writings of Monsignor John A. Ryan" (S.T.D. dissertation,
Catholic University of America, 1973), pp. 114ff.

29. Broderick, *Right Reverend New Dealer*, pp. 31–33.

30. Gearty, *Economic Thought*, pp. 254–297. For a description of
Ryan as a continuing reformer see Neil Betten, "John Ryan and the
Social Action Department," *Thought* 46 (1971): 227–246.

31. Broderick, *Right Reverend New Dealer*, pp. 170–185.

32. John A. Ryan and Moorhouse F. X. Millar, *The State and the
Church* (New York: Macmillan, 1922), pp. 38–39.

33. The best source for the history and description of this move-
ment is Philip Gleason, *The Conservative Reformers: German-American
Catholics and the Social Order* (Notre Dame, Indiana: University of
Notre Dame Press, 1968). For a study of German-American Catholics
in the later part of the nineteenth century see Colman J. Barry, *The
Catholic Church and German Americans* (Milwaukee: Bruce Publishing
Co., 1953). On the particular subject under discussion, but of much
less value than Gleason, see Sister Mary Elizabeth Dye, *By Their Fruits:
A Social Biography of Frederick Kenkel, Catholic Social Pioneer* (New York:
Greenwich Book Publishers, 1960) and Mary Liguori Brophy, *The
Social Thought of the German Roman Catholic Central Verein* (Washington,
D.C.: Catholic University of America Press, 1941).

34. The social thought of the Central Verein was often expounded
in long articles which appeared in installments in *Central-Blatt and
Social Justice*. In addition to Kenkel the most authoritative spokesper-

son was William J. Engelen, S.J., a college professor. See, for example, Engelen, "Social Reflections," *Central-Blatt and Social Justice* 12 (1919–20): 203–205, continuing in twenty installments ending in 14 (1921–22): 178–180; also Engelen, "Social Observations," *Central-Blatt and Social Justice* 14 (1921–22): 219–221, continuing in five installments ending in 14 (1921–22): 357–359.

35. E.g., W. J. Engelen, "Social Reconstruction (VII)," *Central-Blatt and Social Justice* 18 (1925–26): 147–148.

36. Gleason, *Conservative Reformers,* pp. 140–143, 200–203.

37. For an analysis of the German situation see Edgar Alexander, "Social and Political Movements and Ideas in German and Austrian Catholicism (1789–1950)," in *Church and Society,* ed. Joseph N. Moody (New York: Arts Inc., 1953). pp. 325–583.

38. A concise summary of this approach as found in the writings of the German Jesuit Henry Pesch is given in W. J. Engelen, "Social Reconstruction XIII: Rev. Henry Pesch, S.J.," *Central-Blatt and Social Justice* 19 (1926–27): 77–79, 111–112, 147–148, 183–184, 219–220.

39. Frederick P. Kenkel, "Some Arguments against the Proposed Child Labor Amendment," *Central-Blatt and Social Justice* 18 (1925–26): 114–116, 150–152.

40. The best book on the movement in general is William D. Miller, *A Harsh and Dreadful Love: Dorothy Day and the Catholic Worker Movement* (Garden City, New York: Doubleday Image Books, 1974). Additional bibliography may be found there, especially references to books written by Dorothy Day including her autobiographical works and collections of her articles from *The Catholic Worker.* On the particular question of social ethics see O'Brien, pp. 182–211. I am also grateful for help from the research being done at Catholic University by Stuart Sandberg.

41. Neil Betten, "Social Catholicism and the Rise of Catholic Radicalism in America," *Journal of Human Relations* 18 (1970): 710–727; O'Brien, *American Catholics,* p. 211.

42. For my detailed analysis and critique of Furfey's thought see Charles E. Curran, "The Radical Catholic Social Ethics of Paul Hanly Furfey," in *New Perspectives in Moral Theology* (Notre Dame, Indiana: University of Notre Dame Press, 1976), pp. 87–121.

43. Paul Hanly Furfey, *Fire on the Earth* (New York: Macmillan, 1936), pp. 1–21; idem, *Three Theories of Society* (New York: Macmillan, 1937).

44. A sampling of articles from *The Catholic Worker* can be found in *A Penny A Copy: Readings from the Catholic Worker,* ed. Thomas C. Cornell and James H. Forest (New York: Macmillan, 1968).

45. John F. Cronin, *Social Principles and Economic Life,* rev. ed. (Milwaukee: Bruce Publishing Co., 1964), pp. 17–25.

46. John F. Cronin, *Catholic Social Principles* (Milwaukee: Bruce Publishing Co., 1950), pp. 213–253.

47. Cronin, *Social Principles and Economic Life*, pp. 130–140.

48. Ibid., pp. 90ff., 140ff.

49. Gary Wills, *Nixon Agonistes* (New York: Signet Books, 1971), pp. 34–39.

50. John Courtney Murray, "Intercredal Cooperation: Its Theory and Its Organization," *Theological Studies* 4 (1943): 257–286.

51. Paul Hanly Furfey, "Intercredal Cooperation: Its Limitations," *American Ecclesiastical Review* 111 (1944): 161–175.

52. In addition to the articles mentioned in the preceding notes and some other interventions of less importance the debate continued: John Courtney Murray, "On the Problem of Cooperation: Some Clarifications," *American Ecclesiastical Review* 112 (1945): 194–214; Paul Hanly Furfey, "Why Does Rome Discourage Socio-Religious Intercredalism?" *American Ecclesiastical Review* 112 (1945): 365–374.

53. John Courtney Murray, "Leo XIII: Separation of Church and State," *Theological Studies* 14 (1953): 200–201.

54. John Courtney Murray, "Freedom of Religion I: The Ethical Problem," *Theological Studies* 6 (1945): 235.

55. Ibid., pp. 266ff.

56. John Courtney Murray, *The Problem of Religious Freedom* (Westminster, Md.: Newman Press, 1965), pp. 28–30.

57. John Courtney Murray, "The Declaration on Religious Freedom," *Concilium* 15 (May 1966): 11–16.

58. Murray, *Problem of Religious Freedom*, p. 32.

59. John Courtney Murray, "Civil Unity and Religious Integrity: The Articles of Peace," in *We Hold These Truths* (New York: Sheed and Ward, 1960), pp. 59–60.

60. Faith E. Burgess, *The Relationship between Church and State according to John Courtney Murray, S.J.* (Düsseldorf: Rudolf Stehle, 1971), pp. 116–120.

61. John Courtney Murray, "Leo XIII: Two Concepts of Government II: Government and the Order of Culture," *Theological Studies* 15 (1954): 16–21.

62. Burgess, *Relationship between Church and State*, pp. 114–115.

63. Raymond Owen McEvoy, "John Courtney Murray's Thought on Religious Liberty in Its Final Phase," *Studia Moralia* 11 (1973): 240–260.

64. For developments in the conciliar period itself see Richard Regan, *Conflict and Consensus: Religious Freedom and the Second Vatican Council* (New York: Macmillan, 1967).

65. Murray, *We Hold These Truths*, p. 47.

66. Ibid., pp. 327–328.

67. Ibid., pp. 40–41.

68. Ibid., p. 273.

69. Ibid., pp. 334–336.

4. Social Ethics: Future Agenda for Theology and the Church

This chapter will discuss the future agenda for the church in the area of social ethics and the relationship of church and society. The perspective will be that of Catholic social ethics with a realization that a truly Catholic social ethics is ecumenical both in terms of its relation to other Christian thought and action and in relation to all people of good will. We will consider the question against a broad general background but give special importance to the perspective of Catholic social ethics in the United States.

A first consideration logically should focus on the issues involved. What are the particular problems and questions facing the world and the church in the area of social ethics?

One point is certain. There will be no lack of issues. The future agenda can and must learn from what Christians and others have been doing in the past as well as from a true discernment of the problems of the present and the future. The Second Vatican Council grouped the issues of church and society under five headings—marriage and the family, culture, socioeconomic life, life of the political community, and the fostering of peace.[1] The World Conference on Church and Society sponsored by the World Council of Churches in Geneva in 1966 divided its material into four sections—economic development, nature and function of the state, structure of international cooperation, and man and community in changing societies.[2] Recently the "The Call to Action" Conference under the auspices of the American bishops treated the following areas: church, ethnicity and race, family, humankind, nationhood, neighborhood, personhood, work.[3]

Theology as such has no exclusive insight into discerning the social problems facing the world and the church today. Theologians, like all other individuals and groups within society and the church, must try to learn from all possible sources what are the primary issues facing the world and society today. Any true discernment process, recognizing the importance given to participation by Pope Paul VI in *Octogesima adveniens*,[4] must call for the cooperation of all in discerning these problems—especially minorities and those who are oppressed and suffering. Newer problems have emerged in the last few years, but questions concerning peace, the poor and discrimination because of race or sex will continue to be very significant questions.

From the theological perspective the more significant questions concern method—how theology should approach such social questions and how the church should carry out its social mission. These are the two main tasks to be pursued in this study. However, these more methodological questions might best be raised in the context of a particular substantive issue. Social economic issues will be chosen to focus the methodological questions.

In the midst of the myriad social issues facing society, it is difficult to select one issue as primary, but the social economic issue would have to be considered very important, if not primary. The papal encyclicals starting with Leo XIII concentrated on social economic issues; in the United States there was a strong emphasis on social justice in the writings of Catholics. Social economic justice in the encyclicals and in the American Catholic literature centered on the economic questions of safeguarding the rights of workers—a living wage, right to join unions, provision against illness and sudden catastrophe, right to own property.

The changed economic circumstances in the United States obviously influenced a decreased interest in social economic questions in the past few decades. The war economy of World War II artificially solved the problems of the depression.

Catholics who used to be the poor of the land moved into the middle class after that war. The new poor (especially the blacks) were not Roman Catholic, and it was somewhat easy for the church to forget about them. Even the Spanish speaking who are Roman Catholic were easily overlooked. American Catholics struggling to prove they could be loyal Americans tended not to be critical of America the land of opportunity. The post-World War II struggle in which Roman Catholicism and the United States were the two bulwarks of the free world against the Communist menace only served to heighten the identification of American and Catholic and made Catholics less critical of their own society, as was explained in the last chapter.[5]

However, the social economic problem still remains. In the United States such questions as tax reform and welfare reform, although they are not radical questions, show the importance of the socioeconomic sphere. Even more fundamental are the problems of poverty still existing in the United States. The most significant development highlights the worldwide nature of the question.[6] The developing nations of the world feel the inequities of the present economic order. Liberation theology coming from the South American experience calls for a radical change in the economic structures of society. North Americans must look beyond their narrow boundaries to see the problems in their global scale. Issues such as peace, human rights, and sexual equality are always important questions, but the proper distribution of the goods of creation remains very significant. John Coleman Bennett has recently called attention to the importance of economic ethics.[7] Thus social economic questions can well serve as illustrations of how both theology and the church should approach social ethics and social action.

I. Theological Approaches

Various questions of theological methodology and approaches will be raised, but initially some assumptions coming from recent developments in social ethics will be mentioned. First, Catholic social ethics can no longer work out of the model of the nature-supernature, kingdom-world dichotomy which too often characterized Roman Catholic thought in the past. The gospel and the kingdom must be positively related to the world and the social problems facing human existence. The second assumption concerns the need for an historically conscious approach which will be much more inductive.

Both these assumptions are comparatively recent in Catholic social ethics. The Pastoral Constitution on the Church in the Modern World is the first document of the hierarchical magisterium to incorporate such approaches. Note the emphasis on overcoming the dichotomy between faith and the world, the gospel and our daily life, and also observe the methodology which begins the discussion of particular social questions by an inductive reading of the signs of the times. These two approaches are even more evident in the Medellín Documents issued by the South American Bishops in 1968. Although these characteristics did not appear in official Catholic Church documents before 1963, now they can correctly be assumed as necessary aspects of any Christian social ethics.

A third assumption recognizes the need for critical reason and an emphasis on praxis. Moral theology in general and social ethics in particular obviously are more disposed to accept such an emphasis. Again there will be differences in the amount of emphasis given to critical reason and praxis, but still one must underscore the importance of such aspects in social ethics today.

Mediation

Chapter Two has emphasized that Roman Catholic theology has traditionally been characterized by an acceptance of mediation. Catholic theologies of the church and of natural law illustrate this fact. God and God's presence to us is mediated in and through the church. God's plan for human action is primarily known, not directly and immediately from God, but rather in and through our understanding of the human. The divine plan in no way short-circuits the human reasoning process, but precisely in and through human reason reflecting on our existence we arrive at what God wants us to do.

Contemporary emphasis on the gospel and on the kingdom calls for some kind of mediation. The hermeneutic problem in understanding the scriptures recognizes the need for a mediating principle going from the gospel to contemporary existence. How does one go from the gospel or the concept of the kingdom to the particulars of the social, economic and political world in which we live?

Contemporary liberation theologians such as Gutierrez also recognize the need for a mediating principle. Gutierrez acknowledges three distinct levels of liberation which affect each other but are not the same — political liberation, the liberation of man through history and liberation from sin.[8] Gutierrez calls for a mediation through utopias and eschews a politico-religious messianism which does not sufficiently respect the autonomy of the political arena. Faith and political action will not enter into a correct and fruitful relationship except through utopia. Utopia is characterized by three elements — its relationship to historical reality, its verification in praxis and its rational nature.[9] Hugo Assmann calls for a mediation through a sociological analysis based on Marxism[10] and thus seems to argue for a very specific mediation.

Perhaps the American scene can offer another mediating principle — distributive justice. The previous chapter has indicated that the Catholic tradition in the United States has emphasized distributive justice as seen in the significant book of that title by John A. Ryan. Ryan used distributive justice as the canon for the proper distribution of the products of industry among their producers.[11] In contemporary philosophical writing much more importance has been paid lately to questions of justice and distributive justice.[12] The concept of distributive justice thus enables Catholic ethics to enter into dialogue with many other philosophers and people of good will.

The particular social questions that are being raised in the

American context today emphasize problems that readily fit under the category of distributive justice—making medical care available for all, which will be considered at length in a later chapter, income maintenance programs guaranteeing a minimum income for all; an equitable tax system doing away with regressive taxes such as sales taxes or the existing social security tax.[13] The rubric of distributive justice addresses the very significant question of the proper distribution of the goods of this world. Questions of the international economic order can readily be approached in and through this understanding.

Distributive justice as a mediating concept properly emphasizes the biblical concept that the goods of creation exist for all human beings.[14] Too often, especially in the United States, a rugged individualism and a poor concept of freedom have characterized the understanding of the ownership of goods. Distributive justice avoids the pitfalls of a narrowly individualistic concept of justice and rightly emphasizes the Christian belief that God destined the goods of creation for all human beings.[15] The concept of distributive justice remains quite generic, and there can be and will be disagreements about particular ramifications and societal structures. However, it seems to me that distributive justice serves quite well as a mediating concept between the gospel demands and the realities of the present situation.

Mediation and Specificity

The acceptance of mediation recognizes the relative autonomy of the human, human reason and scientific data and their interpretation. Political, social and economic data and their interpretation must be respected by theological ethics in coming to its conclusions. Theological ethics can and should offer guidance for our choices in these societal matters, but such choices are heavily dependent on scientific data and their interpretation, which cannot be short-circuited by theological and ethical judgments. To recognize mediation means that theology cannot say which psychological theory or which sociological interpretation is more adequate for interpreting the reality in question.

Some so stress the autonomy of the human, human reason and human sciences that they contend that theological ethics is imcompetent to draw any such specific conclusions about what should be done in practice.[16] I deny this assertion. Human judgments are not merely economic, social or political judgments. They are truly human and moral judgments, even though they involve a great deal of complex scientific data and interpretation. It is precisely because of being mediated through the specifics of human sciences that particular human, moral and Christian judgments cannot claim to be the only possible Christian interpretation. Sometimes it is rather easy to identify the concrete solution with the Christian approach as in the condemnation of torture or the blatant violation of human rights. But in many cases the Christian solution cannot be so readily identified with any one approach primarily because of the fact that the final judgment relies quite heavily on scientific data and their interpretation. In practice it will often be impossible to claim that there is only one possible Christian solution and no other. This position has been generally accepted in Catholic thought as was mentioned in Chapter Two. Take, for example, proposals made for nuclear disarmament or different ways of providing basic medical care for all.

Eschatology

Eschatological considerations have exerted a strong influence on contemporary theology. In the light of eschatology and of the fullness of the kingdom the present social, political and economic conditions are shown to be imperfect and in need of change. The status quo can never be totally accepted by one who has an eschatological vision. The call to improve the structures of our world must always beckon the Christian.

At the very minimum an eschatological vision provides a negative critique of existing structures. However, ultimately such a critique should also call for a positive response which works to bring about change. The eschatological vision and the understanding of the kingdom can furnish positive aspects in terms of the values, goals, ideals and attitudes that must be present in all Christian approaches. These positive aspects alone do not arrive at concrete solutions. As mentioned above, such values must be mediated through the scientific data and their interpretation in coming to grips with concrete problems.

An eschatological vision calls for a continual effort to change the social, political and economic structures in which we live. However, the fullness of the eschatological vision will never be totally achieved. The Christian recognizes the power of sin in the world and the need to struggle continually against the forces of sin. The kingdom will never be perfectly present in this world; its fullness lies beyond our grasp. Imperfection and lack of completeness will characterize our structures. Likewise, one must reject the naive optimism of Protestant liberalism which identified any change as necessarily good.

Too often in the immediate past some people readily accepted the need for social action and social change, but they quickly became disillusioned when such change did not occur. If the experience of the last decade teaches us anything, it is the need for a long-term commitment to bring about the kinds of social changes which are necessary. Romantic visionaries might be willing to give a bit of their time or a certain amount of effort in trying to bring about change, but they too readily become discouraged in the light of the long-haul situation. Consequently, the virtue of hope strengthens the individual to continue commitment to the struggle even when success seems all too absent. Relatively oppressive and unjust structures will not be changed readily or quickly.

Since the fullness of the eschaton serves as a negative critique on all existing structures, the Christian recognizes that the kingdom cannot totally be identified with any one specific approach. The Christian must always be willing to criticize all things—including one's own vision and tactics in the light of the eschaton. Too often Christians have too readily identified the gospel or the kingdom with their own cause, country or philosophy. American Protestants of earlier generations too readily identified the kingdom of God with the United States.[17] Chapter Three showed that immigrant Catholics at times strained too mightly to prove there was no incompatibility between being American and Catholic.[18]

Such a critical eschatological perspective calls for continual vigilance and self-criticism. The danger, however, always remains that people will use this as an excuse to do nothing and thus accept the status quo. The eschatological vision should never be employed as an excuse for noninvolvement. Christian theology must be willing to criticize all ideologies and their approaches, but there are still some approaches which are more adequate than others and must be adopted in practice. The Christian and eschatological vision must be willing to become incarnate in concrete historical, cultural and political circumstances even though one recognizes the risks involved. In this context I prefer to use the term strategies to refer to the particular approaches that Christians can use in changing social structures. These strategies can and should be very specific, but they can never be absolutized and removed from critical reflection. In this way one avoids the dogmatization of many forms of ideological theories.

An eschatological understanding together with a recognition of mediation also tends to argue against the acceptance of any overly simplistic solutions to social problems. My own innate theological "prejudice" also argues for such complexity. It is too simplistic to reduce all ethical problems to any one type of opposition. Social problems cannot simplistically be reduced to just any one factor be it that of class, sex, race or country. However, it can be that one of these aspects is more significant in a particular situation and thus furnishes the strategy that must be employed in that situation in order to overcome the oppression and injustice.

Although eschatological considerations are most important, I do not think eschatology alone (especially apocalyptic eschatology) can serve as an adequate basis for the development of moral theology or social ethics. I have proposed that the stance or logically first step in moral theology embraces the fivefold Christian mysteries of creation, sin, incarnation, redemption and resurrection destiny. The failure to incorporate all of these aspects stands as a negative critique of such past approaches as Catholic natural law, Lutheran two-realm theory, liberal Protestantism and Neo-Orthodoxy. More positively, such a stance provides the basic horizon or perspective within which moral theology and Christian social ethics should be developed.

Personal and/or Structural Change

Catholic social thought in general and especially since the nineteenth century has emphasized the need and importance of structural change. It is not enough merely to call for personal change and a change of heart. Catholic ethics has traditionally recognized structures and institutions as necessary aspects of human existence, even to call them natural organizations in the sense that human beings are social by nature and thus called to form groups, institutions and structures to creatively accomplish what human beings alone are incapable of doing. Liberal Catholic social thought in the United States has often been associated with the call to reform the social, political and economic structures of society.[19] At times some elements of radical Catholic social reform have so stressed the personal element they have not given enough importance to the need for a change of structures.[20]

From my perspective both changes of heart and changes of structure are necessary in social ethics. Unfortunately these two aspects too often are separated, and the need for both is not stressed. The "Call to Action" Conference sponsored by the American bishops in Detroit in the fall of 1976 rightfully called for structural changes but said little or nothing about the need for change of heart and all the educational and motivational aspects that can help bring about such a change.

The present nature of the economic change required in the world is of such a nature that it cannot be accomplished without a somewhat radical change of attitude on the part of individual persons and especially individual persons existing within the more wealthy nations of the world. When change itself is not too radical, then there is no need for great personal change of heart and attitudes. This has been the assumption and the premise of liberal social reformers in the United States. The myth of ever-greater growth insisted that change means that more people share more equitably in the ever-growing progress—especially material progress. Progress implied more for everyone with no need for anyone to give up what one already enjoys.[21]

Already there are signs even in the United States that such an approach cannot deal with the extent of the problems that are being faced today. The energy crisis might call for a great change in life-styles and attitudes of many Americans. Ecological problems have made us very suspect of the older notion of progress and of the promise that the future will be bigger and better than the present or the past. Especially in the context of the international economic order the rich nations of the world are called to a more radical type of change which cannot be accomplished without a change of heart of individuals and all that is entailed with such a change. Americans must be willing to give up some of their high material standard of living in order that other people on the earth might have an equitable share of the goods of creation. Recent proposals to the effect that small is beautiful remind us of the profound kinds of changes that are necessary. Thus, good theological ethical theory combined with the understanding of the magnitude of the problems that we are facing especially in the areas of socioeconomic ethics reminds us of the need for both personal change of heart and structural change. Any theological ethics which fails to recognize both will tend to be inadequate.

Harmony and Conflict

Catholic social thought, with its traditional emphasis on the natural law as an ordering of reason, has tended to see the world and society in general in terms of order and harmony rather than in terms of conflict and opposition. Catholic theory has seen no true opposition but rather concord between law and freedom. Good law does not restrict our freedom but rather tells human beings to do that which by nature they are called to do. Hierarchical ordering dominated our understanding of human nature as well as our understanding of human society and of the church, with the lower aspects serving the higher. All the individual parts work together in proper coordination and subordination for the good of the whole. When applied to the economic order, this outlook called for the cooperation of all the individual elements and units in the economic order—capital, labor and management—working together for the common good. The corporate society proposed by many Catholic theorists and espoused by Pope Pius XI in *Quadragesimo anno* inculcates such an emphasis on hierarchical ordering and working together for the common good.[22] At times in practice there was an innate realism which recognized the existence of problems and the need for some conflict in such questions as war, strikes and disagreements; but the heavy emphasis in Catholic theory was on order and harmony.

The harmony-conflict question surfaces above all in views of society and the relationship among the classes existing in society. In the economic order Marxism talks about a class struggle between the poor and the rich. How should Catholic ethics look at such conflictual understandings of human existence? In general, Catholic social thought in my judgment must give more importance to conflict with a somewhat decreased emphasis on order and harmony. A recognition of the presence of sin as well as a more historically conscious methodology will put less influence on order and harmony than in the pre-Vatican II Catholic approach. There is also a need to develop a theology of power. However, a greater recognition of the role of conflict does not mean that all social relationships should be seen in terms of conflict or that conflict is the ultimate and most fundamental way of viewing the human scene.

Christianity ultimately calls for love and reconciliation. Love of enemies has been a hallmark of Christian teaching and preaching—if not, unfortunately, of Christian action. Christian social ethics can never forget the appeal to the human person as person to change one's own heart and to work for a change of social structure. Conflict for the Christian cannot be the ultimate nor can it be accepted for its own sake. However, on this side of the fullness of the eschaton, conflict at times can and will be an acceptable strategy in Christian social ethics. As a strategy, it can never become an ideology or an ultimate explanation of reality. However, there will be more conflictual situations than Catholic social ethics was willing to admit in the past. Thus, for example, conflict among classes might be a necessary strategy in bringing about social change, but conflict can never be the first or the ultimate or the most important reality.

Somewhat connected with conflict is the question of violence which must be faced in our contemporary world. Here the Catholic tradition in its just war tradition worked out an understanding that accepted violence in a just cause but at the same time insisted on limiting the violence. There are some today who call for a total pacifism, but I cannot accept such an absolute approach.

Detached and Participant Perspectives

What is the better perspective for arriving at good ethical judgments—that of a participant or that of a detached observer? Emphasis on critical reason and praxis shows the importance of active participation in the ongoing work itself. However, the need for critical reflection on praxis also calls for some type of self-criticism and detachment.

In my judgment there are advantages and disadvantages to both perspectives. History shows that the detached observer does not realize the extent of the problems faced by certain people or societies. White, middle-class, male theologians and ethicists have not been as aware of the injustices existing for other races, the poor and women as they should have been. If one is not involved in the oppression and injustice, there is a tendency not to realize its existence.

On the other hand, the participant can be so involved in a particular struggle that one fails to see other important aspects. I, for example, can never reduce social conflict totally to a struggle of the poor against the rich. I believe that this at times can be very true, but I also believe that there are other social problems such as the evils of sexism and racism. Those who in the past fought the cold war against communism failed to recognize the divergent aspects among different communist countries and also were unwilling to criticize the free world. Advocates of feminine rights correctly recognize the wrongs done to women in society, but at times some tend to overlook the rights of the fetus. The ultimate advantages and disadvantages of both models call for the need for both perspectives in any theological or ethical enterprise.

Social Ethics As a Reflexive, Systematic Discipline

Theological social ethics by its very nature constitutes a reflexive, systematic discipline. Its discourse can be described as second-order discourse as distinguished from first-order discourse (e.g., preaching). Any second-order discourse will not have as immediate an effect upon action and change as first-order discourse. I affirm that social ethics should have some effect on social change, but I recognize there are other realities that have an even greater effect on social change. Every Christian working for justice and social change does not have to be a theologian.

II. Role of the Church

Having treated some questions of theological methodology in the area of social ethics especially in the light of economic questions, this chapter will now consider some ecclesial aspects centering on the social mission of the church. Again, the focus is on the Roman Catholic Church, but what is said applies to all Christian churches. In addition to what is developed in this section there is a great need for ecumenical witness and action in the social mission of the Christian churches.

Importance of the Social Mission of the Church

One cannot stress enough the importance of the social mission of the church. *Justice in the World,* the document released by the Synod of Bishops in 1971, strongly states: "Action on behalf of justice and participation in the transformation of the world fully appear to us as a constitutive dimension of the preaching of the Gospel, or, in other words, of the church's mission for the redemption of the human race and its liberation from every oppressive situation."[23]

The social mission of the church has thus been recognized as a constitutive dimension of the church. The challenge remains to make this a living reality on the pastoral level in the life of the church. Pastoral creativity and imagination must put flesh and blood on the bare bones of this statement. The force of the statement should not be lost—without a social mission the church is not truly church, for it is missing a constitutive aspect. This is true of the church on all levels of its existence but especially on the level of the local church. The parish community must be not only a worshiping community but also a serving community. How to bring this about in practice is perhaps the primary pastoral problem facing the church at the present time.

Peculiar circumstances on the American Catholic scene make this pastoral ministry more difficult but even more imperative. The mainstream of American Catholicism tried to prove there was no basic incompatibility between being American and being Catholic. The older distinction between natural and supernatural was used to point out the different spheres. The great contribution of the American church at the Second Vatican Council was in the advocacy of religious freedom and the separation of church and state. The subtle danger was to separate American and Catholic on the one hand and state and church on the other into two separate spheres. In such a way there was no incompatibility between them, but also the church or the gospel readily lost any influence on the state or the secular. Catholics had a different faith from other Americans, but this did not affect their participation in the national life and questions facing society. There was a fear of admitting anything distinctively Christian or Catholic that one could bring to bear on the social and political orders. The Catholic ethos in the United States tended to eliminate faith, the gospel and the supernatural from political, social and economic theory and life. There is all the more need in the United States for a creative pastoral ministry making the social mission of the church a constitutive part of the church.

There have been some creative developments in the last few years in social ministry. The church and groups in the church can act as catalysts for various forms of community organizations. These community organizations can then work effectively for social change. Here the role of the church is neither patronizing nor paternalistic but rather enabling. Also, church groups can and should act as advocates for the poor and disadvantaged.[24]

Limits on the Social Mission of the Church

The proper understanding of the social mission of the church, as well as the call for creative ministerial intiatives to make the social mission of the church a constitutive part of the church, calls for a recognition of the limitations involved in both comprehending and structuring the social mission of the church. First, the social mission is only a part of the total mission of the church. There are many other aspects of the mission of the church, involving especially the preaching of the gospel and the liturgical celebration of the presence of the risen Lord in our midst with the concomitant hope that he will come again. The social mission should not be seen as opposed to these other aspects, for these other aspects by their very nature call for a social mission dimension. But the church cannot be reduced only to the social mission.

Second, there are many individuals and groups apart from the church who are working for the betterment of society. Catholics and other Christians must avoid the narrow triumphalism of claiming to be the only ones working for social justice and struggling against the forces of oppression. Such a proposed understanding is unfair to all the other individuals and groups who have dedicated themselves to working against injustice.

Third, individual Roman Catholics are not only members of the church community but they belong to many other groups, communities and societies which are also working for the betterment of society. One cannot and should not go back to a Catholic ghetto concept according to which the Catholic does not become involved in ecumenical, secular and other groups working for social change. Any structuring of the social mission of the church must recognize that the social mission of individual Catholics must not be totally or perhaps even primarily in terms of Christian groups or organizations as such. Fourth, there has been much discussion in moral theology in the last decade about the existence of a specifically Christian ethic. My contention is that from the viewpoint of specific moral content as well as that of proximate goals, attitudes and dispositions such as self-sacrificing love, care for the poor and struggling against oppression there is no distinctively Christian social ethical content. Obviously this is a disputed point, but at the very minimum one must be willing to recognize that Christians have no monopoly on social ethical wisdom or insight.

Pluralism

Different aspects of pluralism have been mentioned already in the discussion of theological methodology. First, there can be a legitimate pluralism on the level of theological methodology itself. Many would not agree with the methodology I proposed. Some, for example, would call for a more radical approach that would advocate a Christian witness to peace and voluntary poverty.

Second, there will be a pluralism because of the different possible scientific theories and interpretations of the data involved in complex social ethical questions. Third, on these

specific issues the very complexity of the issues argues against
the possibility of claiming with absolute certitude that there is
only one possible Christian approach or solution.

The history of American Catholic social ethics as developed
in the last chapter reminds us of the pluralism of approaches
that existed even among those who did not accept the status
quo. John A. Ryan put heavy emphasis on the role of the state
to bring about reform. German-American Catholics distrusted
the state and called for a very thoroughgoing reform on the
model of the corporate society. The Catholic Worker Movement espoused a radical personalism that distrusted all organization and even gloried in the name of anarchism. History thus
indicates the pluralism which has existed in social ethics.[25]

It is interesting that Catholic social theory has traditionally
recognized a legitimate diversity or pluralism on concrete
questions facing society.[26]   Elsewhere I have proposed that
dissent, or more positively pluralism, will be increasingly
present on some questions of more personal and individual
ethics such as contraception, sterilization, divorce and even
abortion and euthanasia. The basic reasons stem from the
distance of such questions from the core of faith and from the
complexity of these specific questions because of which one
cannot claim that a particular solution is so certain that it
excludes the possibility of error. One cannot speak about *the*
Christian solution to specific concrete problems as if there
were no other possible Christian alternative. In an era where
pluralism is being recognized even in the area of personal
morality, one cannot logically deny its existence in social ethics.
In both areas theology must continue to discuss the important
question of the limits of pluralism.

Ecclesiological Consequences

My understanding of mediation, eschatology and pluralism
concluded that often Christians and the church can agree in
pointing out what are the problems and difficulties existing in
society (a negative critique). In season and out of season the

whole church should preach and respond to the basic gospel message of conversion which calls for Christians to struggle against the presence of sin not only in our hearts but also in the social structures of society. On the level of the general there should be more agreement among Christians and within the churches on the values, goals and ideals to be present in society, but as one descends to particular plans and strategies, the very complexity of these issues will often mean that it is increasingly difficult to speak about *the* Christian solution.

In this area above all one sees the importance and need for smaller groups within the church. Groups of Christians can and should join together to work for a common purpose and employ a common strategy. In many ways the liberation theology of South America has grown up in the context of such small groups of committed Christians banded together to work for overcoming oppression. In the United States the Catholic Worker movement and other such apostolates illustrate the same basic reality. The peace movement in the United States in a more informal way sponsored the existence of such groups.

Although there have been some such groups present in the United States in the past, it seems that they were not as numerous as in other countries. Perhaps this is because a Catholic Action approach with an emphasis on cell units was not as common in this country as elsewhere. However, I believe it is very important and essential for the good of the church to have a variety of small groups existing within the church.

In the last few years in the United States a number of smaller groups working for social justice and change have come into being. Think, for example, of the Justice and Peace organizations which have sprung up in dioceses and in religious communities. Network, a group of women religious lobbying for social change, has attracted attention and support. There are many different types of groups which can and should exist. At times one might find various church groups on different sides of the same issue as has happened on the Equal Rights Amendment. At times even the bishops can function as such a group within the church.

In this view one sees the church, whether on a local, national or international level, as a larger community in which serious dialogue takes place about what the gospel calls us to do in terms of changing societies. Individuals and smaller groups within the church would be able to do what larger groups and the entire church itself might not be able to do. I would hope that in this way many individual Christians would feel a vocation to join such particular groups in their witness to poverty, peace, social justice, and other vital issues.

There is still at times a role for the total church and its leadership, whether on a local, national or international level, both in terms of teaching and of acting on specific social problems. A whole church body either on a parochial or national or even worldwide basis can and should at times address specific moral questions. However, in so doing there are some cautions that must be taken into account. First of all, since such questions involve technical data and expertise, those who are addressing such problems must make sure that they have competently mastered all the details which are involved. Second, it will be impossible to speak out or act on all the issues facing society because of a lack of expertise, but the more significant questions can and should be chosen. Third, they should recognize that other Christians might disagree with the particular position that is being taken. In this way the position is proposed in the name of the church but with the recognition that even individual members of the church might disagree with a particular aspect of it. Here the moral credibility of the teaching is most significant.

In looking to the question of the future agenda of the church in the area of social ethics this chapter has purposely avoided a substantive consideration of the various issues. Instead, an attempt has been made to consider the theological methodology that should be involved in such discussions and also the ecclesiological implications of the social mission of the church.

NOTES

1. Pastoral Constitution on the Church in the Modern World, nos. 46-93. For a reliable English translation see *The Documents of Vatican II*, ed. Walter M. Abbott (New York: Guild Press, 1966).

2. *World Conference on Church and Society: Official Report* (Geneva: World Council of Churches, 1967).

3. The final recommendations of this conference were printed in *Origins: N.C. Documentary Service* 6, no. 20 (November 4, 1976) and no. 21 (November 11, 1976): 309-340.

4. Pope Paul VI, *Octogesima adveniens*, no. 22. This and other important documents on social justice can be found in *The Gospel of Peace and Justice: Catholic Social Teaching since Pope John*, ed. Joseph Germillion (Maryknoll, New York: Orbis Books, 1976).

5. David J. O'Brien, *The Renewal of American Catholicism* (New York: Oxford University Press, 1972), pp. 138-162.

6. Pope Paul VI, *Populorum progressio*, no. 3, in Gremillion, *The Gospel of Peace and Justice*, p. 388.

7. John C. Bennett, *The Radical Imperative* (Philadelphia: Westminster Press, 1975), pp. 142-164.

8. Gustavo Gutierrez, *A Theology of Liberation* (Maryknoll, New York: Orbis, 1973), pp. 36-37; 176.

9. Ibid., pp. 232-239.

10. Hugo Assmann, *Theology for a Nomad Church* (Maryknoll, New York: Orbis, 1976), pp. 116, 138ff.

11. John A. Ryan, *Distributive Justice* (New York: Macmillan, 1916). See also John A. Coleman, "Vision and Praxis in American Theology," *Theological Studies* 37 (1976): 3-40.

12. John Rawls, *A Theory of Justice* (Cambridge, Mass.: Belknap Press of Harvard University, 1971); Robert A. Nozick, *Anarchy, State and Utopia* (New York: Basic Books, 1974).

13. Bennett, *The Radical Imperative*, pp. 152-154.

14. E.g., Ryan, *Distributive Justice*, p. 358.

15. Recent documents of the hierarchical magisterium have stressed this universal destiny of the goods of creation. See Pastoral Constitution on the Church in the Modern World, no. 69, in Gremillion, *The Gospel of Peace and Justice*, pp. 305-306; *Populorum progressio*, nos. 22-24, in Gremillion, *The Gospel of Peace and Justice*, pp. 393-394.

16. Such an understanding is proposed by Paul Ramsey in his critique of the World Conference on Church and Society held in Geneva in 1967. See Paul Ramsey, *Who Speaks for the Church?* (Nashville: Abingdon, 1967), p. 53.

17. Martin E. Marty, *Righteous Empire: The Protestant Experience in America* (New York: The Dial Press, 1970).

18. O'Brien, *The Renewal of American Catholicism.*

19. Aaron I. Abell, *American Catholicism and Social Action: A Search for Social Justice* (Notre Dame, Indiana: University of Notre Dame Press, 1963).

20. E.g., Paul Hanly Furfey, *Fire on the Earth* (New York: Macmillan, 1936); see also William D. Miller, *A Harsh and Dreadful Love: Dorothy Day and the Catholic Worker Movement* (Garden City, New York: Doubleday Image Books, 1974).

21. Such an assumption in my judgment lies behind many aspects of the social reform ideas of John A. Ryan, especially his theory of underconsumption. See George G. Higgins, "The Underconsumption Theory in the Writings of Monsignor John A. Ryan" (M.A. dissertation, Catholic University of America, 1942).

22. Harold F. Trehey, *Foundations of a Modern Guild System* (Washington, D.C.: Catholic University of America Press, 1940).

23. Justice in the World, no. 6, in Gremillion, *The Gospel of Peace and Justice*, p. 154.

24. For the importance of church organizations as advocates for the poor see *Towards a Renewed Catholic Charities Movement* (Washington, D.C.: National Conference of Catholic Charities, 1971).

25. David J. O'Brien, *American Catholics and Social Reform* (New York: Oxford University Press, 1968).

26. Frans H. Mueller, "The Church and the Social Question," in *The Challenge of Mater et Magistra,* ed. Joseph N. Moody and Justus George Lawler (New York: Herder and Herder, 1963), pp. 13–33. For confirmation of this in recent documents of the hierarchical magisterium see *Octogesima adveniens*, nos. 59–61, in Gremillion, *The Gospel of Peace and Justice*, pp. 510–511; Justice in the World, no. 37, in Gremillion, *The Gospel of Peace and Justice*, p. 521.

5. Religion, Law, and Public Policy in America

The role of religion in American public life has been a perennial question in the American political ethos. The first Amendment of the Constitution prohibits the establishment of any religion and guarantees the free exercise of religion. Throughout the years there have been different topics that have been discussed in relation to this role of religion. A continuing topic of debate is the question of aid to parochial schools. The purpose of this chapter is to investigate two particular contemporary aspects of the question—the controversies over abortion and over the political involvement of some conservative Christians through groups such as the Moral Majority. In the process, criteria and principles will be proposed to govern the role of religion and of church groups in establishing legislation and public policy. The perspective throughout this chapter is that of a Catholic theologian proposing a criterion for the involvement of faith and religion which should be acceptable to all Americans.

I. Abortion Legislation and the Criterion of Political Purpose

The abortion controversy has raised a number of significant issues in the last few years—the morality of abortion, the legality of abortion, the public funding of abortion. Lawyers, courts, philosophers, theologians, churches, and the general public have been discussing all these issues. This chapter addresses a fourth related question—the issue of religious-motivated and church involvement in seeking and lobbying for particular legislation. The specific question has been raised by the contention of the brief for the plaintiffs in *McRae* v. *Califano* that the Hyde Amendment restricting Medicaid funding for abortion violates the nonestablishment clause of the first Amendment by enacting a particular religious view of abortion into law and because the passage of such legislation resulted from religious influence and lobbying, especially by the Roman Catholic Church.[1] Such reasoning has been rejected by both Judge Dooling in his decision in the United States District Court in New York, which declared that the Hyde Amendment is unconstitutional on other grounds, and by the Supreme Court which recently decided that the Hyde Amendment is constitutional.[2] However, the issue as such remains important and significant for our country at large and for those interested in the role of religion and of faith in our religiously pluralistic society.

My perspective in this study is not that of a lawyer but of a Catholic theologian. It seems, at least to this nonlawyer, there exists general agreement among lawyers in discussing questions of the establishment clause of the first Amendment in the light of the criteria proposed by the Supreme Court in the Nyquist case (which dealt with aid to private schools): "To pass muster under the Establishment Clause the law in question, first, must reflect a clearly secular legislative purpose . . . second, must have a primary effect that neither advances nor inhibits religion . . . and third, must avoid excessive government entanglement with religion."[3] Lawyers for both the plaintiffs and the defendants in the *McRae* case argue on the basis of these criteria. My perspective must recognize and accept such legal criteria, but I want to analyze the problem precisely from the angle of faith and religion in American public life and to propose the criterion to govern the involvement of churches and of religion in general.

The question has been proposed in terms of functionally distinguishing between the religious and nonreligious purpose in civil law. I would prefer to rephrase the question: How do we determine if the purpose of the law is truly political? I prefer the term "political" to the term "secular" which is now accepted and used by the courts.

The problem centers around the understanding and the definition of religion. It seems all must admit there are two different ways of understanding religion in this context — a narrow and restricted view and a broader understanding. In the more restricted sense religion is limited to those realities directly and immediately connected with religious belief, worship, practice, and organization. The broader definitions can differ in a number of ways, but in my understanding the broader definition recognizes that religion in some way enters into all aspects of human existence and cannot be divorced totally from the political, cultural, social, and economic aspects of our human existence. At the very minimum one must recognize and clearly differentiate these two understandings of religion, each of which has its proper place in the discussion.

The Supreme Court itself recognizes a narrower and a broader understanding of religion. When the Court discusses questions about the establishment clause, religion is generally understood in the narrower sense. However, in other cases such as *Seeger*, dealing with conscientious objection, the Court has maintained that the concept of religion can be so interpreted that it does not necessarily even include a belief in God as such![4]

From the perspective of my understanding of Christian and Catholic theology there must also exist a broader understanding of religion. The restricted definition of religion readily allows for the distinction between the religious sphere and the secular sphere. However, such a sharp distinction and especially the separation resulting from it are unacceptable to many Christian theologians today. In fact, theologians, churches, and church people are often steadfastly insisting upon the role of the church and of faith in all aspects of our human existence.

Chapter two has strongly defended the thesis that the gospel cannot be restricted to only one small aspect of human life — the religious sphere understood in the narrow sense and confined to the realm of the private. The gospel impels Christians not only to change hearts but also to change the structures of society to serve better the needs of justice and peace. The gospel should have an influence on all aspects of the Christian life. The split between religious faith and daily human existence must be overcome. Such an understanding of the role and function of faith, of the gospel, and of the church can be found especially in recent statements of the World Council of Churches and of the Second Vatican Council.[5] The social mission of the church involving participation in the work of transforming the world and society is a constitutive dimension of the gospel itself and of the mission of the church, as was discussed earlier.

Many Christians insist even more on the social mission of the church in the light of the Marxist critique that religion and Christianity are the opiate of the people. Religion tells people to put up with suffering and injustice in the present world, and their patience will be rewarded with eternal life in the future. Reacting against this criticism, many contemporary Christians have stressed the importance of the church's involvement in the struggle for justice and liberation. The gospel message of freedom affects the whole person in all aspects — personal, social, cultural, economic, and political. Perhaps the strongest apologetic for the Christian faith today is the fact that practicing Christians are concerned and trying to do something about the problem of the oppressed, the poor, and the needy.[6]

From the perspective of the American self-understanding, both definitions of religion must be retained. Theoretically the American proposition recognizes religious pluralism and proclaims that civil unity can and should exist side by side with religious pluralism. Many people who profess different religions or no religion at all join together to form a civic unity. The nonestablishment clause of the first Amendment safeguards this reality. In this respect there is a proper place for the more limited and restricted definition and understanding of religion.

However, the American system does not exclude religion or faith understood in the broader sense from affecting society. Ours is not a professedly atheistic society in which there is no room for faith and belief in God, even though some people may be atheists, and their right to such a position must be scrupulously protected and safeguarded. American democracy differs considerably from the Continental liberalism of the nineteenth century which proclaimed there was no room for religion and faith in society. Religion was relegated to a personal and private role. Our system professes the incompetency of the government and of the state in religious matters (understood in the strict sense) and protects the religious freedom of all citizens, but it still recognizes that religion in the broader sense can and should have a role in society and even in legislation and government.[7] Chapter three developed the theory of John Courtney Murray in this matter.

Especially in recent times our American experience testifies to this theoretical understanding. The two most significant social problems faced by our nation and involving government legislation and action in the last few decades have been the questions of racial discrimination and war. In both these issues the churches have contributed heavily to changing our laws and our public policy. In fact, there were a number of voices in society and in the church who condemned the churches for not being in the forefront of the movements for racial equality and for an end to the unjust war in Vietnam. There are many other issues on which religious people and churches, committed to their religious beliefs, have sought an impact on legislation and society — questions of poverty and welfare, gun control, the acceptance of the Panama Canal treaty and of the Salt II treaty, nuclear weapons and defense, nuclear power, capital punishment, women's rights, and many other such questions.

Both American theory and American practice recognize that religion, understood in the broad sense, can and should influence not only society but also government and legislation. Christian theology also argues strenuously for the involvement of individuals and churches in influenceing government and the state. For these reasons I strongly oppose the contention that the Hyde Amendment is unconstitutional because it legislates one religious view or because of the lobbying effort of the Catholic Church. If this principle were accepted, faith and the churches could no longer make a contribution to government and legislation.

However, one must recognize that there are also illegitimate and unacceptable ways in which religion and churches might influence government and legislation. (I am not talking now about what might be called imprudent and therefore wrong

ways. For example, one cannot say that single-issue politics
is unconstitutional, but in my judgment it is politically imprudent and wrong.) Think, for example, of prohibition laws
or of laws against selling contraceptives. It is necessary to have
some criterion, then, to distinguish legitimate and illegitimate
involvement of religion and of the churches in the political
process.

To phrase the question in terms of distinguishing religious
and nonreligious purpose is not felicitous because of the different ways in which religion can be understood and because
of the danger that religion in the broad sense will be excluded
from the sphere of influencing the state and legislation. Likewise, the criterion of secular purpose seems to promote a
dichotomy between the secular and the religious and thereby
fails to recognize the influence religion in the broad sense of
the term can and should have. I prefer the criterion of truly
political purpose. Note that we are talking about the specific
question of the impact of religion and faith on the state,
government, and legislation and not about the broader question of its influence on society in general.

When dealing explicitly with the question of restricting the
freedom of all people in society, there are three principles
which spell out the meaning of truly political purpose and
should guide the role of religion and of the churches in determining what is truly political purpose.

First, the freedom of human beings is to be respected
as far as possible and curtailed only when and insofar as
necessary.

Second, the principle for state action or restriction of freedom is the public order, which is a much more restricted concept than the common good. The public order is the narrow
area in which the coercive power of the state appropriately
functions. There are three aspects that make up the public
order — an order of justice including social justice and human
rights, an order of public morality (this refers to the morality
necessary for prople to live together in society), and an order
of public peace. The state should intervene to protect basic
human rights, to promote the economic rights of all in society, and also to prevent public disturbances of the peace.

Third, any legislation involving a restriction of freedom must be good law in the sense that it is equitable and enforceable.

There can and should be much discussion about the extension and application of the three principles which are proposed here, but the basic principles supply a framework which all religious people and churches can use in discerning on what issues they try to influence the state and its laws.

Note that in these principles no mention is made of the motivation or ultimate grounding of what constitutes the threefold aspect of the public order. Some might oppose stealing on the basis of the Judeo-Christian tradition, on the grounds of Muslim teaching, or on any number of different philosophical systems. The only determining factor is the end or purpose — a truly political purpose which concretely means a demand of the public order with its threefold aspects of justice, of public morality, and of peace.

In this brief schematic presentation I have purposely tried to present only the theory and not become involved in the origin of the theory and in its application to the particular question of abortion. The theory proposed here is fundamentally that found in the Declaration on Religious Liberty of the Second Vatican Council, which itself is heavily based on the work of John Courtney Murray.[8] One important aspect has been added — the insistence on social justice as a legitimate and necessary function of government and of law. Neither Murray nor the Vatican declaration (perhaps because of the limited subject matter of religious freedom) gave enough importance to the role of the state in preserving and promoting social justice. Unfortunately, this proposal found in official Catholic documents has not always been followed even in other Catholic documents such as the Declaration on Procured Abortion issued by the Sacred Congregation for the Doctrine of the Faith in 1974.

How would I apply these principles to the issues raised by abortion? From the perspective of the morality of abortion I believe that truly individual human life is present from the fourteenth to the twenty-first day after conception, and after that time only the life of the mother or a reason commensurate with life could morally justify an abortion. Legally, in the light of the divisions in our society and on the basis of the presumption in favor of freedom found in the first principle, I have opposed efforts to overturn the 1973 Supreme Court decision by amending the Constitution. However, I defend the right of all people who believe that truly human life is present in the fetus to work to amend the Constitution because the protection of human life is the most basic right in society. The motivation or the ultimate grounding for one's decision as to when human life does begin cannot be a basis for denying the right of people with such a judgment from working for a law that protects what they believe is human life. As for public funding, I have concluded that a creative politics should be able to find a way in which tax payers opposed to abortion would not have to support it. However, if there is no other alternative, I would reluctantly accept the public funding of medically indicated abortions for the poor.[9] Yes, people can employ the same criterion and come to different conclusions on controversial issues such as abortion. But all should admit in theory and in practice that the criterion for allowing state intervention is a truly political purpose, spelled out in terms of public order and applied in the light of the presumption in favor of freedom and of the requirements of good law.

Although my personal position is generally opposed to abortion in the moral arena, I do not advocate working for a constitutional amendment to restrict abortions legally because I give great weight to the first principle of political purpose which in the midst of public disagreement establishes a presumption in favor of no coercion. The American Catholic bishops emphasize the second principle which justifies the intervention of law to protect what one believes to be truly human life. In addition to this theoretical argument I have a practical objection to attempting to amend the Constitution. There are two possible avenues of approach — a states' rights amendment or a federal amendment declaring the fetus to be a truly human being with all the protection of law. Any attempts for such amendments will be both divisive and futile. A states' rights approach will mean that many states will ultimately choose to allow some abortions as certain states did before the 1973 Court ruling. In addition, I fear that in advocating a states' rights approach I would be aligning myself with many people who over the years have obstructed the struggle for social justice in the United States. An amendment to the Constitution to protect the fetus will not be successful. Although many people, perhaps even a majority, may be opposed to the Court decision, it will be impossible for three-fourths (38) of the states to agree on the question of when truly human life begins. Some will argue for conception; some for segmentation; some for brain waves; some for twelve weeks after conception. In the light of the existing differences it will be impossible to find the political agreement necessary to support a constitutional amendment saying at what time the fetus is a truly human being.

There are weaknesses in my position. I accept the existing pluralism in our society, so that the prophetic, or teaching, aspect of law is greatly reduced. Some argue against my position by pointing to the past denial of civil rights to blacks. However, in abortion there are serious reasons for recognizing some difficulties in proving the true humanity of the fetus, whereas in the case of blacks serious reasons did not exist for denying their humanity. Likewise the quantity and quality of the persons denying the true humanhood of the fetus must be acknowledged even if not accepted. A practical political argument can also be raised against my position. Perhaps a constitutional amendement will not succeed, but this is one form of exerting pressure which will bear fruit in other areas such as the 1977 Court ruling on funding. In my judgment none of these reasons is strong enough to overturn my position.

It does not follow that the prolife adherents should do nothing in society to promote their position. The theory explained above, and developed in chapter three, recognizes an important difference between the state and society. The prolife adherents and the Roman Catholic Church could and should still try to influence society in the matter of abortion choice. I have advocated a nationally coordinated program voluntarily supported by Roman Catholics and others, if they wish, to publicize that the Catholic Church will guarantee for any pregnant woman the financial, psychological, medical, and social help needed to carry her child to term and to care for that child after birth. Through its resources, both financial and especially in terms of persons willing to do volunteer work, the Catholic Church (and others) could establish a program that would both be effective in preventing some abortions and at the same time bear witness and be prophetic within society without causing the excessive divisiveness of futile efforts to amend the Constitution.

One specific question about abortion arose in the context of the 1980 elections. Cardinal Medeiros of Boston urged the defeat of candidates in the primary and general elections who had supported the legalization of abortions.[10] As mentioned above, my position accepts the present law on abortion, but Catholics and others are within their American rights and operating on the solid criterion of political purpose if they work for a constitutional amendment to overturn the present abortion law. However, in my view it is ordinarily a violation of political prudence to vote for legislators only on the basis of one issue. All the more so, a Catholic bishop should not officially call upon Catholics to act in this manner. In this case, in fact, it seems that Cardinal Medeiros acted contrary to the position proposed by the American Catholic bishops as a whole. The Catholic bishops issued a statement in November 1979, based on a previous statement made in 1976, calling for Catholics to consider a number of important issues in deciding how they should vote. The issues included abortion, arms control and disarmament, capital punishment, the economy, education, food and agricultural policy, health care, housing, human rights, mass media, and regional conflict in the world. Thus the American Catholic bishops as a whole have opposed single-issue voting.[11]Abortion and the role of Catholic bishops were discussed at length in the 1984 election campaign, but again the bishops as a whole, despite significant individual exceptions, came out against single-issue voting.

II. The Moral Majority

One of the new phenomena arising in American politics in the last few years and especially at the time of the 1980 and 1984 political campaigns has been the organized efforts of conservative evangelical Christians to work for the political causes which will counter political liberalism. The question naturally arises about the legitimacy and propriety of such involvement. This discussion has made even more important the need for criteria and principles which religious groups can and should use in determining their political involvement. Too often there exists the danger of some religionists defending their own involvement in public policy questions but accusing the opposing group of violating the American understanding of the role of separation between church and state.

There are a number of different groups which belong to what has been called by some the New Christian Right. Since it is impossible to describe all these different groups, our consideration will be limited to the Moral Majority, an organization headed by Dr. Jerry Falwell. The Reverend Falwell is pastor of the Thomas Road Baptist Church in Lynchburg, Virginia. Falwell is perhaps best known and most effective through the "Old-Time Gospel Hour," a Sunday religious service carried by almost 700 TV and radio stations and reaching an estimated 21 million people. Our consideration of Falwell's position will be on the basis of his book *Listen, America!*[12] The dust cover describes the Moral Majority as a "non-profit organization intended to counter political liberalism. Its aim is to mobilize at least two million Americans to work for pro-God, pro-family policies in government, so that, according to *Conservative Digest*, 'clear-cut moral choices can be offered to the American voters for the first time in decades.' "

Falwell, in keeping with his fundamentalist theology, calls his approach "a biblical plan of action" (pp. 245-254). Our country was once great but is now sick because of permissiveness and moral decay. The moral majority must work together to overcome these problems. His first chapter describes the malaise or crisis in the military, economic, and political orders. For the first time in our lifetime America is no longer the military might of the world. Economically a growing welfare system threatens our country with bankruptcy. The free-enterprise system as found in America is clearly outlined in the Book of Proverbs. Furthermore, there is a vacuum of political leadership (pp. 8-23). The concluding chapter summarizes our five major national sins — abortion, homosexuality, pornography, humanism, and the fractured family. He is strongly opposed to communism (even defending the

Rhodesia of Ian Smith and South Africa), socialism, redistribution of wealth, ERA, the no-win war strategy which we pursued in Vietnam, humanism and liberalism, the Salt II Treaty, the Panama Canal Treaty, government bureaucracy and intrusion into all aspects of life, especially education with laws on busing, school prayer, and regulations against Christian schools. The names most frequently cited in the book include Milton Friedman and Senator Jesse Helms.

Honesty compels me to admit that I have many differences with Dr. Falwell's approach, but it is important to recognize the different types of disagreements. It is grossly unfair to accuse Falwell of violating the American system of church and state merely because on religious grounds he advocates many proposals for legislation or public policy with which I disagree. As an American I have to recognize that he has the right to propose many of these positions even though I have my right to disagree both as an American and as a Christian believer. Three areas will be touched upon in the following discussions — my theological differences with Falwell; the question of the proper criterion governing the involvement of religious individuals and groups as well as all other individuals and groups in proposing legislation and public policy; discussion of particular issues.

Theological Differences

From the perspective of Christian theology my greatest area of disagreement with Dr. Falwell centers on his understanding of the role and use of scripture. My Catholic theological tradition has justly been criticized in the past for not giving enough importance to the scriptural witness. Catholic moral theology at the present time is rightly trying to incorporate a more scripturally oriented vision and grounding to its approach. However, I am in total agreement with the traditional Catholic opposition to *sola scriptura* (the scripture alone). In my judgment the *and* in Catholic theology has been most important and points to an emphasis on mediation as the basic characteristic of the Catholic theological tradition. The Catholic tradition has recognized the importance of *and*: scripture and tradition; faith and reason; Jesus and the church. Too often in the Catholic tradition the second element has been seen as too absolute and independent of the first, but the second element in these pairs must be seen in relationship to the first. The Catholic tradition in moral theology should be criticized for not giving enough importance to the scriptures, but the scriptures are not the only source of ethical wisdom and knowledge available to the Christian. Human reason understood in the broadest possible way remains an important source of ethical wisdom and knowledge for Christian social ethics. All the human sciences of politics, economics, sociology, and others are necessary in coming to specific judgments and conclusions in the area of Christian social ethics. To incarnate Christian values and attitudes in concrete reality one needs the input of all these other sciences.

Dr. Falwell seems to indicate that his whole approach is biblical. The concluding section of his book begins with a section on "A Biblical Plan of Action." Falwell nowhere explicitly admits the need or existence of sources of wisdom for Christian social ethics other than the scriptures. However, it seems that some form of human reason in general and the interpretations of many other human sciences are involved in the very fact that he has strong convictions on such specific questions as the Panama Canal Treaty and Salt II. I do not see how it is possible to claim that there is a biblical solution to these questions without recognizing an important role for human reason and the human sciences as mediating the biblical values and message.

My understanding of the use of the scriptures in determining Christian social morality differs greatly from the approach proposed in *Listen, America!* According to Falwell "The Bible is absolutely infallible, without error in all matters pertaining to faith and practice, as well as in areas such as geography, science, history, etc." (p. 63). My approach would accept the tools of biblical criticism and the importance of hermeneutics in understanding the Bible and using its teaching in forming contemporary Christian social ethics. The hermeneutic aspect recognizes that one cannot go immediately and directly from a text embedded in one historical and cultural period to an application in possibly different historical and cultural circumstances. Think, for example, of the biblical teaching on slavery. The New Testament does not seem to oppose the institution of slavery, but today most Christian theologians would strongly oppose slavery.

Criterion of Political Purpose

The criterion of political purpose was proposed to guide the involvement of religion, faith, and the churches in matters of legislation and public policy. The basic thrust behind such a distinction is the fundamental and absolutely necessary distinction between the realm of Christian moral teaching and the realm of legislation and public policy. Falwell's book does not explicitly deal with this question. One can understand that a particular book cannot mention all aspects of the question. However, in the context of our religiously pluralistic society Falwell and other leaders of the so-called New Christian Right must expressly deal with these questions.

Falwell explictly recognizes and upholds the separation of church and state, but he claims such an understanding does not mean a government devoid of God and the Bible (p. 53). I too can agree with that understanding in general, but it would be helpful for Falwell to develop this relationship with as much precision as possible. Our author's staunch support for the nation of Israel and his prayer for God's continuing blessing on this miracle also indicate that he accepts the separation of church and state (pp. 107-113). However, there are emphases in the book which can raise some questions about his acceptance of religious pluralism and the separation of church and state. The major thesis of the book maintains that America is suffering from moral decay and permissiveness, with the root cause in sin. Before there can be a revival, there must be an awareness and conviction of the problem of sin (p. 68). The answer to every one of our nations' dilemmas is a spiritual one. We as a nation must acknowledge God as our creator and Jesus Christ as the savior of mankind. Such an acknowledgment will turn our nation around economically and in every other way (p. 81). The book contains some startling statements, such as: "If a person is not a Christian, he is inherently a failure" (p. 62). Since nothing is said explicitly to the contrary, one could be left with the impression that the function of law and politics is to assist in and even legislate totally in accord with this view of spiritual renewal. Such statements come close to identifying the unity of the City of God with the unity of the City of Man. At the very minimum Falwell must deal more explicitly and precisely with this question of religious pluralism in America and the distinction between church and state.

There is no discussion in Falwell's book on the distinction between morality and legality. Such a distinction is basic to any recognition of the need for determining a criterion to direct and justify religious involvement in legislation and public policy. The frequent citations of biblical texts on particular issues can readily give the impression that one can move directly from the level of the revealed morality of the Bible to the level of the political and legal. A real difference between morality and legality must be recognized especially in the matter of what is often called private morality. Here, as pointed out above, the first rule of jurisprudence calls for as much freedom as possible and as little restraint as necessary. Falwell must deal more explicitly and precisely with these questions.

Particular Issues

In terms of political discourse the central focus of my disagreements with Falwell is on many specific issues, as illustrated in the description of his position, which he supports on the basis of biblical warrants. I disagree on most of these issues both in regard to the substance of the issue and with the contention that these are Christian or biblical approaches. My differences with Falwell are not based on the accusation that he is violating the spirit or letter of the American separation of church and state by supporting these issues in the name of the Bible. It is impossible to discuss all these particular issues, but I will mention three very significant areas of disagreement — the use of military force, the distribution of the goods of creation, and the role of America in the plan of God.

Falwell decries the decline in our military power, our appeasement vis-à-vis communism, our attempts at disarmament, and our no-win war policies. He justifies the use of the sword by government as revenging and executing God's wrath on those who do evil (e.g., p. 98). Much has been written about the Christian and biblical approach to peace and war. At the very minimum Falwell gives no attention to the many sayings attributed to Jesus (he would have to maintain they are literally the statements of the historical Jesus) about peace and mercy. On the basis of the scriptures some Christians are convinced pacificists. Even those who have accepted war, as in the theory of just war, stress that war is always a last resort, and there are limitations on the ways in which war can be waged. Falwell's approach to military might and strength seems to be opposed to the approaches taken by most of the Christian tradition.

Falwell strongly defends free enterprise, laissez-faire capitalism, and a limited and decentralized government (p. 72). "The free-enterprise system is clearly outlined in the Book of Proverbs in the Bible. Jesus Christ made it clear that the work ethic was a part of his plan for man. Ownership of property is biblical. Competition in business is biblical. Ambitious and successful business management is clearly outlined as part of God's plan for His people" (p. 13). Many Christians would rightly disagree with some of the above statements and emphases. Again, it is impossible to develop a full Christian approach to the economic and political orders. However, in my judgment the very first thing that a Christian must say about worldly goods is that the goods of creation exist to serve the needs of all. This is the understanding found in recent documents of the World Council of Churches and of conciliar and papal Catholic social teaching. Pope Paul VI in his encyclical *Populorum progressio* asserted, "All other rights whatsoever, including those of property and of free commerce, are to be subordinated to this principle."[13]

Although Falwell finds decay and weaknesses in contemporary America, he basically sees America as God's chosen people. "I love America because, she, above all the nations of the world, has honored the principles of the Bible. America has been great because she has been good" (p. 263). Falwell speaks out "against Godless communism which would seek to destroy the work of Christ that is going out from this base of America" (p. 106). Falwell too readily identifies the cause of the United States with the cause of God and God's plan.

The Judeo-Christian tradition has always nourished within itself a prophetic aspect and an eschatological aspect which calls on all believers to reexamine their own lives, causes, and nations. Arrogance and not biblical teaching is the source of the identification of America with the cause of God.

In conclusion, I agree with Falwell that faith and religion should not be excluded from our laws and public policy. However, it is incumbent upon him in the future to spell out more clearly what is the relationship between the two. I have attempted to do so with the criterion of political purpose and the three principles which spell out the meaning and applications of political purpose. Falwell must clearly distinguish between morality and legality in what are often called questions of private morality. In the meantime in the area of private morality he is vulnerable to the charge of not distinguishing properly between the role of the church and of the state. On most of the specific issues of public policy which Falwell endorses I do not dispute his right as an American to propose such positions and even to base them on his understanding of the Christian faith. My disagreement with the founder of the Moral Majority is on the substantive positons he takes and the Christian and biblical warrants he gives for those positions. I think he is wrong both with regard to most of his positions and with regard to his claim that these represent Christian or biblical teaching.

This study has dealt with the problem of the relationship between faith or religion and American political life. Two emotionally charged issues have been considered. There is always the danger in such an atmosphere of accusing those who disagree with my position of violating the American principle of the separation of church and state, while at times I use religious reasons to support the public policy I agree with. There is need for consistency, discipline, and restraint in our argumentation. The criterion of political purpose determines what constitutes a legitimate involvement of religious ideas into the political arena. In the light of this criterion it is legitimate for people on the basis of their religious and philosophical principles to work for legislation which forbids abortion or the public funding of abortion. Note, however, that for a number of reasons I do not favor such action. Dr. Falwell needs to explain more clearly how he understands the relationship between religious beliefs and principles and political life in our country. Although on many issues such as defense, military, and economic policies his religiously grounded positions do not violate the American understanding of the relationship between church and state, nevertheless, in my judgment his positions are often erroneous. Hopefully these considerations might contribute to a better understanding of the relationship between religion and politics and to a more precise and accurate public discourse.

NOTES

1. Copies of the brief can be obtained from Center for Constitutional Rights, 853 Broadway, New York, New York 10003.

2. *Harris v. McRae*, 48 USLW 4941, June 30, 1980. For different reactions to the decision of the Supreme Court, see John T. Noonan, Jr., "The Supreme Court and Abortion: Upholding Constitutional Principles," *The Hastings Center Report* 10, 6 (December 1980), 14-16; David Mechanic, "The Supreme Court and Abortion: Sidestepping Social Realities," *The Hastings Report* 10, 6 (December 1980), 17-19.

3. *Committee for Public Education v. Nyquist*, 413 U.S. 756, 773 (1973).

4. *United States v. Seeger*, 380 U.S. 163 (1965). For a discussion of the question of selective conscientious objection, see John A. Rohr, *Prophets Without Honor: Public Policy and the Selective Conscientious Objector* (New York: Abingdon, 1971).

5. Paul Bock, *In Search of a Responsible World Society: The Social Teaching of the World Council of Churches* (Philadelphia: Westminster, 1974); *Renewing the Earth: Catholic Documents on Peace, Justice and Liberation*, eds. David J. O'Brien and Thomas A. Shannon (Garden City, New York: Doubleday Image Book, 1977).

6. Such themes are often found in contemporary political and liberation theology. See Dorothy Soelle, *Political Theology* (Philadelphia: Fortress Press, 1974); Gustavo Gutierrez, *A Theology of Liberation* (Maryknoll, New York: Orbis Books, 1972).

7. John Courtney Murray, *We Hold These Truths: Catholic Reflections on the American Proposition* (New York: Sheed and Ward, 1960).

8. John Courtney Murray, *The Problem of Religious Freedom* (Westminster, Md.: Newman Press, 1965), pp. 40-45.

9. Charles E. Curran, *Ongoing Revision in Moral Theology* (Notre Dame, Indiana: Fides/Claretian Publication, 1975); pp. 107-143; *Transition and Tradition in Moral Theology* (Notre Dame, Indiana: University of Notre Dame Press, 1979), pp. 207-250.

10. "Abortion and the Elections: Cardinal Medeiros," *Origins: N.C. Documentary Service* 10 (September 25, 1980), 239.

11. United States Catholic Conference Administrative Board, "Political Responsibility: Choices for the 1980s," *Origins: N.C. Documentary Service* 9 (November 15, 1979), 349-355. See also *Origins: N.C. Documentary Service* 6 (September 30, 1976), 236.

12. Jerry Falwell, *Listen, America!* (Garden City, New York: Doubleday, 1980). Page numbers in the subsequent paragraphs will refer to this book.

13. Pope Paul VI, *Populorum Progressio*, par. 22, in *Renewing the Earth*, p. 320.

6. Saul D. Alinsky, Catholic Social Practice, and Catholic Theory

Many contemporary theologians understand theology as reflection on the living of Christian life. Gustavo Gutierrez[1] has described liberation theology as critical reflection on praxis. On the Catholic scene liberation theology has been one of the most distinctive developments in the post-Vatican II period. This theology comes out of the struggle for liberation of the economically, politically, and socially oppressed people of Latin America, just as black liberation theology or feminist theology has developed in North America. There has been much talk about what liberation theology would look like in a North American context, but all recognize that the North American experience is quite different from the South American experience.[2]

The theological literature is silent about any such distinctive movements or approaches in the United States to social justice with the exception of the Catholic peace movement in the 1960s and early 1970s.[3] However, as a matter of fact, there has been something new and distinctive in the practical approach to social justice in North American Catholicism which has surfaced since the Second Vatican Council. I refer to the community organization approaches developed by Saul D. Alinsky. Unfortunately, the theological and the ethical communities in Roman Catholicism have not reflected on this phenomenon. I say Catholic theological literature purposely, because there was a significant discussion about Alinsky's approach to community organization in Protestant literature in the late 1950s and the 1960s.[4]

Catholic theological, ethical, and pastoral disciplines are

not the only ones which have neglected to reflect on the Alinsky approach to community organization. A recent sociological article is entitled "Saul D. Alinsky: A Neglected Source but Promising Resource."[5] The authors maintain that the sociological literature has failed to deal with the organizing methods of Alinsky, who in the turbulent sixties was one of the best-known community organizers in the country and whose approach offers great promise for the future, especially in the light of reduced federal support.

I

The first step is to prove that support of Alinsky-style community organizations is the most distinctive practical approach taken to social justice by the Catholic Church in the United States. At first sight this fact seems to be quite implausible. Alinsky was an agnostic Jew who in his own person illustrated the importance he attached to irreverence as a primary virtue in the organizer. Alinsky, who gloried in calling himself a radical, often tweaked the nose of all establishments, including the Roman Catholic Church. Alinsky was born in Chicago in 1909 and did graduate work in criminology at The University of Chicago. Later he worked with prisoners and released prisoners at Joliet State Prison. He was attracted by the labor union organizers of the CIO and later even wrote a biography of John L. Lewis. In the late 1930s he organized the Back of the Yards area in Chicago which had been the scene of Upton Sinclair's *Jungle*. This launched his lifelong work in community organization which was carried out through the Industrial Areas Foundation which he began in 1940. Alinsky and his staff of trained organizers worked quite frequently in Chicago areas, but now their work touches all parts of the country. Alinsky himself died in 1972, but the Industrial Areas Foundation is continuing his work of training community organizers.[6] As implausible as it might seem, this man and the organization he founded, the Industrial Areas Foundation, have had more impact on grass-roots Catholic work for social justice than any other person or group in the United States in the last few decades.

In May 1969 the American Catholic bishops passed a resolution that led to the creation of the Campaign for Human Development. The Catholic bishops recognized the great work that had been done in the past by the human services provided under church auspices, but something new was needed in the light of the problems of urban America in the late 60s. The whole purpose of the campaign was to make funds available for organized groups of white and minority poor to develop economic strength and political power in their own communities. A collection has been taken up in all Catholic churches in the United States for the campaign which has averaged over 7 million dollars a year since its inception in 1970. In addition to funding community organizations the Campaign for Human Development also has an educational campaign aimed at making Catholics and others more aware of the problems of poverty. The vast majority of the funding goes to self-help projects involving community organizations using conflictual means in an attempt to bring about substantive changes within the social, economic, and political system. The conflictual character of these community organizations indicate that they are based on the Alinsky model of community organization.[7]

For anyone with a slight understanding of Alinsky's history the fact that the Catholic Church would officially support his approach to community organizations is not totally surprising. The Catholic Church has in many ways been a source of strong financial and moral support for Alinsky over the years. Alinsky's first work as an organizer was in bringing together the Back of the Yards Council in Chicago in the late 1930s. Since the neighborhood was heavily Catholic, he had to work with the Catholic pastors and churches. In this work he was helped and supported by Bishop Bernard Sheil, the auxiliary bishop of Chicago.[8] Chicago remained a strong base for Alinsky's work. There are at least four Alinsky-style community organizations in

Chicago — the Northwest Community Organization (NCO), the Southwest Community Congress (SCC), Organization for a Better Austin (OBA), and The Woodlawn Organization (TWO).[9] Much of Alinsky's funding in the Chicago area in the 40s and 50s came from the Catholic Church. The archbishop of Chicago supported Alinsky's projects and even had him on the diocesan payroll for some time.

In the early 40s Alinsky began a rather close and lasting relationship with Monsignor John O'Grady, the secretary of the National Conference of Catholic Charities. O'Grady invited Alinsky to give an address at the 1942 annual meeting of the National Conference of Catholic Charities. The two collaborated on a number of organizing projects. So close was the relationship that Alinsky, who had previously written a biography of John L. Lewis, wanted to write a biography of John O'Grady. A draft was apparently written, but the project was abandoned.[10]

Although the Catholic theological, ethical, and pastoral literature has persistently ignored Alinsky, the Protestant literature in the late 50s and early-to-mid 60s followed his work with great attention. In general, the editors and writers in the *Christian Century* strongly disagreed with Alinsky, whereas *Christianity and Crisis* supported him.[11] One of the most significant aspects discussed in the Protestant debate was the Catholic Church's support for Alinsky. Charles Silberman, in his popular *Crisis in Black and White*, strongly supported Alinsky and his organizational tactics but pointed out that Alinsky was attacked as "a dupe of the Catholic Church, the mastermind of a Catholic conspiracy."[12]

Alinsky's most ardent Protestant opponents, Harold Fey, the editor of the *Christian Century*, and Walter Kloetzli constantly emphasized Catholic support for Alinsky.[13] Stephen Rose writing in *Christianity and Crisis* supported Alinsky, but the first charge he attempted to refute was that the IAF was dominated by Roman Catholic interests.[14] Thus Catholic support for Alinsky was well recognized. However, in the 1960s in Chicago, Rochester, and throughout the country Protestants also gave very significant moral and financial support to Alinsky's organizing approaches.

There can be no doubt that many people might be surprised by the thesis that Alinsky-style people's organizations are the most distinctive approach to social justice involvement by the Catholic Church in the United States in the last few decades. There are a number of reasons contributing to this lack of awareness. Very little attention has been given by Catholic theologians and ethicists to what has occurred on the American Catholic scene in general. The Campaign for Human Development itself is concerned that the struggle for social justice by means of community organizations using conflict approaches might alienate some church members. The continued financial backing for CHD indicates that the average Catholic still supports the program. However, CHD obviously does not want to call undue attention to the conflictual aspects that are by definition a part of its organizing the poor and powerless.[15] Perhaps the greatest reason for the lack of awareness of Catholic Church involvement in supporting Alinsky-style community organizations comes from ignorance. Even professionals in the church are really not aware of what has been happening. Fortunately, in the near future a new book by P. David Finks, which has been painstakingly researched over a good number of years, will help in making people more aware of the contribution Alinsky has made to new approaches to social justice in the Catholic Church in the United States.[16]

II

The next step is to explain very briefly the Alinsky approach to community organization. Saul Alinsky wrote two books about his approach — *Reveille for Radicals*, first published in 1946 and republished in 1969 with a new introduction and afterword, and *Rules for Radicals: A Practical Primer for Realistic Radicals*, published in 1971.[17] Alinsky referred to himself as a radical in his earlier writings, but in the early 1960s his self-description as a realistic radical was used to distinguish himself from the radicals of the new left.

Our author, in response to his own question, defines a radical as a person to whom the common good is the greatest personal value. The radical wants a world in which the worth of the individual is recognized. All human beings should be economically, politically, and socially free. According to Alinsky a political radical is passionately devoted to democracy. Tocqueville is frequently cited in his writings. Democracy, however, is much more than just voting once a year. The whole purpose of community organization is to enable the powerless and the have-nots to participate in determining their lives.[18]

Alinsky's radicalism can better be understood in the light of his strong opposition to three other groups—liberals, social workers, and the new left of the sixties. From the beginning of his organization of local communities our author contrasted his own approach to that of liberals. As in much of his writing and speaking, Alinsky in this discussion often shows his own irreverence, his tendency to polarize issues, and some hyperbole which can only infuriate his opponents. Liberals like people with their heads, but radicals like people with both their heads and their hearts. Liberals are well-balanced, impartial, and objective; whereas radicals are passionate partisans for the poor and the victims of injustice. The issue of power constitutes a fundamental difference between radicals and liberals. Liberals fear power; they often agree with goals but will never use conflict and power tactics to achieve these goals. Radicals use power and conflict and actually precipitate the social crisis by their actions. There are as many clear lines of distinction between radicals and liberals as there are between liberals and conservatives.[19] It is obvious that Alinsky often found himself at odds with liberals, who agreed with him at least in theory about the existence of the problems and the goals to be achieved, but who strongly disagreed with his tactics.

From the very beginning of his organizing work Saul Alinsky differed with social-work theoreticians and practitioners whom he accused of welfare colonialism. Their approach involves handouts and band-aids but brings about no real structural change. The have-nots still remain powerless. Mass community organizations want to change the system so that the people govern themselves. The establishment is always threatened by such an approach because they must ultimately give up and share some of their power. Fundamental, structural, and truly democratic changes are not going to be brought about by committees and councils composed of professionals and by centralized bureaucracies.[20]

After the mid-60s a new group of opponents appeared on the scene — the radicals of the new left. Pragmatic radicals, unlike the new left, begin with the existing system because there is no other place to begin. A true political revolution (a true democracy) will occur only if there is the supporting base of a popular reformation. To build a popular mass organization is tedious and takes time, but there is no real alternative to working within the system. The new left offers only a mess of rhetorical garbage and meaningless slogans. The American system might have its problems and difficulties, but at least there exist some freedom and the possibility to bring about change.[21]

In a democratic society the people are the motor, and the organizations of people are the gears. The power of the people is transmitted to the gears of their own organizations, and democracy thus moves forward. Democracy is truly a warfare and involves conflict between different power groups. Most of the conflict takes place in orderly and conventionally approved legal procedures. But the building and development of a new power group — a people's organization — is a threat to the existing establishment and power structure.[22]

The purpose of a people's organization is to enable the people to participate in governing themselves and thus to make democracy truly work. Alinsky's people's organization is composed of representatives from smaller organizations or institutions in the neighborhood — clubs, churches, etc. Every year there is a convention at which policy is set in a democratic way. The organized community thus is able to obtain power for itself and its members who heretofore were powerless. The radical organizer frequently mentions that a people's organization must be broad enough to include all the issues facing the neighborhood. Single-issue community organizations cannot last. A people's organization must be broad, deep, and all inclusive.[23]

Alinsky is primarily an organizer and trainer of organizers. The organizer gradually withdraws from the organization as it becomes a vital and living reality. The most controversial aspects about Alinsky are the tactics and approaches he recommends for the organizer and the organization. In building up a mass community organization with indigenous leadership our radical appeals to power, conflict, self-interest, ego, and compromise.[24]

The organizer recognizes that the people in a particular neighborhood are powerless; apathy, resignation, hopelessness, resentment, and despair are the characteristics that mark the people. These are the have-nots or the have-too-littles of our society who truly are excluded from the power structure of political, social, and economic life. At best the professionals, the school boards, and the planning commissions service these people in the name of welfare colonialism, but the people are unable to truly participate. There is no structural change occurring.[25]

The organizer is an outsider coming into such a local neighborhood situation and trying to build ultimately a truly participative community based on the real needs of the community and involving indigenous leadership. The organizer must overcome the suspicion that he or she is an outsider. In the very beginning the organizer wants to manipulate and provoke the establishment into attacking the organizer. This tactic makes the local people sympathize with and identify with the organizer against the establishment. In the early stages it is important also to bring about a victory for the have-nots which will show that they can achieve their goals through the power of the organization.[26]

The first step in community organization is community disorganization—the disruption of the present organization of power. The organizer "must first rub raw the resentment of the people of the community; fan the latent hostilities of many of the people to the point of overt expression." The organizer searches out issues and conflicts, stirs up discontent and dissatisfaction, and provides a channel into which people can angrily pour their frustration. The organizer is an agitator.[27]

In selecting issues Alinsky gives succinct advice: "Pick the target, freeze it, personalize it, and polarize it." In reality nothing is 100 percent good or bad, but in organizing one must act as if the issue is 100 percent. Through such tactics the organizer goads the enemy into a response. The response often involves a tactical blunder on the part of the establishment which helps both the organizer and the incipient community organization.[28]

As might be expected, Alinsky spends much time concentrating on explaining tactics. Tactics are nonviolent but conflictual and imaginative. Ridicule, irony, and forcing the enemy to live up to the enemy's reputed value systems are important. The threat is often more significant than the reality itself, especially if the tactic is consonant with the experience of the have-nots but goes outside the experience of the establishment.[29]

One example illustrates some of the rules for tactics given by Alinsky. Alinsky's organizers brought together a black ghetto community in Rochester, New York. Alinsky polarized the target as Eastman Kodak Company and the local power establishment. One suggested tactic was to buy one hundred tickets to the opening performance of the Rochester Symphony Orchestra, a cultural jewel highly prized in the city. The tickets would be given to one hundred ghetto blacks, who would first be entertained at a dinner party lasting three hours, served in the ghetto and consisting solely of baked beans. In the end Alinsky never carried through on the tactic, but the threat alone accomplished much. One can see here the importance of threats, ridicule, polarization, and targeting the opposition. Above all such a tactic illustrates a very important Alinsky rule — a good tactic is one your people enjoy.[30]

Alinsky was in the business of training organizers but was always afraid that people would merely copy some of the tactics that had been used in the past. There are a number of qualities that are essential for a good organizer — curiosity, with the attendant approach of asking questions, a fair and open mind, an organized personality, a blurred vision of a better world, imagination, irreverence, and a sense of humor. The organizer must come to know the local community; understand the basic issues; spot and support the indigenous leaders; use all one's skill to put together an effective organization with broad-based support from all the different groups in the community; and be willing to play a behind-the-scenes role that is ulitmately to be phased out in favor of the organization once it comes into being.[31]

The most significant attribute in the organizer is a deep faith in the people. The whole purpose of community organizations is to enable the people truly to participate in governing themselves. Never forget that democracy is one of the greatest revolutions in human history. The fire, the energy, and the life of democracy is popular pressure. A people's organization is the machinery through which the people can achieve their program. An all-inclusive organization overcomes all artificial barriers, sectarian interests, as well as religious, national, and racial distinctions. The task of building such organizations is dirty, tedious, and heartbreaking, but only through such organizations can the revolution of democracy survive and prosper. It is only in such a truly democratic atmosphere that the values we cherish can flourish.[32]

III

This section will develop a theological and ethical evaluation of the Alinsky approach to community organization. First, a comparison will be made between the South American liberation theology and Alinsky's approach. Second, Alinsky's theory and practice will be judged in the light of the traditional Catholic understanding of political and social ethics.

There are many similarities between Alinsky's community organization approach and liberation theology, but there are also significant differences. An important similarity concerns the basic understanding of sociology and epistemology. Liberation theology rightly reacts against a value-free sociology with its claim of arriving at totally objective truth and its emphasis on quantitative analysis. A value-free approach by its very nature tends to identify with and reinforce the *status quo*. Knowledge is not as objective and independent of human involvement as a classical understanding once thought. The sociology of knowledge reminds us that all knowledge is situated and subject to prejudice. One must approach all existing realities and thought patterns with some ideological suspicion.[33]

Saul Alinsky is not primarily interested in writing for the academic community, but he stresses in his own way a hermeneutic of suspicion and opposes the myth of knowledge as objective and value free. All of life is partisan. There is no dispassionate objectivity.[34] Rationalization is an important human reality with which any organizer must come to grips. Rationalization not only affects the establishment and those who are committed to the *status quo* but also the have-nots in society. The have-nots need rationalization to explain away and justify the fact that they have not tried to do anything to change their situation.[35]

On the basis of its gospel values liberation theology opts for the poor. Such a partisan approach is in keeping with the understanding of sociology and of epistemology mentioned above. The option for the poor has become very central in both the praxis and theory of liberation theology.[36]

This same option for the poor, especially understood in terms of the powerless, characterizes the Alinsky method of community organization. Alinsky definitely sides with the powerless—the have-nots—in their struggle. Objectivity, like the claim that one is nonpartisan or reasonable, is usually a rationalization used to defend the *status quo*.[37] Alinsky also emphasizes the need to work with the middle class. The great danger is that once the have-nots begin to achieve something, they become counterrevolutionary. Our realistic radical frequently points out that organized labor in the United States has lost its reforming zeal and has become self-defensive and protective.[38] His lifelong commitment was to work to empower the powerless.

Liberation theology gives great importance to Paulo Friere's pedagogy of the oppressed. In the process called "conscientization," through an unalienating and liberating cultural action, the oppressed person perceives and modifies one's relationship to the world. The person thus moves from a naive awareness to a critical awareness.[39]

Although Alinsky does not use the word "conscientization," there is no doubt that such a process is the cornerstone of his method. The powerless must have their consciousness raised. The first step in the process is to become aware of their situation of powerlessness. The organizer must break through the people's own rationalizations of accepting their condition so that they can truly confront their own problems. In the beginning it is very important that the people acquire a sense that the can change things if only they come together to use their power. The organizer must astutely arrange a confrontation with the establishment which can easily be won by the people so that their organizing momentum can continue. An early defeat would cripple further development of a people's organization. The people must learn that through their power they can bring about change.[40]

Raising consciousness is a part of Alinsky's overarching commitment to popular education. "In the last analysis the objective for which any democratic movement must stand is the ultimate objective implicit within democracy — popular education." Our agnostic radical is a romantic Jeffersonian in his praise for popular education. All the teachers, libraries, and buildings will not help if the people do not have a desire for education. A people's organization is constantly searching for approaches to create an ethos receptive to learning and education. Alinsky the optimist puts his faith in people and education.[41]

Liberation theology accepts a conflictual model of social analysis and praxis. The option for the poor means that the true Christian is partisan in the struggle against systematic oppression and injustice. So too Alinsky uses a conflictual approach and emphasizes the conflictual nature of the tactics to be employed by a successful people's organization. The use of conflict and conflictual tactics distinguishes the radical from the liberal. Very often in his writings Alinsky describes the strategy of a people's organization in terms of warfare and uses metaphors derived from war. However, this constant conflict will be nonviolent and usually occur within the parameters of the law.[42]

The whole purpose of a people's organization is to bring about change through the use of power. Those in the establishment who have power will naturally resist very strongly any attempt to change the power structure. The very first step in community organization is community disorganization. The organizer is immediately confronted with the need to stir up dissatisfaction and discontent — to first rub raw the resentment of the people of the community.[43]

In describing rules for tactics our organizer constantly refers to "the other" as the enemy. The first rule, for example, states: "Power is not only what you have but what the enemy thinks you have." Perhaps the most famous and distinctive rule is the thirteenth: "Pick the target, freeze it, personalize it, and polarize it." The author of this rule recognizes that in reality no issue is 100 percent good or bad! Conflict requires such an all-or-nothing attitude. In all the theorizing about tactics never forget that the real action is the enemy's reaction. Provoking the enemy into a costly mistake will ultimately play into your own hand.[44] There can be no doubt that power and conflict are fundamental aspects of Alinsky's practice.

Although there are strong similarities between South American liberation theology and the community organization approach used by Saul D. Alinsky in the United States, there are also significant differences. Some liberation theologians adopt a Marxist sociological analysis to understand what is happening in society. One must be careful to note here the different levels of expression of Marxism. Liberation theologians do not accept all the theological and philosophical aspects of Marxism, but many, like Juan Luis Segundo, do use a Marxist analysis and make an option for a type of socialism.[45] Alinsky, on the other hand, defines his radicalism in terms of its commitment to true democracy.

In describing the ideal organizer Alinsky really describes himself as having "one all consuming conviction, one belief, one article of faith — a belief in people." If people have the power and the opportunity to act, in the long run and most of the time they will make the right decision. There are no other alternatives to democracy because all the other alternatives entail rule by one elite or another over other human beings.[46] The people have not only been the strength of the democratic ideal but also its weakness. Alinsky is greatly concerned about the vast masses of our people who because of lack of interest or of opportunity do not truly participate in their life as citizens. Alinsky eloquently maintains that there can be no darker or more devastating tragedy than the death of a human being's faith in oneself and in one's power to chart one's own future. Citizens who cannot or do not participate in their role of being the government sink further into apathy, anonymity, and depersonalization.[47]

The realistic radical's later writings are very clear and vocal in their denunciation of the ideology of the new-left radicals. There is no alternative to working within the system to change it. Alinsky employs all his ridicule and sarcasm against the rhetorical garbage of the new left. One must start with the system and the people, for there is no other place to start except political lunacy. Since democracy must be from the bottom up, Alinsky not only opposes totaltitarianism but also rejects any planning from the top down.[48]

An organizer operating in an open society is a political relativist who realizes that everything is relative. The organizer's most frequent question is "Why?" The primary virtue is irreverence, which never ceases to ask questions and poke fun at all those realities that are absolutized by people. Insistence on constant questioning goes against any fixed ideology. However, Alinsky himself recognizes that he has his own absolutes or his own basic commitment even if he does not want to call it an ideology. The radical has ultimate faith in the people and is committed to true democracy, which is literally and truly of, by, and for all the people. Alinsky, however, recognizes that democracy itself is only a means and not an end. It is the best means of achieving the values proposed by the Judeo-Christian and the democratic political traditions — equality, justice, freedom, peace, and the preciousness of human life with its basic rights.[49]

Alinsky's commitment to these basic values and to true democracy as the means to achieve them colors and influences many other aspects of his thought and differentiates some of these aspects from the approach taken by liberation theology. At times there can be in some liberation theologies a danger of emphasizing just one issue or aspect to the detriment of others. No one can doubt that race or sex or economic structures are the most important aspects for certain people, but there is a danger of so absolutizing one aspect that other aspects of oppression or issues are not given sufficient importance.

In both his books our pragmatic radical insists that single-issue community organizations are doomed to failure. There are both practical and theoretical reasons against a single- or limited-issue(s) organization. Practically, such an approach limits one to a small organization, and recent history shows that such organizations will not last. Problems such as crime, health, unemployment, and poverty cannot be isolated because they have the same basic cause. The underlying cause of all these problems must be overcome. In addition, individuals within the community have a number of different loyalties to diverse organizations and causes — churches, athletic groups, nationality associations, benevolent societies, recreational groups, fraternal lodges, political parties, business and labor organizations. The multiple interests of the individual must be recognized in any successful community organization. But more important than all these reasons is the fact that a democratic community organization must deal with all the concerns of a broad-based membership.[50]

The commitment to democracy and the values it protects also nuances Alinsky's approach to power. On the one hand, Alinsky constantly insists on the importance of power. It is impossible to conceive of a world without power. Life without power is death; a world without power would be a ghostly wasteland.[51] However, the radical organizer had to come to grips with the abuse of power even in his own organizations. The Back of the Yards community organization which he began in the late 1930s had become segregationist in the 50s.[52] So from personal experience with his own community organizations and from observing other institutions and organizations Alinsky knew the abuses of power.

Power must always be limited and controlled. The guiding star for the organizer is the dignity of the individual. Any program or organization that opposes people because of religion, race, creed, or economic status must be opposed. People must come to learn and appreciate the basic values of democracy. Without such a learning process the building of an organization becomes merely the substitution of one power group for another.[53] Power is not an absolute but is in the service of the other values and must be controlled by them.

The realistic North American radical shares with South American liberation theology an emphasis on conflict. Both have been accused of positions incompatible with Christianity with its stress on love and reconciliation. At the minimum Christians would generally have to agree that conflict cannot be an absolute or an ultimate. Catholic moral theology in its traditional approach to just war and strikes has always recognized that conflict can be an acceptable and legitimate tactic for Christians even though the Christian is committed ultimately to love and reconciliation.

Alinsky's dedication to democracy is what justifies the role of conflict but also at the same time limits conflict to a tactic and prevents its ever becoming an ultimate. Democracy by its very nature is going to involve the struggle among different groups and interests in society. The radical organizer refers to democracy as a warfare. We should not criticize lobbies and pressure groups but rather build our own pressure groups. There is no true democracy without conflict. There can be no doubt that the irreverent Alinsky takes personal glee in stressing the conflictual approaches used by a community organization.[54] However, the very nature of democracy keeps conflict from being absolutized and limits it to the role of a tactic. Alinsky recognizes that conflictual tactics will be more prominent in building up the people's organization. However, even in the beginning of a community organization there are limits on conflict. Recall that Alinsky recognizes that most issues are not 100 percent good or bad. Since a community organization must always be broad-based, multi-issued, and truly democratic, there must be room for compromise within the organization. Later on and in dealing with the broader society there will even be more need for compromise.

Saul Alinsky's fundamental commitment to democracy grounds the need for compromise. In dialogue with the new left in the 1960s our author gives even more attention to compromise. Compromise is now linked with power, self-interest, and conflict as the central concepts in our author's approach even though these words and the realities behind them are often looked upon as evil and wrong by many in society. To some, compromise has connotations of weakness, vacillation, and betrayal of ideals and principles. But to the organizer compromise is a key and beautiful word. A democratic society is truly an ongoing conflict interrupted periodically by compromises. A society devoid of compromise is totalitarian. In the light of this dialectic and rhythm of conflict and compromise the organizer must be a well-integrated political schizoid. On the one hand, the organizer polarizes the issue 100 percent to zero and leads the forces into conflict, all the while knowing that when the time comes for negotiations, there is probably only a 10 percent difference with the opposition.[55]

There is a second very profound difference between the Alinsky approach and that of liberation theology. Alinsky does not base his theory on explicitly religious warrants even though he occasionally mentions them. Liberation theologies have emerged in a South American context which is predominantly Christian and Catholic and in which the Catholic Church is the only force in society large enough to challenge the political and economic structures. The United States is a pluralistic society in religion and in many other ways. An effective organization attempting to embrace all cannot have a narrow or sectarian grounding. Catholic acceptance of Alinsky-style community organization involves a commitment to working with all others in the society for the common good. The theory and practice of such an approach must be ecumenical in the broadest sense of the term.

Traditional Catholic social teaching provides another perspective from which one can analyze and evaluate Alinsky's approach. Catholic theory has always seen the state and the political order as based on human nature itself. Human beings are called by their very nature to come together in political society so that they can achieve through their common political efforts what they cannot achieve as individuals for themselves. The goal of society is the common good which flows back on all the individuals who are part of the social whole. The limited end of the common good grounds social ethics and distinguishes social from individual ethics. Intimately connected with this understanding is the recognition that human beings are called to their own fulfillment. The Catholic tradition has never looked upon love of self as something bad or opposed to love of God and of neighbor. The Catholic theological tradition has tried to harmonize and bring into a unity the proper love of God, neighbor, and self.

By appealing both to the common good and to self-interest Saul Alinsky shows himself to be in line with the traditional Catholic understanding even though he does not develop his theory in any depth. The radical "is that person to whom the common good is the greatest personal value." The challenge for our society is to build people's organizations which are all-inclusive of both the people and their many organizations and institutions. The organizer aims to unite all the different people with their different organizations through a common interest that far transcends individual differences.[56] The common good can call for sacrifices on the part of some individuals in order to guarantee ultimately their own freedom and the freedom of all.[57]

The strong appeal to self-interest is constantly stressed but with the recognition that true self-interest must be seen in terms of the common good. Recall that *Rules for Radicals* devotes one chapter to the words prevalent in the language of politics, such as power, self-interest, compromise, and conflict. Many people reject the morality of self-interest by making it synonymous with self-centeredness and opposed to altruism and love. Alinsky firmly believes that self-interest is a very important factor in political life, but it is also a morally good factor. In no way should one condemn acting out of self-interest in the political order, but at the same time there is no incompatibility among morality, the common good, and self-interest properly understood. For this reason Machiavelli's understanding of self-interest as divorced from morality cannot be accepted.[58]

In his typical irreverent and hyperbolic way our author refers to his approach as the low road to morality—but there is no other way. It is not our better nature but our self-interest that demands that we be our brothers' and sisters' keeper. In our world no one can have a loaf of bread when one's neighbor does not. Alinsky the pragmatist maintains that the more practical life is the moral life and that the moral life is the only road to survival.[59]

Even though our pragmatic radical was an agnostic Jew,

he had some understanding of both Catholic and Protestant theology. In addition, at least into the mid-60s, he had been most often supported by the Catholics and attacked by some Protestants. There can be no doubt that he saw his approach as being in conformity with Catholic self-understanding and opposed to some Protestant positions. "The myth of altruism as a motivating factor in our behavior could arise and survive only in a society bundled in the sterile gauze of New England puritanism and Protestant morality and tied together with the ribbons of Madison Avenue public relations. It is one of the classic American fairy tales."[60]

The difference between some Protestant approaches to social ethics and one based on a theory of the common good with its acceptance of self-fulfillment and self-interest properly understood was briefly noted by Alinsky. Writing about the same time, John Courtney Murray from his perspective as a Catholic theologian developed the same point at great length. Murray describes Protestant ethical thought as vacillating between an idealistic approach (the Social Gospel, although he does not use the name) and a realistic or ambiguous approach which admits complexity (Christian Realism, but again he does not use the name). Both of these approaches assume a need to overcome any differences between individual and social morality, reject the pursuit of self-interest in social ethics, and have difficulty seeing power as anything but evil. On the basis of the natural-law tradition Murray sharply disagrees with the way in which both forms of Protestant ethics handle these three issues which he calls pseudoproblems. Civil society and the state are natural societies with limited functions and are not coextensive with the ends of the human person as such. With this limited understanding of the nature of the state one should not attempt to see its morality as univocally the morality of personal life. Self-interest is a very legitimate concern of the state, but in foreign affairs the national interest must always be seen in terms of the needs of the universal world community. There is no dichotomy because national unity is achieved only interior to and as a part of the growing international order. Murray also maintains that there is no politics without power to promote it. All politics is power politics—up to a point. Thus Murray substantiates in the light of the Catholic tradition the point that Alinsky was making against the approach of some Protestants. Political action based on self-interest properly understood is morally good, and politics and power cannot be separated.[61]

Catholic social ethics has always tried to hold on to both the dignity of the individual and to the social nature of the person. The Catholic position historically tried to find a middle ground or a third way between the extremes of individualistic capitalism and totalitarian socialism. Capitalism so stresses the individual that it forgets the social nature of all human beings and denies that to live in political society is natural for all human beings. Socialism so stresses the society that it downplays the natural rights and dignity of the individual person. In Catholic thought the principle of subsidiarity mediates this tension between the individual and the social aspects of human existence. In the political order the smaller groupings should be allowed to do all they can, while the state should step in only when this is necessary to do what smaller groups and organizations cannot accomplish.

There can be no doubt that Alinsky's thinking is totally in accord with that of the Catholic tradition on these points. Our pragmatic radical is deeply committed to the basic rights of individuals but recognizes the significant role of the state in working for the common good. The term "the principle of subsidiarity" does not appear in *Reveille* or in *Rules*, but the reality is ever present. The basic need is for all to participate in self-rule. Today our country and our cities lack citizen participation on the local level. Self-government will perish unless individual citizens are regularly involved. Democracy must be built from the bottom up and not from the top down. In spelling out what a radical stands for, *Reveille* clearly describes significant applications of the principle of subsidiarity. Human rights are more important than property rights. Free universal public education should be available to all. The radical opposes federal control of education in favor of local control, but national governmental authority must be able to eradicate abuses that can occur on the local level. In general the radical fights to defend local rights against usurpations by the centralized federal bureaucracy, but recognition of the use of local or states' rights by Tory reactionaries makes the radical constantly shift now from one side to the other in the controversy over local versus federal power.[62]

In developing his theory Alinsky incessantly underscores the importance of the freedom, equality, and participation of all citizens. The Catholic tradition historically did not emphasize these aspects, but lately special attention has been paid to them. In *Octogesima Adveniens* in 1971 Pope Paul VI describes two aspirations that have come to characterize human beings in our contemporary situation — the aspiration to equality and the aspiration to participation, two forms of human dignity and freedom.[63] Thus the papal tradition has come to accept and articulate human dignity in a way which was defended earlier by Saul David Alinsky.

Intrinsic evidence thus shows that Alinsky's basic theory is in accord with the Catholic understanding of the political order. In addition, what might be called external evidence also supports this basic compatibility. I refer here above all to the relationship between Alinsky and Jacques Maritain, the most famous Catholic philosopher in the Thomistic tradition in the twentieth century. Available sources occasionally refer to this relationship. The first blurb on the back cover of the Vintage book edition of *Reveille* comes from Jacques Maritain: "I consider him [Alinsky] to be one of the few really great men of our century." Stephen Rose, a Protestant who was generally supportive of Alinsky, refers to this friendship between Maritain and Alinsky and relates how, through Maritain, Alinsky spent a week talking with Archbishop Montini of Milan about the social problems of the archdiocese before Montini became Pope Paul VI.[64] P. David Finks' study documents in great detail the friendship and personal involvement between the two. Obviously this friendship also included the sharing of a basic vision about the political life.

Maritain's 1951 book *Man and the State* twice quotes *Reveille for Radicals*.[65] Even more significant is the fact that Maritain's approach to the question is very similar to Alinsky's and gives theoretical support for what Alinsky tried to do in his people's organizations without, however, explicitly saying so. One might even go further and suggest that perhaps Alinsky had even influenced Maritain's understanding and approach.

The themes stressed by Alinsky are also emphasized throughout Maritain's book—democracy is the best form of government; education and trust in people are necessary to make democracy truly work; democracy must be built from the bottom up. In describing morality and means in political life the French Thomist insists on the need to avoid the extremes of hypermoralism and Machiavellianism. There is a political ethics, but political ethics is not the same as individual ethics. Political ethics is concerned with a limited end in a given order—the terrestrial common good. This end is more limited and restricted than the end governing individual morality. The order of means must correspond to the order of ends. Given the end of politics as the terrestrial common good, then realities such as power, force, self-assertion, some distrust and suspicion, the recognition of the principle of the lesser evil, and other realities are ethically grounded.[66]

Maritain recognizes that for a democracy to exist it is necessary for the people to control and participate in the state. The first means for such control by the people is through the right to vote. In the second place the people also use the means of communication to express public opinion and thereby influence the state. The third means involves pressure groups that agitate and act upon the government and the state. The Catholic philosopher refers to these groups and their means as the "flesh and bone means of political warfare."[67] Immediately after this statement Maritain cites Alinsky and takes from him a long quote by Toc-

queville. Later on *Man and the State* devotes a section to "prophetic shock minorities" which are absolutely necessary for
democracy to truly function.[68] There can be no doubt that
Alinsky's people's organizations fit under what Maritain
calls the third way by which the people can control government and also fit under the category of prophetic shock
minorities. One can only speculate if Maritian would have
written about these things if there had been no personal and
intellectual relationship with Alinsky.

Without a doubt the most questioned aspect of Alinsky's
theory and practice has been the area of means. However,
Maritain cites Alinsky precisely in his chapter on means and
thereby seems to give implicit approval, at least in general,
to Alinsky's approach in this area. On the very second page
of the long chapter "Of Means and Ends" in *Rules* Alinsky
himself quotes Maritain as saying: "The fear of soiling
ourselves by entering the context of history is not virtue but
a way of escaping virtue."[69] Alinsky gives no exact citation
to Maritain's quote, but it comes from the chapter in *Man
and the State* on "The Problem of Means."[70]

I for one would not agree with all that Alinsky writes in
his chapter on means and ends in *Rules*, but the disagreements are few. Again one must remember that Alinsky is not
writing primarily for ethicists or philosophers; in fact, he
chides the intellectual who sits back and condemns the
means used by pragmatic radicals who are getting their
hands dirty. However, Alinsky does recognize that there are
limits in the means to be employed. Means are related to
values, and the realistic radical insists on a commitment to
the complex of high values that a democracy serves. Even in
discussing warfare Alinsky recognizes some, but in my judgment not enough, limits — in war the end justifies almost any
means."[71] Thus I would nuance some of Alinsky's seemingly
absolute utilitarian statements on means and ends and also
disagree with a few of his examples, especially on limits of
war. However, in general, and following in the footsteps of
the best-known Catholic Thomistic scholar in this century,
I find myself in basic agreement with Alinsky's practice and
theory about people's organizations and the means they use.

IV

Many other questions can be asked about Alinsky-type community organizations. Studies have pointed up some problems and weaknesses in his approach.[72] The approach has been most successful in middle-class neighborhoods. Alinsky talks about the need for coalitions with other organizations and groups on a broader level, but how effective have they been in practice? Other questions include the practical one of making sure that both conflict and compromise are able to coexist in such democratic organizations. Once the community organization is built and conflictual tactics are less prominent, how can one insure that the continued participation in the democratic process does not wane? The ongoing life of any community or organization is never as dramatic or as interesting as its beginning.

I think there is also a danger in exaggerating what such community organizations can do. They are themselves only a means to a further end which is a truly participative democratic society. Even the democratic ideal itself is only a means to deal with content problems and issues facing society. There are substantive issues involving such important topics as equitable distribution of goods, taxation, health care, education, rights of the poor, military defense, etc. that must be addressed. Not all people in even the most true democracy are going to agree on all these issues. There are also questions of political and economic structures that must be resolved more equitably. Community organizations are limited in what they can do. Substantive and structural questions cannot be ignored. However, Alinsky-style people's organizations are one very important way of trying to make our present system truly more democratic.

The purpose of this study has been twofold. First, this essay has called attention to the fact that Alinsky-style community organizations have been the most distinctive contribution to Catholic social action in the United States in the last few decades. Second, such an approach commends itself to Catholic theology and ethics. Hopefully in the future

more discussion will take place on this very important but
neglected development in American Catholic social practice.

NOTES

1. Gustavo Gutierrez, *A Theology of Liberation* (Maryknoll, NY:
Orbis Books, 1973), pp. 6ff.

2. See, for example, Sergio Torres and John Eagleson, eds.,
Theology in the Americas (Maryknoll, NY: Orbis Books, 1976);
Brian Mahan and L. Dale Richesin, eds., *The Challenge of Liberation
Theology: A First World Response* (Maryknoll, NY: Orbis Books,
1981).

3. See Charles A. Meconis, *With Clumsy Grace: The American
Catholic Left, 1961-1975* (New York: Seabury Press, 1979).

4. For a Protestant view which claims to be "objective" and
which reviews much of the Protestant debate about Alinsky, see
Lyle E. Schaller, *Community Organization: Conflict and Reconciliation*
(New York: Abingdon Press, 1966). For essays on both sides of
the debate in American Protestantism see John R. Fry, ed., *The
Church and Community Organization* (New York: National Council of
Churches, 1965).

5. Donald G. Reitzes and Dietrich C. Reitzes, "Saul D. Alinsky: A Neglected Source But Promising Resource," *The American
Sociologist* 17 (February 1982): 47-56.

6. At the present time there is no biography of Alinsky. The
data mentioned here can be found throughout his own writings
and in the other bibliography mentioned in the notes. Fortunately, Paulist Press will soon publish a very significant biography
and study of Alinsky by P. David Finks. I am personally most
grateful to Finks for first making me aware of Alinsky's work and
for keeping me abreast of his own research on Alinsky.

7. Bernard F. Evans, "Campaign for Human Development:
Church Involvement in Social Change," *Review of Religious Research*
20 (1979): 266, 267.

8. Alinsky frequently refers to his work with the Back of the
Yards Council in his two books: Saul D. Alinsky, *Reveille for
Radicals* (Chicago: University of Chicago Press, 1946); Saul D.
Alinsky, *Rules for Radicals: A Practical Primer for Realistic Radicals*
(New York: Vintage Books, 1972). References in this chapter to

Reveille will use the Vintage Book edition of 1969 which includes a new "Introduction" and a new "Afterword."

9. For a favorable study of Alinsky's work in Chicago with special emphasis on the Organization for a Better Austin, see Robert Bailey, Jr., *Radicals in Urban Politics: The Alinsky Approach* (Chicago: University of Chicago Press, 1974). For a popularly written and very sympathetic account of Alinsky's work with The Woodlawn Organization, see Charles E. Silberman, *Crisis in Black and White* (New York: Vintage Books, 1964).

10. Thomas W. Tift, "Toward a More Humane Social Policy: The Work and Influence of Monsignor John O'Grady" (Ph.D. diss., The Catholic University of America, 1980), pp. 6, 32, 667, 675.

11. For a summary of this debate see Schaller.

12. Silberman, *Crisis in Black and White*, p. 322.

13. Harold Fey, "Editorials," *The Christian Century* 78 (1961): 579, 580; 79 (1962): 879, 880; 81 (1964): 195-197; 82 (1965): 827, 828; Walter Kloetzli, *The Church and the Urban Challenge* (Philadelphia: Fortress Press, 1961).

14. Stephen C. Rose, "Saul Alinsky and His Critics," *Christianity and Crisis* 24 (July 20, 1964): 143-152.

15. Evans, "Campaign for Human Development," pp. 277, 278.

16. See note 6.

17. See note 8.

18. *Reveille*, pp. 15ff.

19. *Reveille*, pp. 18-23.

20. *Reveille*, pp. 64-69, 174-180.

21. *Rules*, pp. xvi-xxii; *Reveille*, "Afterword to the Vintage Edition," pp. 223-235.

22. *Reveille*, pp. 46-48, 132ff.

23. *Reveille*, pp. 53-63.

24. *Rules*, pp. 48-80.

25. *Reveille*, pp. 38-50, 225ff.

26. *Rules*, pp. 98-104.

27. *Rules*, pp. 116, 117.

28. *Rules*, pp. 130ff.

29. *Reveille*, pp. 89-154; *Rules*, pp. 126-164.

30. *Rules*, pp. 136-140.

31. *Rules*, pp. 63-80. ·

32. *Reveille*, pp. 190-204.

33. Juan Luis Segundo, *The Liberation of Theology* (Maryknoll, NY: Orbis Books, 1976), pp. 7-68.

34. *Rules*, p. 10.

35. *Rules*, p. 116.

36. Matthew L. Lamb, *Solidarity with Victims: Toward a Theology of Social Transformation* (New York: Crossroad, 1982).

37. *Reveille*, p. ix.

38. *Rules*, pp. 194-196; *Reveille*, p. 200, 234-235.

39. Paulo Freire, *Pedagogy of the Oppressed* (New York: Herder and Herder, 1970); Gutierrez, *A Theology of Liberation*, pp. 91-92, 113-117, 269-270.

40. *Rules*, pp. 109-115.

41. *Reveille*, pp. 155-173. The citation is the very first sentence in his chapter "Popular Education."

42. *Reveille*, pp. 132-135.

43. *Rules*, pp. 115-119.

44. *Rules*, pp. 126-138.

45. Alfred T. Hennelly, *Theologies in Conflict: The Challenge of Juan Luis Segundo* (Maryknoll, NY: Orbis Books, 1979), pp. 157-175.

46. *Reveille*, p. xiv.

47. *Rules*, pp. xxv, xxvi.

48. *Rules*, pp. xx, xxi.

49. *Rules*, pp. 10-12; *Reveille*, pp. 1-23.

50. *Reveille*, pp. 56-63; *Rules*, pp. 76-78.

51. E.g., *Rules*, pp. 49-53.

52. *Reveille*, pp. xi-xiii.

53. *Rules*, pp. 122, 123.

54. *Reveille*, pp. 190-204.

55. *Rules*, pp. 48-62, 78, 79; *Reveille*, p. 225.

56. *Reveille*, pp. 15, 205.

57. *Rules*, p. xxv.

58. *Rules*, pp. 53-59.

59. *Rules*, p. 23.

60. *Rules*, p. 53.

61. John Courtney Murray, *We Hold These Truths: Catholic Reflections on the American Proposition* (New York: Sheed and Ward, 1960), pp. 275-294.

62. *Reveille*, pp. xxv, xxvi, 16, 17; *Rules*, pp. xxii-xxvi.

63. Pope Paul VI, *Octogesima Adveniens*, par. 22, found in *Renewing the Earth: Catholic Documents on Peace, Justice, and Liberation,*

ed. David J. O'Brien and Thomas A. Shannon (Garden City, NY: Doubleday Image Books, 1977), p. 364.

64. Rose, *Christianity and Crisis* 24 (July 20, 1964): 143-152.

65. Jacques Maritain, *Man and the State* (Chicago: University of Chicago Press, 1951), pp. 66, 68. References here will be to the Phoenix edition of 1956 of the University of Chicago Press.

66. Ibid., pp. 62, 63.

67. Ibid., p. 66.

68. Ibid., pp. 139-146.

69. *Rules*, pp. 26, 27.

70. Maritain, *Man and the State*, p. 63.

71. *Rules*, p. 29.

72. For a summary of some questions and evaluations see Reitzes and Reitzes, "Saul D. Alinsky," pp. 52-55.

7. An Analysis of the American Bishops' Pastoral Letter on Peace and War

On May 3, 1983, the American Catholic bishops, by a vote of 238 in favor to 9 opposed issued a pastoral letter on peace and war entitled "The Challenge of Peace: God's Promise and Our Response."[1] A committee of bishops chaired by Archbishop (now Cardinal) Bernardin of Chicago began working on the document in spring of 1981. The committee had many meetings, heard testimony from over thirty-five expert witnesses, and issued a first draft in June 1982. A second draft was sent to the bishops in October 1982 and discussed at the annual bishops' meeting in Washington in November. The third draft was issued in early spring of 1983 and served as the basis for the final document approved at the May meeting of the bishops.[2]

Synopsis of the Pastoral Letter

In my judgment there are three realities that set the perspective and background for the teaching found in the letter. The letter begins with a recognition of what might be called the most significant of the signs of the times — we live in a moment of supreme crisis because of the possibility of the destruction of our world through the use of nuclear weapons. This present-day reality is balanced off by the call for peace as both a gospel imperative and a moral challenge arising from the interdependent world in which we live. In the present situation nations still retain as a last resort the right to self-defense within moral limits, but all of us are called to work for peace. The building of peace is the way to prevent war.

The pastoral letter is divided into four parts. In proposing ways of building peace "Part III: The Promotion of Peace: Proposals and Policies" appeals to the need for structural change, while "Part IV: The Pastoral Challenge and Response" calls for a change of heart and education. Catholic teaching consistently recognizes the international common good and calls for structures commensurate to that good. We can begin by strengthening existing structures such as the United Nations. The absence of adequate structures at the present time places an even greater responsibility on the part of the individual states who are called to interpret their own national interest in the light of the larger global interest. One must realistically assess the contemporary world situation dominated by the superpowers in a divided world. The bishops recognize the fact of a Soviet threat and a Soviet imperial drive for hegemony in some regions of major strategic interest. We as a nation have failed at times to live up to our own ideals, but at least we do enjoy political freedom. Although there are major differences between American and Soviet philosophies and political systems, the undeniable truth is that objective mutual interests do exist between the superpowers. These mutual interests furnish the starting point for structural change, beginning with negotiations between the superpowers, which can and must occur in order to insure peace. Nonviolent means of conflict resolution must also be developed. Part four insists on the importance of change of heart and education, and concludes by addressing the many different individuals involved in the work for peace — pastoral ministers; educators; parents; the young; men and women in the military, in defense industries, in science, and in the media; public officials; and Catholics as citizens.

The challenge to work for peace exists side by side with the justification for governments to go to war in self-defense as a last resort and in a limited manner. We Christians must recognize the reality of the paradox we face in our world as it exists. We must continue to recognize our belief that peace is possible and necessary and yet acknowledge that limited force in self-defense might be justified. The first two parts of the letter consider the Christian approaches to the use of force and to nuclear deterrence.

"Part I: Peace in the Modern World: Religious Perspectives and Principles" begins by justifying the need for such a document, by differentiating the different levels of teaching authority in the letter, and by briefly describing the methodology to be used and the audiences to be addressed. A scriptural section is followed by a description of our eschatological situation in the "already but not yet of Christian existence." The moral choice for the kingdom involves a commitment to work for peace, but the preservation of peace and the protection of human rights are to be accomplished in a world marked by sin. There is always a strong presumption in favor of peace, but limited self-defense cannot be denied to nations in our world. While governments must defend their people against unjust aggression, individuals may either be pacifists or support a legitimate use of limited force in self-defense. The document then spells out the just-war criteria under the traditional headings of *jus ad bellum* (just cause, competent authority, comparative justice, right understanding, last resort, probability of success, and proportionality) and of *jus in bello* (principles of discrimination and proportionality). A final section justifies nonviolence as a choice for some individuals. Pacifism and just war are distinct but interdependent methods of evaluating warfare, with each contributing to the full moral vision we need in pursuit of human peace.

"Part II: War and Peace in the Modern World: Problems and Principles" applies these principles of a just war to the contemporary scene. Since this section will be analyzed later in greater detail, a brief description will suffice. In the light of the distinctive capability of nuclear weapons we are faced with the necessary and urgent task of saying no to the use of nuclear weapons. The pastoral letter takes three positions on the use of nuclear weapons: no use of nuclear weapons against civilian population targets; no first use of nuclear weapons; while highly skeptical of the possibility of limiting any nuclear war, the bishops do not absolutely reject the use of counterforce nuclear weapons (as distinguished from counterpopulation or countervalue) in response to a nuclear attack. The letter gives a strictly conditioned moral acceptance of a limited nuclear deterrence which can never be the basis for a true peace. More specifically the bishops accept a limited counterforce deterrent which is not destabilizing, does not possess hard-target kill capability, and is limited to preventing nuclear war and not to fighting a limited nuclear war. Sufficiency to deter a nuclear war and not superiority in the arms race is another limiting criterion of moral deterrence.

The primary purpose of this study is to give an analysis of the pastoral letter. The first section will discuss the various tensions that arose in writing the drafts of the letter. The second and longest section will analyze the ethical teaching on just war and its application to nuclear use and deterrence. The third section will briefly consider the ecclesiological aspects of the document.

Tensions Experienced in the Drafting

Throughout the drafting process the bishops were in dialogue with and even opposed by a number of different groups within the church and without. Within the church the relationship with Rome and with other national hierarchies was a predominant consideration. The Vatican Council and the popes have spoken on these issues. Obviously the American bishops were not going to be in opposition with the official teaching of the universal church. However, the early drafts clearly indicated that the pastoral letter intended to be more specific and concrete than the earlier documents of the universal church. At the same time there was a possible tension with other national hierarchies, especially those within

Europe. It was well known that some French and German bishops were opposed to the condemnation of the first use of nuclear weapons since both the NATO and the French defense systems rely on the threat of limited nuclear weapons to deter attack even by conventional forces of the enemy. The universal church obviously is concerned that different national hierarchies might come to different moral conclusions on these issues.

These possible tensions with Rome and with other European hierarchies occasioned a special consultation in Rome among representatives of the American bishops' conference, European bishops' conferences, and officials of the Vatican. A synopsis of the meeting written by the Reverend Jan Schotte of the Pontifical Commission on Justice and Peace was sent to all American bishops in March 1983 and subsequently has been published.[3] Cardinal Ratzinger, the prefect of the Congregation for the Doctrine of the Faith, chaired this meeting and proposed five points for discussion: bishops' conferences as such do not have a *mandatum docendi*; the need to be clear when the bishops are speaking as bishops and invoking their teaching authority; the use of scripture in the American document; the presumption of a dualism involving both a just-war tradition and a nonviolent tradition in the church; and the application of fundamental moral principles to the nuclear-arms issue, especially taking into account the geopolitical context.

Within the church itself in the United States, as might be expected, there were disagreements with the proposed draft from both the "left" and the "right." Both positions were somewhat vocal during the drafting process. The "left" wanted a more prophetic statement based on gospel values which would not compromise and would forthrightly condemn all use of nuclear arms and call for unilateral nuclear disarmament.[4] In the end many advocates of this position were somewhat satisfied with the bishops' pastoral because they understood the document as moving somewhat in this direction and as taking a negative stand against the existing deterrent policy of this country. Numerically speaking the "right" was stronger than the "left." On a somewhat general level they questioned the competency of the bishops to become involved in such complex political issues. More specifically there was a feeling that the draft was too idealistic and did not recognize the complexities and realities in the existing world situation with the resulting need at times to use and to threaten to use nuclear weapons. The most significant statement of this position was a draft pastoral letter written by the lay theologian and philosopher Michael Novak, which was signed by a number of Catholics and published in its entirety in both the *National Review* and *Catholicism in Crisis*.[5]

Another source of tension involved the relationship between the American bishops and the American government. Stories appeared in the press that the American government was trying to go to Rome to force the American bishops to soften some of the earlier drafts. The press tended to see the changes made in subsequent drafts primarily in terms of the relationship between the bishops and the administration. Although the bishops do not call for a unilateral disarmament, they certainly are critical of many aspects of American policies. Reagan administration spokespersons tended to criticize very strongly the second draft of the letter but then were much less negative about the third draft. In my judgment this change on their part was more of a tactical maneuver. There can be no doubt that by their opposition to the second draft they gave more importance and significance to the bishops' document. The reaction by the administration and the press to the third draft was such that Archbishop Roach, the president of the American Bishops' Conference, and Archbishop Bernardin issued a news release pointing out the many areas in which the third draft disagreed with American policy.[6] The third draft did back down somewhat by substituting "curb" for "halt" with reference to bilateral agreements on the arms race, but the substance of the third draft was basically the same as the second. Despite the addition of some more "realistic" wording, and a few corresponding changes, the third draft went beyond the second draft and condemned counterpopulation deterrence. The final document clearly shows that the American bishops no longer feel the need to prove their loyalty and patriotism by an uncritical acceptance of American policy. Within the last few years this critical attitude of the American bishops toward the American government has been growing, but the pastoral letter marks a very significant development in this movement.[7] A further tension involved ethical theory and will be discussed in detail in the following section.

Ethical Analysis of the Teaching on Nuclear Use and Deterrence

The pastoral letter recognizes that individuals within the church can follow either a pacifist approach or the just-war theory. Despite some questioning in the Roman meeting that nonviolence has not been a second tradition within the church alongside the just-war theory, the final document is very strong in its suppport of nonviolence.[8] The bishops affirm that the theme of Christian nonviolence and pacifism has echoed and reechoed, sometimes more strongly and sometimes more faintly, from the beginning of the Christian tradition down to our own day. The specific section in the pastoral on the value of nonviolence twice quotes the Pastoral Constitution on the Church in the Modern World. The text refers to the praise that the Council Fathers gave "to those who renounce the use of violence in the vindication of their rights." However, the pastoral letter in this its major discussion of nonviolence does not add the condition found in the very same sentence of the Constitution on the Church in the Modern World (n. 78), namely, "provided this can be done without injury to the rights and duties of others or of the community itself." There can be no doubt that the bishops are quite absolute in their acceptance of pacifism as one option for the individual Catholic conscience and insist that such an option has been a tradition in the church. However, the pastoral letter recognizes that governments have an obligation to defend their people against unjust aggression and cannot adopt a totally pacifist perspective.

The letter addresses the question about the use of nuclear weapons in the light of the just-war theory. The third draft made one curious addition to the criteria related to the *jus ad bellum* which was not found in the second draft and is usually not found in the tradition—comparative justice. Under this criterion the draft recognizes defects in the American system but insisits there is a greater justice in our society in which basic human rights are at least recognized as compared to tyrannical and totalitarian regimes.[9] The final document retains this curious criterion but eliminates the assessment that our political system is comparatively more just and uses the category to emphasize the presumption against war.[10] Thus the bishops finally retain this criterion but use it differently from the purpose it seems to have had in the third draft.

The most significant question in ethical theory concerns the relationship between nuclear use and deterrence. This chapter will briefly explain, analyze, and criticize the different drafts of the letter on this important point. On the question of the use of nuclear weapons the drafts show relatively little change.[11] Step one consistently condemns the use of nuclear weapons or any weapons used against population centers or civilian targets. Step two condemns the first use of nuclear weapons. The third draft abhors the concept of initiating nuclear war on however restricted a scale. Such a war is an unjustifiable moral risk because of the danger of escalation. However, obviously in response to the concerns of some European bishops, the draft goes on to say, "Therefore, a serious moral obligation exists to develop defensive strategies as rapidly as possible to preclude any justification for using nuclear weapons in response to non-nuclear attacks." One could conclude that until such defense strategies are developed the first use of nuclear weapons might not be completely ruled out. Cardinal Ratzinger has interpreted the document in this way.[12] The final version is somewhat changed. The first sentence, as a result of an amendment made by Archbishop Quinn in Chicago, reverts to the language of the second draft and reads: "We do not perceive any situation in which the deliberate initiation of nuclear warfare on however restricted a scale can be morally justified." However, the same paragraph still contains the first part of the statement as found in the third draft maintaining that a serious moral obligation exists to develop nonnuclear strategies as rapidly as possible. There could very well be a contradiction between these two sentences in the same short paragraph. The new opening sentence seems to say that no situation can justify first use, but the final sentence could be interpreted to leave open the possibility of such use until one has fulfilled the moral obligation of developing nonnuclear defensive strategies. Perhaps this possible contradiction indicates one of the problems in trying to amend a document in a meeting of three hundred people.

The third step in the use of nuclear weapons deals with what is technically called retaliatory (as distinguished from first use) counterforce (as distinguished from countercity, counterpopulation, or countervalue) use. The first draft recognizes that Christians and others of good will may differ as to whether nuclear weapons of this type may ever be used. I describe the position taken here in the first draft as a reluctant noncondemnation of such use, with the major problems being the difficulty of keeping such use limited and the danger of accident or misjudgment. The subsequent drafts are in basic continuity with the first but somewhat more skeptical about even the possibility of keeping a nuclear war limited. In the final version there is no absolute moral condemnation of retaliatory counterforce use of nuclear weapons, but like the third draft, the final document remains highly skeptical about keeping such use of nuclear weapons limited.

What about the consistency of the bishops' position on the use of nuclear weapons? An argument can certainly be made for consistency. In the case of a defensive retaliatory use of counterforce nuclear weapons there might be a proportionate reason justifying the risk that nuclear war will become unlimited, while there is no proportionate reason that could justify the first use of such weapons. However, the whole thrust of the letter insists on the impossibility of keeping nuclear war limited. Also in the case of retaliation why are counterforce nuclear weapons necessary if conventional weapons could often accomplish the necessary purpose? Can the bishops perceive any situation in which the retaliatory use of counterforce nuclear weapons on however restricted a scale could be morally justified? I think the whole thrust of the bishops' argument goes against any use of counterforce nuclear weapons as first use or in retaliation. However, in fairness, the pastoral letter does not advocate such retaliatory counterforce use but rather does not absolutely rule out such use.

There is another very important reason why the pastoral letter does not absolutely rule out all counterforce nuclear weapons. The position on deterrence is intimately connected with the position on use. The bishops do not want to demand unilateral disarmament because it would be destabilizing. They are willing to accept some nuclear deterrence in a conditioned way. In many ways it is this position on deterrence which logically has a great effect on their not categorically condemning all counterforce use of nuclear weapons. Here we enter the very difficult ethical problem of the relationship between use and deterrence. There has been much development within the drafts of the pastoral letter on the kind of deterrence acceptable, the relationship between use and deterrence, and the moral theory governing these considerations.

The first draft proposes a unique two-tiered approach to deterrence.[13] The first tier is a marginally or barely justifiable deterrent policy. The draft explicitly recognizes that it has left the door open and has not absolutely condemned counterforce use in order to justify some deterrence. The draft maintains that it is wrong to threaten to do what you cannot morally do. Here the draft quotes the 1976 pastoral letter issued by the American bishops "To Live in Christ

Jesus." Consequently it is wrong to threaten to attack civilian population centers or to threaten to initiate nuclear war. Since some retaliatory counterforce use might be justifiable, one can legitimately threaten and deter with such counterforce nuclear weapons.

The second tier of deterrence in the first draft is the toleration of countercity or counterpopulation deterrence. The draft, quoting from official government documents, assumes that American policy involves a counterpopulation deterrence which cannot be approved outright. The draft then justifies the toleration of such an evil on the basis of the lesser of two evils in order to avoid the greater evil of destabilizing the international ordering by requiring the unilateral disarmament of our counterpopulation deterrence. In arriving at this judgment the draft quotes extensively from the testimony of Cardinal Krol before the Senate Foreign Relations Committee in 1979 on the SALT II treaty. The draft does not approve such deterrence but merely tolerates it as long as there is hope that negotiations will lead to meaningful and continuing reduction of nuclear stockpiles.

The second draft drops the two-tiered approach to deterrence.[14] The discussion of deterrence on the basis of the *US Military Posture Statement for FY 1983* understands American deterrent policy as involving the willingness to threaten and strike targets of value in the Soviet Union. Such targets of value either explicitly include the civilian population or include individual targets which essentially would involve killing a large number of civilians.

The document recognizes the moral and political paradox of deterrence which by threatening the use of such nuclear weapons has apparently prevented their use. The Pastoral Constitution on the Church in the Modern World is then cited in this regard. The draft quotes the pertinent parts of the 1976 bishops' pastoral letter "To Live in Christ Jesus"—not only is it wrong to attack civilian populations but it is also wrong to threaten to attack them as part of a strategy of deterrence. Then the Krol document is cited with its toleration, but not approval, of countervalue or countercity deterrence provided through negotiations there is meaningful progress toward reducing and phasing out altogether nuclear deterrence and the threat of mutual assured destruction.

The second draft goes on to quote something new, the June 1982 address of Pope John Paul II to the United Nations. (The address was actually given by Cardinal Casaroli, who read the Pope's document.) The Pope said: "In current conditions deterrence based on balance, certainly not as an end in itself, but as a step on the way toward a progressive disarmament may still be judged morally acceptable." The draft in the light of this gives a strictly conditional moral acceptance to deterrence and later develops the limits of deterrence. There are negative elements connected with deterrence including "the intention to use strategic nuclear weapons which would violate the principles of discrimination and proportionality." This fact and other negative dimensions make the arms race with deterrence as its key element a sinful situation which must be changed. However, such a situation can still be morally acceptable provided it is a step toward progressive disarmament. Note the reasoning is basically the reasoning of the 1979 Krol testimony, but the conclusion is taken from the Pope.

However, there is a serious ethical problem in the Krol testimony. The 1976 pastoral letter "To Live in Christ Jesus" deals with all aspects of the moral life and devotes only a few paragraphs to the nuclear question.[15] However, this document contains a sentence that has not been in previous statements of the universal hierarchical magisterium or of the American bishops — not only is it wrong to attack civilian populations but it is also wrong to threaten to attack them as part of a strategy of deterrence. This sentence caused no great excitement at the time, but it was to have a great influence later. This statement basically maintains that it is morally wrong to threaten to do what you cannot morally do, apparently because the threat involves the immoral intention to do the moral evil. One could thus logically conclude that counterpopulation deterrence is morally wrong and must be condemned.

The Krol testimony in 1979 tries to answer the dilemma.[16] Deterrence aims to prevent the use of nuclear weapons, but it does so by an expressed threat to attack the civilian populations of the adversaries. This wrong declared intention explains the Catholic dissatisfaction with deterrence. As the second draft says explicitly, for this reason such deterrence cannot be accepted but only tolerated.

However, the Krol testimony involves a novel use of toleration. Yes, the Catholic tradition has traditionally recognized especially in social and political ethics that one can tolerate an evil in order to avoid a greater evil or to bring about a greater good., The classic example is the toleration of laws allowing public prostitution. However, in the Krol testimony one is tolerating one's own immoral intention to do moral evil. To intend to do moral evil in the Catholic theological tradition is morally wrong. It cannot be approved or tolerated; it must be condemned.

Moral theologians identified with a more conservative approach to moral theology accused such an approach of consequentialism.[17] The moral evil of an immoral intention is justified by the good effects that come from such deterrence — namely, the prevention of the use of nuclear weapons. Such an ethical theory, it was pointed out, would put the bishops in support of revisionist Catholic moral theology which accepts the morality of contraception and sterilization, and questions the absolute condemnation of direct abortion. The revisionist position says that these evils which are called premoral or nonmoral evils can be justified by a proportionate reason. Obviously the framers of the bishops' letter did not want to be accused of proposing a moral theory that would logically lead them to justify positions contrary to hierarchical magisterial teaching in the area of sexual morality.

However, revisionists do not necessarily accept the reasoning of the Krol testimony and of the second draft. The novel use of tolerating one's own moral evil was pointed out by revisionists. Most revisionists would agree that one cannot intend to do moral evil. The theory of proportionalism maintains that one can do premoral evil if there is a proportionate reason but not moral evil. To do moral evil or to intend to do moral evil is always wrong.[18] Thus revisionists too pointed out problems in the reasoning of the Krol testimony and of the second draft. It is wrong to identify such reasoning with the revisionist theory of proportionalism.

Such intramural Catholic debate pointed out the ethical problem in the theory proposed in the Krol testimony which was accepted somewhat in the first draft (the second tier of tolerated deterrence) and wholeheartedly accepted in the second draft. Archbishop Bernardin alluded to these problems on a number of occasions. At the discussion of the second draft at the November 1982 meeting of the American bishops and at the January 1983 meeting in Rome, Bernardin indicated that the committee was not yet totally satisfied with the theoretical argument in the second draft on the morality of deterrence.[19]

One other important change occurred during the time of preparation of the third draft. The tension between the early drafts and American policy has already been pointed out. It was well known that the Reagan administration was somewhat upset with the drafts. The administration and the bishops' committee were in dialogue. There was a very significant letter of William Clark, the national security advisor, to Cardinal Bernardin on January 15, 1983. The letter stated very clearly, "For moral, political, and military reasons the United States does not target the Soviet civilian population as such." We target only the war-making capability of the Soviet Union — its armed forces and the industrial capacity to sustain war.[20] This letter is very important. In the Krol testimony and in the first and second drafts the bishops assume and cite official documents to show that the United States deterrent policy involves countervalue and not just counterforce deterrence. Now they have a document asserting that the United States nuclear deterrence is counterforce and not counterpopulation.

All the above considerations set the stage for the third draft. In the third draft the section on deterrence in principle and practice begins with an explanation of the concept and development of deterrent policy.[21] Particularly significant is the relationship between "declaratory policy" (the public explanations of our strategies, intentions, and capabilities) and "action policy" (the actual planning and targeting policies to be followed in a nuclear attack). Without going into detail the letter recognizes that there has been substantial continuity in American action policy despite real changes in declaratory policy. (However, as will be highlighted below, the bishops themselves thought there was a different targeting policy in their earlier drafts.)

The section on the moral assessment of deterrence begins by citing the Second Vatican Council and discussing various aspects of the question. The 1976 pastoral letter and the Krol testimony are both mentioned and summarized together in one short papagraph with no mention of the teaching on the specifics of deterrence and the moral theory behind it. Pope John Paul II's address to the United Nations in June 1983 is quoted at length as are other statements by the Pope. The draft concludes that in light of the need to prevent nuclear war from ever occurring and to protect and preserve justice, freedom, and independence, deterrence not as an end in itself but as a step on the way to progressive disarmament may be judged as morally acceptable. However, there are moral limits to deterrence just as there are to use. Specifically, it is not morally acceptable to intend to kill the innocent as part of a strategy of deterring nuclear war. The draft appreciates the clarifications given in the letter from William Clark and in the annual report of Secretary Weinberger to Congress maintaining that it is not American policy to target enemy populations. Although such a policy does not go against the principle of discrimination, there still remains the question of proportionality, namely, that attacks on military targets would involve massive and disproportionate civilian casualties.

The third draft like its predecessors then spells out the implications of its strictly conditioned moral acceptance of deterrence. Proposals for fighting a limited nuclear war are not acceptable, for the whole purpose of deterrence is to prevent the use of nuclear weapons. Sufficiency to deter and not superiority must be the moral criterion. Any theoretical or practical changes must be assessed on whether they aid or impair steps toward progressive disarmament. The document then goes on to spell out some specifics in the light of this understanding. Basically the draft calls for a conditioned acceptance of limited counterforce deterrence, with no ap-

pearance of first-strike capability, not possessing hard-target
kill capability, which is aimed at preventing nuclear war and
not at fighting a limited nuclear war.

The final version of the letter approved by the bishops is
in basic and almost verbal agreement with the moral theory
and general judgments about deterrence found in the third
draft.[22] There are only comparatively minor changes from
what has been outlined above. The final letter does include
a citation from the Krol testimony, but the quote does not
deal with toleration or the moral theory behind toleration.
The final version relegates the Clark letter and the
Weinberger report to the footnotes but explains their content in the text as no targeting of civilian populations.

One can understand better the position of the pastoral letter on deterrence by comparing it with the conciliar and
papal statements so often cited in the document itself. It is
true that the bishops do not go against the papal and conciliar teaching, but they do take significant steps beyond
such teaching. The pope and the council never directly opposed countercity or counterpopulation deterrence. The
bishops now, at least on the level of targeting policies, oppose counterpopulation deterrence. The pope has never accepted the principle that countercity deterrence involves the
immoral intention to do what is morally wrong. The bishops
accept the principle and therefore cannot accept counterpopulation deterrence. The pope consequently has not ruled
out the moral acceptance of a bluff strategy, but the bishops
do not accept any bluff strategy in terms of targeting policies of deterrence. These are three significant differences between the papal position and that of the American bishops.

The bishops in the course of their drafting process changed
their ethical theory and their position on counterpopulation
nuclear deterrence. The unanswered question is, Why? Our
analysis has shown that the two most important factors were
the recognition of the problem connected with the theory of
toleration of such deterrence and the changed factual
recognition that American deterrence was not targeted on
population centers as such.

The theory of toleration proposed in the Krol testimony

and in the first draft does have some problems in terms of the Catholic theological tradition. However, the bishops could have rejected this theory and still accepted a counter-city deterrence. Logically they would then have to reject the 1976 statement that one cannot threaten to use what one cannot morally use. Pope John Paul II has not condemned countercity deterrence. They could have used the general arguments proposed by the pope without getting into the particulars which caused the problem in the Krol testimony and in the first two drafts. Did they change because of their changed understanding of the factual situation? Once they realized that American policy does not involve the targeting of population centers, then they would not run into much American opposition in condemning countercity deterrence. However, the bishops were certainly willing in many other instances to oppose American and NATO policy.

Perhaps they changed because they came to realize that a limited counterforce deterrence is sufficient to achieve the purpose of deterrence—to prevent the use of nuclear weapons. Perhaps they are merely following through on the logic of their argument to limit deterrence as much as possible. What they did not think was sufficient in the first draft they decided to be sufficient deterrence by the time of writing the third draft.

Another question can be raised. The final document ties use and deterrence very closely together by maintaining that one cannot threaten to do what one cannot morally do. Another ethical option is to claim that there is a great separation between the order of deterrence and the order of use. So great is this distinction that to threaten to deter does not necessarily involve a moral intention to use. Such a position is maintained by those who accept, in one way or another, a theory of bluff. Such a theory could maintain an absolute prohibition against all use of nuclears (a position perhaps logically contained in the bishops' own argument on use) but still accept some deterrence. I personally lean toward this position, even though it is not without its own problems.

The very fact that the bishops have related use and deterrence so very closely raises other problems for the bishops. Is it the need to hold to some deterrence that prevents their total condemnation of the use of nuclear weapons? If this is so, perhaps they should give this as one of their reasons. A second question concerns the exact relationship between use and deterrence. The pastoral letter wants to put the two together, but the final document seems to allow room for much greater deterrence (granted it is still quite limited) than it does for use.

This analysis has shown that the greatest changes in the course of drafting the document involve the theory about deterrence and the substantive question of countercity deterrence. The thorny question of deterrence and the ethical theory supporting it will continue to be the most important subject for further ethical investigation.

Ecclesiological Aspects

A somewhat brief and final consideration must be directed to the ecclesiological implications of this letter. In this light two aspects — the process itself and the recognition of the possibility of dissent from specific teaching — deserve attention. The process itself was quite different from that followed in most previous documents put out by the American bishops, although there has been a refreshing attempt to have broad-based consultation in some catechetical documents. In this case there were meetings of the committee with people involved on all sides of the issue. The people consulted represented all shades of opinion, and no position was a priori excluded. The first draft was sent to all the bishops and marked confidential. However, within a few days the content of the pastoral letter was published in the media. The second and third drafts were publicly released to the press and the general public after they were sent to the bishops. Likewise the final meeting in Chicago, at which amendments were proposed, voted on, and the final document approved, was open to the press. Many bishops in their individual dioceses encouraged study and discussion of the various drafts as they were proposed. Often in the past, episcopal statements—especially those dealing with questions of social ethics—were prepared with no participation from outside and very little involvement by the individual bishops. As a result, even the bishops themselves did not really "own" these documents. Many Roman Catholics today are very surprised to learn about the existence of the body of teachings which the American bishops have issued on social questions in the last fifteen years.[23]

The process itself greatly helped and abetted the purpose of making Catholics and the general public much more aware of the moral issues involved in this question. The best teaching device is no longer merely a letter coming from on high which will probably be read and studied by very few. The public and participatory process thus enhanced the teaching aspect and the influence of the letter, to say nothing about the internal strength of the document itself.

Perhaps even more importantly the process has set a precedent for the future. The consultative process indicates that the whole church was involved in preparing the document. If further documents on other subjects are to be credible, they must be willing to follow the same process. Unfortunately, in other areas of morality there has not been as great a willingness to bring about a dialogue involving the whole church.

A second ecclesiological implication concerns the possibility of dissent and the existence of pluralism within the church on specific ethical issues. At the Rome meeting in January 1983 great emphasis was attached to the need to distinguish the different levels of authoritative teaching involved in the document. The third draft and the pastoral letter itself distinguish universally binding moral principles, statements of recent popes and of Vatican II, and the application of moral principles to particular judgments. In the application of principles the letter realizes that prudential judgments are involved based on circumstances which can be changed or be interpreted differently by people of good will. Such moral judgments made in specific cases do not bind in conscience but are to be given serious attention and consideration by Catholics in making their moral choices.[24]

Such an ecclesiology recognizes a "big church" in that there will always be room for disagreement, pluralism, and dissent on specific complex questions, although the letter carefully avoids using the term "dissent." The bishops rightly insist that the unity of the church is not to be found on such specific questions. The basic principle behind such a statement is that in these areas one cannot attain a certitude that excludes the possibility of error. In my judgment such an approach logically must recognize the possibility of dissent in other areas of church teaching where one cannot claim to preclude the possibility of error. The following chapter will develop these ecclesiological aspects in greater detail.

This study has attempted to analyze the American bishops' pastoral letter on peace and war. The content of the teaching was briefly explained and some of the tensions in the drafting process were mentioned. The major section involved an ethical analysis of the document concentrating on the theory and the teaching on nuclear use and deterrence. A final short section considered the ecclesiological implications of the document. In conclusion, I do not think that it is an exaggeration to say that this letter is perhaps the most important and significant document ever issued by the American bishops.

NOTES

1. "The Pastoral Letter on War and Peace: The Challenge of Peace: God's Promise and Our Response," *Origins* 13 (1983): 1-32.

2. "First Draft: Pastoral Letter on War and Peace," *National Catholic Reporter* 18 (July 2, 1982): 11f; "Second Draft: Pastoral Letter on War and Peace," *Origins* 12 (1982): 305-328; "Third Draft: Pastoral Letter on War and Peace," *Origins* 12 (1983): 697-728. For the sake of clarity I have used the similar generic title for the different drafts.

3. "Rome Consultation on Peace and Disarmament: A Vatican Synthesis," *Origins* 12 (1983): 691-695.

4. Arthur Jones, "What Is Evil Is Evil: An Alternative Pastoral Letter," *National Catholic Reporter* 19 (April 15, 1983): 14.

5. Michael Novak, "Moral Clarity in the Nuclear Age: A Letter from Catholic Clergy and Laity," *Catholicism in Crisis* 1 (March 1983): 3-23.

6. National Catholic Office for Information, "News Release," April 8, 1983.

7. J. Brian Benestad and Francis J. Butler, eds., *Quest for Justice: A Compendium of Statements of the United States Catholic Bishops on the Political and Social Order 1966-1980* (Washington, D.C.: United States Catholic Conference, 1981).

8. *Origins* 13 (1983): 12, 13.

9. *Origins* 12 (1982): 707.

10. *Origins* 13 (1983): 10.

11. *National Catholic Reporter* 18 (July 2, 1982): p.11; *Origins* 12 (1982): 314, 315; *Origins* 12 (1983): 711, 712; *Origins* 13 (1983): 14-16.

12. *N.C. News Service*, Thursday, May 19, 1983, p. 1.

13. *National Catholic Reporter* 18 (July 2, 1982): 11, 12.

14. *Origins* 12 (1982): 315-318.

15. Benestad and Butler, *Quest for Justice*, pp. 43-45.

16. Cardinal John Krol, "SALT II: A Statement of Support," *Origins* 9 (1979): 195-199.

17. Germain Grisez, "The Moral Implications of a Nuclear Deterrent," *Center Journal* 2 (Winter 1982): 9-24.

18. Richard A. McCormick, "Ambiguity in Moral Choice" and "A Commentary on the Commentaries," in *Doing Evil to Achieve Good: Moral Choice in Conflict Situations*, ed. Richard A. McCormick and Paul Ramsey (Chicago: Loyola University Press, 1978), pp. 7-53 and 193-267.

19. Archbishop Joseph Bernardin, "Address to the November 1982 Bishops' Meeting," *Origins* 12 (1982): 397; *Origins* 12 (1983): 692.

20. *Origins* 12 (1983): 714.

21. Ibid., pp. 713-716.

22. *Origins* 13 (1983): 16-19.

23. Benestad and Butler, *Quest for Justice*.

24. *Origins* 12 (1982): 700; *Origins* 13 (1983): 2, 3.

8. Roman Catholic Teaching on Peace and War in a Broader Theological Context

This chapter will continue to examine the positions on peace, war, deterrence, and disarmament proposed in the Roman Catholic Church. The previous chapter proposed an ethical analysis of the teaching of the American bishops' pastoral letter on nuclear weapons. This chapter will proceed in a different manner. The first part will briefly summarize the present teaching of the Roman Catholic Church as this is found in the documents of the universal hierarchical teaching authority and in the statements representing the American bishops as a whole. Then the main body of the chapter will analyze the official Roman Catholic teaching on peace, war, and disarmament in the light of the broader perspective of moral theology by giving special attention to three important areas — ethical theory, eschatology, and ecclesiology.

I. Official Roman Catholic Teaching

The most authoritative recent statement of the teaching of the Roman Catholic Church on peace and war is found in the Pastoral Constitution on the Church in the Modern World of the Second Vatican Council. There have been and continue to be discussions about the exact teaching of Vatican II, but the main outlines of these teachings are, in my judgment, clear. The document calls on Christians to cooperate with all people in securing a peace based on justice and love. The constitution, known by its Latin name *Gaudium et Spes*, stresses the need for peace rooted in the hearts of all but also recognizes the need to set up structures and institutions to bring about that peace. Since human beings are sinful, "the threat of war hangs over them and will hang over them until the return of Christ."[1] However, it is our duty to work for the time that war will be completely outlawed by international consent. This goal requires the establishment of some effective universal public authority to safeguard peace.[2]

The council further recognizes that the savagery and horror of war are magnified by the new weapons of massive destruction and devastation. "All these considerations compel us to undertake an evaluation of war with an entirely new attitude."[3] The exact meaning of this sentence is not clear. The footnote is to the statement of Pope John XXIII in the Encyclical *Pacem in Terris* which maintains war is no longer an apt means of vindicating violated rights. There has been some doubt about the interpretation of this particular passage from *Pacem in Terris*, but it seems that the pope was not taking away the right to war as a means of self-defense but only as a means of vindicating rights which had already been violated.[4] In the text itself of *Gaudium et Spes*, after the statement about the need for an entirely new attitude, the pastoral constitution applies without explicitly saying so the just-war principle of discrimination to the use of nuclear weapons.

There are some significant new developments in the teaching of the Catholic Church as found in this document. For the first time pacifism and nonviolence are recognized as acceptable approaches within the Roman Catholic Church. *Gaudium et Spes* also calls for the state to make humane provisions for those who because of conscience refuse to bear arms provided they accept some other form of service to the human community. No distinction is made between conscientious objection and selective conscientious objection.[5]

However, the document does not abandon the just-war tradition and obviously employs that tradition in its approach. Since war has not been rooted out of human affairs and since there is no effective international institution, governments cannot be denied the right to legitimate defense once every means of peaceful settlement has been exhausted. Even in self-defense there are limits on the ways in which war and violence are employed.[6] The strongest condemnation of the whole council is an explicit application of the just-war principle of discrimination. "Any act of war aimed indiscriminately at the destruction of entire cities or of extensive areas along with their population is a crime against God and humanity. It merits unequivocal and unhesitating condemnation."[7] Note that the condemnation does not include all nuclear weapons but only indiscriminate weapons.

The arms race is condemned as an utterly treacherous trap and one which affects the poor to an intolerable degree. It is not a safe way to preserve a true peace. The peace of a sort resulting from the present balance is not authentic and true peace.[8] In light of the present world realities all must work to end the arms race and "to make a true beginning of disarmament, not indeed a unilateral disarmament, but one proceding at an equal pace according to agreement, and backed up by authentic and workable safeguards."[9] Subsequent papal teaching has been in continuity with the proposals of the Second Vatican Council.[10]

In the light of the teaching of the Vatican Council and of other subsequent papal utterances, the American bishops have made corporate statements about the issues. The most significant statements according to Archbishop Bernardin, the chair of the committee which drafted the pastoral letter, are the pastoral letter "Human Life in Our Day" (1968), the pastoral reflection "To Live in Christ Jesus" (1976), Cardinal Krol's congressional testimony representing the official policy of the United States Catholic Conference on the SALT II treaty (1979), and the Administrative Board's statement on registration and the draft (1980).[11]

"Human Life in Our Day" and subsequent statements acknowledge the continuing legitimacy of service in the military as a service to society. However, in accord with the Vatican Council document, the bishops also accept the legitimacy of Christian pacifism and call for the recognition of both conscientious objection and selective conscientious objection by our legal system.[12]

While half the pastoral letter "Human Life in Our Day" is addressed to the family of nations and the issues of peace and war, the pastoral reflection "To Live in Christ Jesus" discusses all aspects of the Christian life and devotes about two pages to peace issues.[13] This document succinctly summarizes the material found in the universal and American documents already considered. Chapter Seven has discussed the one new aspect found in this document—the claim that it is not only wrong to attack civilian populations but it is also wrong to threaten to attack them as part of a strategy of deterrence. The document does not explicitly raise the questions of how deterrence can continue to exist in the light of this or how deterrence can be effective without someone's having the intention to use the weapons.

Cardinal Krol's congressional testimony in 1979 on the ratification of the SALT II treaty discusses the nuclear question at greater length.[14] The cardinal is very precise and exact in introducing his testimony. On such specific issues as the SALT treaty there is a divergence of views within the Roman Catholic Church. The position he adopts is not the unanimous position of all the bishops or of all Catholics, but it is the official policy of the United States Catholic Conference. The testimony maintains that the first and primary moral imperative is to prevent the use of any nuclear weapons. The previous chapter has discussed Krol's approach to deterrence. Likewise there is no need to repeat here the summary of the American bishops' pastoral letter on peace and war.

The main thrust of this chapter is to analyze this teaching in the light of the broader perspective of Catholic moral theology. Three areas of moral theology will be considered—

ethical theory, eschatology, and ecclesiology. Is this approach to peace and war intimately related to and even grounded in broader theological understandings in the Roman Catholic theological tradition?

II. General Ethical Theory

In my judgment the most distinctive aspect of Roman Catholic ethics is the insistence on mediation. Mediation is characteristic of Roman Catholic theology in general. Karl Barth maintained that his biggest problem with Roman Catholicism was its *and*.[15] This comment points to the Catholic insistence on *and*—Scripture and tradition, faith and reason, God and human beings, faith and works, Jesus and the church. The Catholic tradition has opposed the axiom "the Scripture alone," because the Scripture must always be made concrete and contemporary through the continuing work of the Spirit in the church in the light of the historical, cultural, and social circumstances of the times. Catholic theology has rejected the axiom "to God alone belongs the glory," because the human being is a sharer and participator in the glory of God. Catholic ecclesiology insists on the church as a visible society mediating the word and work of the risen Lord. The believer is a part of this community of the church and through the church community is related to the risen Lord.

Major problems have occurred in the Catholic tradition when the true concept of mediation was forgotten. At times the second element in the couplet was given independent value and seemed to exist on its own apart from the first. Think of the older Catholic approach to Scripture and tradition as two different sources of revelation. An older apologetic thought that reason could conclusively prove the existence of God. A previous morality so emphasized work that the charge of Pelagianism was rightly raised because of the failure to see faith being active in works. An older ecclesiology absolutized the institution of the church and in its triumphalism failed to see that the whole reality and meaning of the church are in terms of mediation. However, all these abuses were abuses precisely because they forgot the reality of mediation or participation.

As applied to moral theology, mediation can be seen in a number of different ways. The traditional natural-law theory, especially from the perspective of theology, well illustrates the reality of mediation. To know what human beings are to do, this approach does not appeal immediately and directly to God or God's plan or will. Yes, the plan of God is the ultimate norm of human morality, but the natural law is precisely the participation of the eternal plan in the rational creature. Human reason reflecting on human nature can arrive at the plan of God. In a similar manner, Catholic theology maintains that the faith vision of the Christian is mediated in and through human reason and human sciences. In the best of the Catholic tradition there can never be a dichotomy or opposition between faith and reason. If anything, the older manuals erred by absolutizing human reason in itself and failing to understand reason as mediating faith. In this light, approaches to the realities of peace and war often prescinded from faith and scriptural perspectives. However, these faith perspectives cannot exist alone but must be mediated through human reason. One cannot jump immediately from scriptural citations to complex specific moral issues without the mediating use of reason.

This emphasis on mediation in Catholic social ethics is illustrated in the tradition by the tendency for moral theology to give a very specific and minute analysis of moral questions. Compare, for example, *A Living Wage* published by John A. Ryan in 1906 with *Christianity and the Social Crisis* written by Walter Rauschenbusch in 1907.[16] These two men were the leading figures in the Roman Catholic and Protestant social ethics of their day. Rauschenbusch's book deals in a very broad way, as the title indicates, with Christianity and the social crisis. Ryan deals with one comparatively small concern — a living wage. The Catholic author discusses various theories of wage justice and argues for a living wage by insisting on the fact that God created the world for the sustenance of all and that access to the bounty of the earth becomes available to most people only through the expenditure of useful labor. In addition to a thorough and detailed form of reasoning, Ryan also employs economic theory and statistics in his book. A living family wage for an average size family of four or five children is at least six hundred dollars a year in American cities, and more is needed in the larger cities. Ryan makes out a family budget to prove his contention. Ryan's work well illustrates the fact that Catholic moral theology has used reason and the sciences as mediating realities in coming to its specific ethical conclusions. Obviously there are other factors such as confessional practice which also strongly influence the Catholic tendency to be quite specific in its ethical analysis and conclusions.

The recognition of mediation means that morality becomes very concrete but also that moral appeals must employ and appropriate the data of all the human sciences. Too often there has been a tendency to claim that many issues involve only economic or political decisions and not moral decisions. However, there is a moral aspect to these decisions, and most truly human decisions are moral decisions even though they involve much data from the human sciences. John Ryan can again illustrate the Catholic tradition in this regard. The very first sentence in Ryan's unpublished licentiate dissertation makes the point: "Every free economic action has ethical relations, and is subject to ethical laws."[17] Thus in the contemporary discussions of peace and war, the issues of deterrence and disarmament are not merely political problems but are truly moral and ethical issues.

A mediated ethic which recognizes the need to become concrete and specific through the use of the data of the sciences must logically acknowledge that solutions employing such data cannot claim too great a degree of certitude. The human sciences are not able to provide certitude without the fear of error. Church teachings in moral theology must recognize the inability to achieve absolute certitude on complex specific issues. This realization lies behind the caution given by Cardinal Krol when he testified for the United States Catholic Conference on the SALT II treaty. The testimony supported the treaty but also recognized many shortcomings in it. The cardinal distinguished between the principles of Catholic morality and the positions taken on a particular issue such as the SALT II treaty. Krol carefully recognized that his testimony did not represent the unanimous position of all Catholics or of all the Catholic bishops or even of the Administrative Board of the Catholic bishops. It was nonetheless the official policy of the United States Catholic Conference.

The outstanding characteristic of all the drafts of the pastoral letter of the American bishops, especially in comparison with the documents of the universal church, is the emphasis on specifics. In this sense the pastoral letter goes beyond but not necessarily against the papal and conciliar statements. The pastoral letter explicitly calls attention to the specific character of many of its proposals and distinguishes these proposals from the broader level of moral principles. Such specific proposals are prudential judgments which cannot and do not claim to have the same moral and doctrinal authority as the more general moral principles. Catholics can legitimately disagree with these judgments. The principle of mediation thus recognizes that on a specific complex issue or judgment one cannot claim a certitude that excludes the possibility of error.

The traditional Catholic emphasis on mediation in moral theology, together with other influences, recognizes that social reform and social justice require not only a change of heart but also a change of institutions and structures. This emphasis has always been present in Roman Catholicism with its integral vision of the world and is illustrated in the social teaching of the popes beginning with the encyclical *Rerum Novarum* of 1891. Change of heart alone is not enough, but a change of institutions and structures is also necessary. In fact, the official Catholic social teaching in the last century could rightly be criticized for not giving enough importance to interior dispositions, or the change of heart.

Documents such as *Rerum Novarum* concentrate on structural change and only at the very end briefly mention the need for interior personal change. This recognition of the need for both a change of heart and a change of structures is also present in the official Catholic teachings on peace, war, and deterrence. *Gaudium et Spes* sees peace as resulting from justice and love and as being deeply rooted in the hearts of individuals. However, to bring about peace in our world certain political structures are required. The goal of completely eliminating war requires the establishment of some universal, public authority acknowledged as such by all and endowed with effective power. In the meantime, everything must be done to strengthen trust in existing institutions and structures. The rejection of a call for unilateral disarmament echoes the need for systems and institutions which can assure the peace. The structural aspect of securing peace is most important. Part three of the pastoral letter entitled "The Promotion of Peace: Proposals and Policies" stresses the structural changes necessary, whereas the fourth part, "The Pastoral Challenge and Response," emphasizes the need for conversion and education.

The discussion of Catholic ethical theory has thus far concentrated on the characteristic aspect of mediation and its consequences for ethics in general and specifically for official Catholic teaching on peace, war, and disarmament. There is one other aspect of Catholic ethical thinking which should be mentioned—the contemporary debate about the existence and grounding of norms. Within the discussion about peace and war in the Catholic tradition there can be no doubt that a very strong pacifist tendency has emerged during the last few years.[18] This pacifism takes many different forms and has many different groundings and formulations. One form of pacifism is the pacifism of the Catholic Worker movement associated with Dorothy Day and such "traditional" Catholic pacifists as Gordon Zahn.[19] In my judgment their approach can best be described as Christian witness pacifism. The gospel calls the Christian to bear witness to Jesus who did not take up arms or engage in violence. The primary emphasis is on bearing witness.

The Christian is not primarily concerned with efficacy, for in the end results are in the hands of God. The Catholic action communities of the 1960's, often called in the media the Catholic left, also held pacifist positions but in a different way.[20] They were totally committed to nonviolence but saw nonviolence not primarily as a witness but as an effective and efficacious means of social change. A third group might be called nuclear pacifists, but the term pacifists is here used in a very equivocal manner because many of these people are not absolute pacifists. The growth and influence of the pacifist movement in Roman Catholicism are readily evident. The conditioned acceptance of pacifism by Vatican II as a legitimate Catholic option both has been brought about by this contemporary movement and has also contributed to the growth of the pacifist movement.

While pacifism has been growing within Roman Catholic circles, another development has occurred in Catholic ethical theory which in general tends to argue against an absolute pacifism. Since the middle 1960s a growing number of Catholic moral theologians have questioned the existence and grounding of absolute moral norms.[21] The revisionists maintain that the older approach has often identified the human moral act with the physical stucture of the act. The physical structure, in such instances as contraception and the concept of directly doing evil, constitutes a premoral evil which can be justified for a proportionate reason. Sometimes the terms deontological and teleological are used to describe the two approaches. The older, or deontological, approach maintains that certain actions are always wrong no matter what the consequences. The teleological approach maintains that premoral evil can be done if there is a proportionate reason. I prefer to describe the revisionist approach as emphasizing a more relational understanding which refuses to absolutize any one value.

The revisionist approach to the moral theory about the existence and grounding of norms tends to be in opposition to the growing emphasis on pacifism in the literature dealing only with peace and war issues. Peace and no killing are absolutized; violence is never permitted. The revisionist approach would see violence or killing as a premoral evil which could be justified by a proportionate reason. Peace exists in relationship to other values or virtues; sometimes in the name of justice, for example, violence might become morally acceptable. These two different developments — one in the specific question of peace and war and the other in the area of moral theory — have been growing in the last few years without any interaction. Those writing on pacifism tend to be interested only in the pacifism issue and have not entered into the current methodological discussion in Catholic moral theology. As a proponent of a revisionist approach in moral theory I see such an approach as another reason why I personally or the church as a whole cannot accept an absolute pacifist position.

The revisionist approach to the grounding and existence of norms, however, must come to grips with the just-war principle which traditionally has forbidden the direct killing of noncombatants. Can such killing be only a premoral evil which is justified for a proportionate reason? Many of the revisionists have explicitly considered this question and concluded that there is a moral norm in this case because there is no proportionate reason that could ever justify such killing in warfare.[22] More dialogue and discussion would be helpful in this area.

In general there appears to be a consistency between the Roman Catholic teaching on peace, war, and disarmament and the understanding of Roman Catholic ethics as accepting the reality of mediation with all of its ramifications. In addition recent revisionist developments in ethical theory also argue against an absolute pacifism and seem to be opposed to the line of reasoning proposed by the growing number of recent Catholic advocates of pacifism.

III. Eschatology

Eschatology has been a subject of increasing interest in the last few decades in Christian theology especially in terms of such discussions as secularization, the meaning of history, and the social mission of the church. My own approach to eschatology is in terms of the fivefold stance I propose for moral theology.[23] The Christian looks at the world and reality in terms of the fivefold mysteries of creation, sin, incarnation, redemption, and resurrection destiny. Creation reminds us of the goodness and finitude of all that was made by God. Sin affects everything human but cannot totally destroy the goodness of creation. The incarnation recalls that God has destined all of created reality to be joined in the work of Jesus. Redemption means that the saving love of God is already present in our midst, but the fullness of the eschaton always remains future and will never occur in this world. In general terms this eschatological vision corresponds to the type proposed by H. Richard Niebuhr of Christ transforming culture.[24]

What has been explained above in terms of eschatology can also be expressed in other theological terms and under other aspects of theology. The doctrine of God corresponding to this eschatological approach understands God's action in terms of creating, preserving, and redeeming. The corresponding theological anthropology sees the Christian person in the light of all these different mysteries.

In the discussion on peace and war, especially in *Gaudium et Spes*, the Catholic teaching seems to adopt such an eschatology. Some of the other parts of *Gaudium et Spes* (especially chapters 1, 2, and 3 of part I), with their intention of emphasizing the christological aspect of reality, so overstress the resurrection and redemption that they fail to recognize that the fullness of the eschaton will always lie outside history. The discussion of the nature of peace seems to present a more adequate eschatology in keeping with the stance mentioned above.[25] Peace results from the harmony built into human society by its divine founder and actuated by human beings as they thirst after greater justice, but because of the presence of sin this is not enough. Peace is likewise the fruit of love which goes beyond what justice can provide. This earthly peace results from the peace of Christ, who through the cross reconciled all to God. Because of our sinfulness the threat of war will hang over us until the return of Christ. There are some indications that perhaps the fullness of the eschaton as future is somewhat slighted in these formulations, but on the whole the eschatological vision of this paragraph of *Gaudium et Spes* coheres with the stance mentioned above.

A significant change between the first and the second drafts of the pastoral letter of the American bishops underscores the need for such an eschatological perspective. The first draft begins with an introduction based on the Scriptures giving a picture of the kingdom as embracing peace and the living out of the Sermon on the Mount. The next section treats of peace in the modern world and the different stands that Christians take toward peace and violence in this world.[26] The second draft, after the biblical section entitled "Peace and the Kingdom," adds an important section on "Kingdom and History" which recognizes the imperfect and sinful realities of the present in relation to the eschatological fullness.[27] Only in the light of this eschatological perspective does the draft then develop the different approaches which Christians take with regard to peace and force in our world. The second and subsequent drafts also have, near the very beginning, a short section describing the Catholic social tradition. Here the letter refers to the biblical vision of the world created and sustained by God, scarred by sin, redeemed in Christ, and destined for the kingdom, which is at the heart of our religious heritage. It is the task of theology to elaborate, explain, and apply this vision in each age.[28]

The general consequences of such an eschatological vision center on the tensions created by it. The believer and the believing community will always experience the tension between the imperfections of the present and the fullness of the eschatological future. The perennial temptation consists in trying to deny or collapse this tension. One can collapse the tension by stressing either pole to the detriment of the other. The one approach expects the fullness of the kingdom to come quickly, readily, and easily, thereby forgetting the struggle and the pilgrim nature of the Christian life. The other extreme forgets the pull of the future and merely accepts the status quo without any impulse to change and transform it.

This eschatological vision also serves as a basis for the tension which exists between the believing community and the culture around it. In the words of H. Richard Niebuhr's model, the Christian and the believing community are always striving to transform the culture or society in which they live.[29]

At times because of the finitude, sinfulness, and lack of eschatological fullness present in our world and culture, the church should oppose what is happening in the contemporary society. Too often in the American ethos there has been the tendency for all churches to be too conforming and not to critique certain aspects of the culture. There are different explanations for the general conforming propensities of the mainline American churches, but the immigrant status of Roman Catholicism helped to frame a mentality which tried to show that one could be both Catholic and American at one and the same time. The mainstream of Roman Catholicism from the last part of the nineteenth century adopted such a posture, and this characterized most of the Roman Catholic Church until recent times.[30]

Not only do finitude, sin, and incompleteness mark our contemporary world and ethos, but the goodness of creation, the destiny of the incarnation, and the grace of the resurrection are also present. The Christian believer and the believing communities work with all other individuals and groups within society to try to bring about a greater peace and justice in our world. The relationship of the believing community to the world will always be complex. At times Christians must strongly criticize. At other times Christians can and will learn from the society. However, at all times the believing community must work with all other human beings to achieve a greater but always imperfect peace and justice in our world.

Eschatology's relationship to social ethics takes on a number of different forms. The fullness of the eschaton serves as a negative critique of all existing human institutions and structures. However, such an understanding cannot result in a hands off, "plague on both your houses" type of approach. As Karl Barth phrased it, even in the dark of night not all cats are gray.[31] The negative critique should include the positive commitment to change and transform the existing situation.[32]

The eschatological vision also presents the positive values at which we aim — in this specific case the realities of peace and justice. This utopia or vision gives a general sense of direction to what Christians and the Christian community should try to do.

At times the eschatological vision means that the Christian and the Christian community must reluctantly accept or tolerate some nonmoral evils. Sometimes one must make the prudential judgment that half a loaf is better than none. There are many examples of accepting something less than perfect and of toleration in the strict sense in Catholic teaching and theology. Thomas Aquinas' approach to civil law furnishes a good example. According to Aquinas the civil law is based on the natural law. However, the civil law can permit some evils. Laws are imposed on people according to their condition, but the greater part of human beings are not perfect in virtue. Human law, consequently, should not prohibit all vices from which the virtuous are able to abstain but only those more serious vices which the greater part of human beings can avoid.[33] In discussing whether or not the rights of infidels can be tolerated, Aquinas briefly develops his theory about tolerating evil. Human rulers and human governments are derived from divine government and should imitate the divine example. However, the Almighty God permits certain evils to occur in the universe which could be prohibited, lest in prohibiting them greater good would be taken away or greater evil would follow. Thus human government or rulers can tolerate some evils lest certain goods be impeded or worse evils occur.[34] The Thomistic recognition that evil can be tolerated logically coheres with the eschatological vision proposed above. The previous chapter dealt more specifically with the kind of evil that can be tolerated.

Reactions within the Roman Catholic community to the SALT II treaty also illustrate the tension created by the imperfections of the time in which we live. Opponents to the treaty claimed that it failed to really reduce arms and therefore did not merit a positive reception.[35] Proponents of the treaty, including the official position of the United States Catholic Conference, recognized the very significant limitations of the treaty but endorsed it as a step toward continuing negotiations and the reduction of arms. They obviously maintained that half a loaf is better than none.[36]

Another example has recently occurred in the Roman Catholic Church in the United States. The Roman Catholic bishops have been very public and visible in their support for a constitutional amendment to overturn the 1973 ruling of the Supreme Court on abortion. The bishops never said specifically what type of amendment they supported, but their opposition to all direct abortion was well known.[37] In fall 1981 the American bishops officially supported the Hatch Amendment which provides that a right to abortion is not secured by the constitution. Congress and the states have concurrent power to restrict abortion, but a provision of a law of a state which is more restrictive than a conflicting provision of a law of Congress shall govern. Some Catholic bishops and others involved in the right-to-life movement were upset by such support. Were the Catholic bishops backing down from their strong antiabortion position?[38] Without a doubt if the Hatch Amendment were to become law, there would still be a large number of abortions performed in the United States, but the number would be much less than at present. Obviously the bishops based their decision on political expediency—in the best sense of the term. An amendment prohibiting almost all abortions except in very limited circumstances apparently has no chance of becoming law at the present time. According to the thinking of its supporters there is the possibility that the Hatch Amendment can be passed, especially with strong support from the American bishops. (My own position has been opposed to any attempt to change the ruling of the Supreme

Court by a constitutional amendment both for theoretical reasons and for concerns of feasibility and practicality.)

These eschatological considerations show that the Christian believer and the Christian community will always experience the tension between the now and the eschatological future. This same tension is manifest in the church's relationship to society and culture with the result that the church can never be a total opposition movement nor can it be uncritical of the imperfections and evils of the society in which it lives. The eschatological tension means that the church will always try to transform the present reality, but at times the church will have to settle for something less than the perfect good or will have to tolerate some evil in order to avoid greater evils.

The teaching on peace and war found in the official Roman Catholic teaching well illustrates this eschatological tension. The just-war theory itself expresses such a tension by trying to limit both the right to go to war and the ways in which even just wars are fought but at the same time recognizing that in our present world nations still have the right to go to war in self-defense provided such violence is a last resort and is conducted in a just way. The pastoral letter disagrees with American policy by opposing the first use of nuclear weapons. The bishops do not call for unilateral nuclear disarmament but conditionally accept limited counterforce deterrence provided such deterrence exists only to prevent the use of nuclear weapons and is accompanied by meaningful steps toward negotiated reduction in arms and disarmament. While conditionally accepting some limited deterrence, the pastoral letter continues to criticize significant aspects of both Soviet and American deterrence policies.

IV. Ecclesiology

The ecclesiology to be proposed here is in keeping with the traditional Roman Catholic self-understanding, is consistent with the ethical and eschatological concerns already discussed, and is coherent with the teaching on peace, war, and deterrence discussed in the first part of this paper. This section will discuss the church as a community intimately involved in the life of society and will devote most of its space to a consideration of pluralism within the church on specific social issues such as those under discussion.

The church is a community involved in the struggle for justice and peace in the world. At times the church can and must be critical of the society, but it can never find its total identity as a sectarian movement always opposed to and separated from political life and institutions. The history of the Roman Catholic Church illustrates such an approach. The eschatological considerations discussed in the previous section form the basis for such an understanding of the church. The whole tradition of the church's dealing with the issues of peace and war support such an understanding of the church.

Within the church there exists a pluralism of acceptable positions on specific concrete social questions. The Catholic Church is also catholic — with a small "c." There is a universality about it and a willingness to recognize diverse possible options within the church on specific and complex social questions such as war, peace, and deterrence. Obviously there are limitations to this pluralism, but the Catholic Church in respect to social issues is a "big church" with room for diversity. The historical and existential self-understanding of Roman Catholicism recognizes this pluralism. The Catholic Church community has been big enough to include a Francisco Franco and a Julius Nyerere. American Catholicism embraced both a Dorothy Day and a Father Coughlin. The Catholic teaching on peace and war in both its universal and American contexts recognizes such pluralism and diversity. Both pacifism and just-war theories are acceptable. A complete and unlimited bellicism is outside the pale of Catholic options, but there will always be the possibility of pluralism on issues such as arms reduction treaties. The American bishops explicitly recognize a legitimate pluralism within the church on prudential judgments such as no first use of nuclear weapons.

This pluralism of options within the church is grounded in the ethical and eschatological approaches discussed earlier. Ethical theory recognizes the epistemological problem that in the midst of complexity one cannot attain a certitude that excludes the possibility of error. Since Catholic social teaching recognizes the need to mediate the evangelical vision through reason and the human sciences, it also recognizes the lack of absolute certitude in such specific areas. In addition, the eschatological tension also acknowledges a pluralism of approaches. At times some might be willing to tolerate certain evils which others would not. A further justification for pluralism within the church on specific and complex social issues is a theological reason recognizing the legitimate freedom of the believer. Roman Catholic theory has not given much explicit attention to this reality, but concern for such freedom has existed, even when that freedom was narrowly circumscribed. The theory of probabilism, for example, safeguards the freedom of the individual Catholic against a rigoristic tutiorism or probabiliorism. No confessor can take away the freedom of the individual to follow an opinion which is truly probable even though the contrary opinion might be safer or more probable.[39] Cardinal Krol in his testimony before Congress on the SALT II treaty was very careful to recognize implicitly the freedom of the believer within the Catholic Church community. The Roman consultation in January 1983 mentioned respect for the freedom of the Christian as the first reason calling for a distinction among the various levels of teaching authority found in the American bishops' letter.[40]

Pluralism within the church in dealing with complex social issues cannot be merely a flabby pluralism, for there are definite limits to legitimate pluralism within the church even on issues of peace and war. Even within the limits of legitimate pluralism there are important truth claims involved in the positions taken. One should strive to convince others of the truth of one's own position, but one cannot claim that an opposing position places one outside the church. Since there are a number of different legitimate positions within the church, the church itself must often be seen as a community of moral discourse rather than as a provider of answers for its members in all such cases.

One of the most striking illustrations of this pluralism within Roman Catholicism has been the cautious official acceptance of a pacifist position, which appeared for the first time in *Gaudium et Spes*. As noted in the last chapter, the American bishops are even stronger in their acceptance of pacifism as an individual option within the church. In my judgment there must always be in the church a place for the pacifist position, but the whole church cannot be pacifist in our present circumstances. All the aspects mentioned previously — ethical theory, eschatology, and a catholic ecclesiology — argue against the fact that the whole church can be pacifist today. However, before talking about the different positions within the church, one must always recognize and emphasize the common ground which exists between the pacifist and others in the Christian community. All are called to work for peace. Change of heart, nonviolent approaches, and changes of structures to make peace more of a reality in our world can and should be acknowledged by all. War and violence can never be accepted as anything more than a last resort — an *ultima ratio*. Within the pluralism of the believing community the different positions must realize in theory and in practice that they share much in common.

However, the question remains: If the whole church cannot be pacifist, how can there be a place, even an important place, for pacifists within the church? Note that here we are dealing very much on the level of principle and not just the level of prudential judgments. I think that from within the Catholic tradition an analogy can and should be made with the concept of vocation to religious life. It seems, in a way similar to the stance of Reinhold Niebuhr, that there is a place and a need for a vocation to pacifism within the church community.[41] Religious life rests on a commitment to one or other of the basic Christian values and virtues of poverty, chastity, or obedience. Peace is also a very important value in human existence. Just as in the case of religious life, so too there can and should be vocations in the Christian community through the gift of the Spirit for people to bear witness to the value of peace. Commitment to peace and bearing witness to it constitute a very significant vocation for some Christian people today. Also this vocation serves a purpose for the total Christian community by calling to mind the importance of this value and especially the danger of abuses of violence which all too often have occurred.

Is pacifism a higher calling or something closer to the gospel than the reluctant acceptance of violence as a last resort in the quest for justice? The analogy to religious life in the Roman Catholic tradition might lead one to this conclusion. However, I personally disagree with the older Catholic theology that claimed religious life was a higher state of life. Even in accord with aspects of traditional Catholic theology one can maintain that life according to the religious vows is not a higher form or better grade of Christian existence. According to Thomistic theology the goal of the Christian life is charity—love of God and neighbor. The vows concern only means to an end.[42] An older theory wrongly absolutized these means rather than seeing them as mediations of charity. In the practice of religious life absolutized vows were considered in themselves apart from their primary function to be mediations of charity. All Christians have the same goal, and there is no better or higher way to achieve that goal. In other theological terminology, the primary vow of the Christian is the baptismal vow. All other subsequent vows add nothing to this basic commitment but only specify it.

From a more evangelical perspective one might maintain that pacifism is closer to the gospel ideal of peace and hence something higher and better. However, the Scriptures also need a hermeneutic and must be interpreted in the light of the eschatological tension and signs of the time. Here again I do not think one can talk in terms of a better or higher way. Paul Ramsey, from his perspective on Christian ethics, has tried to indicate that one and the same agape can justify both pacifism and the acceptance of violence as a last resort in protecting the neighbor in need. Agape can take either fork in the road, but one way cannot be necessarily better than the other.[43] My understanding of pluralism thus recognizes an important place for a vocation to pacifism within the church, even though the whole church today cannot be pacifist and pacifism is not necessarily a higher calling.

A final consideration involves the understanding of the prophetic role in the church. This prophetic role stresses the leadership of the church in speaking God's judgment against injustices and evils in the world, often in a very concrete and specific manner. What is the relationship between a church recognizing the pluralism of different options in the area of peace, war, and disarmament and a prophetic church? There can be no doubt that my view of the church in its relationship to the particular questions under discussion and to social teaching in general is much less prophetic than many approaches to church today. Sectarian understandings and an emphasis on a small elite church result in a more prophetic church. At times I have the feeling that some Roman Catholics calling for a more prophetic church still suffer from the genetic disease that constantly threatens all Roman Catholics — triumphalism. This newer form of triumphalism maintains that the church must be the leader in all things and must be there as the "firstest with the mostest." On the other hand, I do not want to leave the impression that the church does not have a prophetic function.

The prophetic function of the church is nuanced and contextualized in the light of the other considerations already developed. The ethical perspective calls to mind the complexity of specific social issues and the difficulty of achieving certitude in these areas. This lack of certitude is bound to temper the prophetic aspect of the church in dealing with specific moral problems. From an eschatological viewpoint the church will always experience the tension between the imperfection of the now and the fullness of the eschaton. The acceptance of a lesser good or the toleration of evil is at times necessary and required. An ecclesiology which stresses a "big church" is also going to limit the prophetic aspect of the church. A big church is comprised of both saints and sinners. In a sense the church itself is always *simul justus et peccator*. The church can never be reduced to an elite of any type. The big church has many functions — the prophetic, the reconciling, the healing, the forgiving, the challenging.

Prophetic is a word which everyone wants to claim for one's self in these days. For that reason I think theologians should be very careful in using the word. It is very interesting to me that in the contemporary life of the Roman Catholic Church the word prophetic often appears in two very different contexts. Some people urge the church to be prophetic and come out in favor of unilateral nuclear disarmament. Anything short of that is seen as being unprophetic and not living up to the fullness of the gospel.[44] The other context in which the word is frequently used is in the defense of the teaching of *Humanae Vitae* on artificial contraception. The proponents of this teaching have frequently referred to it in the last few years as prophetic.[45] From my perspective the prophetic can never be in opposition to what is reasonable. The Catholic tradition has insisted that morality in general and social morality in particular must be in accord with reason.

The prophetic, nonetheless, remains a significant function and reality in the church, but there are different ways in which the truly prophetic aspect can and should become real in the church. In terms of the preaching and acting of the whole church a prophetic criticism of existing structures in the light of the gospel is always called for. Also in words, symbols, and acts the whole community must stress the goal commandments of Christian existence. However, on specific complex issues such as those under consideration one must always recognize the legitimate diversity and pluralism within the church even though one should be strongly committed to one's own position.

Smaller groups and individuals within the church can have a prophetic witness (with emphasis on witness) to one or other important values or aspects of the Christian life even though the total church cannot act in this way. This function has been carried out well in the church by small groups such as the Catholic Worker movement in the United States.[46]

Conclusion

The Roman Catholic teaching on peace, war, and disarmament in the documents of both the universal and the American Church has been studied not primarily in terms of an in-depth analysis of the teaching itself but rather in terms of the relationship of this teaching to broader aspects of moral theology.

The ethical, eschatological, and ecclesiological implications of the official teachings on peace and war are consistent with the general Catholic understanding of these realities. The just-war approach used in these documents, together with the recognition of a vocation to pacifism for some, is thus firmly grounded in Catholic moral theology in general. This just-war theory continues to serve its purpose of both justifying some wars and condemning others while at the same time placing significant limits on the way in which even a just war can be waged.

Obviously, within the parameters of these ethical, eschatological, and ecclesiological dimensions there is room for different approaches to specific questions and to prudential judgments. One, for example, with the same theological perspectives could oppose a bilateral nuclear freeze. Since the theory involved and the general outlines of the approach taken to peace and war in these official Catholic documents are so intimately connected with a broader Catholic theological self-understanding, one can conclude that the same general approach will continue to direct Roman Catholic teaching in the future.

NOTES

1. *Gaudium et Spes*, n. 80. For an English translation of the Vatical II documents see Walter M. Abbott, ed., *The Documents of*

Vatican II (New York: Guild Press, 1966). In subsequent references n. will refer to the paragraph in the document, and page references to Abbott will also be given.

2. Ibid., n. 82; Abbott, p. 295.

3. Ibid., n. 80; Abbott, p. 293.

4. For a defense of this interpretation see Paul Ramsey, *The Just War: Force and Political Responsibility* (New York: Charles Scribner's Sons, 1968), pp. 192-197.

5. *Gaudium et Spes*, n. 78; Abbott, p. 291.

6. Ibid., n. 79; Abbott, p. 293.

7. Ibid., n. 80; Abbott, p. 294.

8. Ibid., n. 81; Abbott, pp. 294-295.

9. Ibid., n. 82; Abbott, p. 296.

10. J. Bryan Hehir, "War and Peace: Reflections on Recent Teachings," *New Catholic World* 226 (March/April 1982): 60-64.

11. Archbishop Joseph Bernardin, "Studying War and Peace," *Origins* 11 (1981): 403-404.

12. "Human Life in our Day," in *Quest for Justice: A Compendium of Statements of the United States Catholic Bishops on the Political and Social Order 1966-1980*, ed. J. Brian Benestad and Francis J. Butler (Washington, DC: United States Catholic Conference, 1981), pp. 57-69. Subsequent references to American episcopal documents will be made to this compendium as *Quest for Justice*.

13. *Quest for Justice*, pp. 43-45.

14. Cardinal John Krol, "Salt II: A Statement of Support," *Origins* 9 (1979): 195-199.

15. From a Catholic perspective see Hans Urs von Balthasar, *The Theology of Karl Barth* (New York: Holt, Rinehart and Winston, 1971), pp. 40-41.

16. John A. Ryan, *A Living Wage* (New York: Macmillan, 1906); Walter Rauschenbusch, *Christianity and the Social Crisis* (New York: Harper Torchbook, 1964).

17. John A. Ryan, "Some Ethical Aspects of Speculation," (S.T.L. dissertation, The Catholic University of America, 1906), p. 1.

18. Joseph Fahey, "Pax Christi," in *War or Peace: The Search for New Answers*, ed. Thomas A. Shannon (Maryknoll, NY: Orbis Books, 1980), pp. 59-71; Patricia F. McNeal, *The American Catholic Peace Movement, 1928-1972* (New York: Arno Press, 1978), pp. 123-299.

19. E.g., Gordon C. Zahn, "The Berrigans: Radical Activism

Personified," in *The Berrigans*, ed. William Van Etten Casey and Philip Nobile (New York: Avon Books, 1971), pp. 97-112.

20. Charles A. Meconis, *With Clumsy Grace: The American Catholic Left, 1961-75* (New York: Seabury Press, 1979).

21. For readings on this debate, see eds., Richard A. McCormick and Paul Ramsey, *Doing Evil to Achieve Good: Moral Choice in Conflict Situations* (Chicago: Loyola University Press, 1978); eds., Charles E. Curran and Richard A. McCormick, *Readings in Moral Theology No. 1: Moral Norms and Catholic Tradition* (New York: Paulist Press, 1979).

22. See, for example, McCormick in McCormick and Ramsey, *Doing Evil to Achieve Good*, pp. 259-261; Curran in Curran and McCormick, *Readings in Moral Theology*, pp. 345ff.

23. Charles E. Curran, *New Perspectives in Moral Theology* (Notre Dame, IN: University of Notre Dame Press, 1976), pp. 47-86.

24. H. Richard Niebuhr, *Christ and Culture* (New York: Harper Torchbook, 1956).

25. *Gaudium et Spes*, nn. 77-90; Abbott, pp. 289-305.

26. "First Draft: Pastoral Letter on War and Peace," *National Catholic Reporter* 18 (July 2, 1982): 11, 12. Note that for the sake of consistency the pastoral letter and its drafts will be referred to in this manner.

27. "Second Draft: Pastoral Letter on War and Peace," *Origins* 12 (1982): 309-311.

28. Ibid., p. 307; "Pastoral Letter on War and Peace," *Origins* 13 (1983): 3.

29. Niebuhr, *Christ and Culture*, pp. 190-229.

30. David J. O'Brien, *American Catholics and Social Reform* (New York: Oxford University Press, 1968), pp. 212-227; O'Brien, *The Renewal of American Catholicism* (New York: Oxford University Press, 1972), pp. 138-162

31. Karl Barth, *Community, State, and Church* (Garden City, NY: Doubleday Anchor Books, 1960), p. 119.

32. Joseph Jankowiak, *Critical Negativity and Political Ethics* (Rome: Pontifical Gregorian University Press, 1975).

33. Thomas Aquinas, *Summa Theologiae* (Turin and Rome: Marietti, 1952), $I^a II^{ae}$, q. 96, a. 2.

34. Ibid., $II^a II^{ae}$, q. 10, a. 11.

35. Thomas J. Gumbleton, "Chaplain Blessing the Bombers: Is SALT Worth Supporting? No!" *Commonweal* 106 (1979): 105-106.

36. Krol, "Salt II," *Origins* 9 (1979): 195-199.

37. James T. McHugh, *The Relationship of Moral Principles to Civil Laws with Special Application to Abortion Legislation in the United States of America, 1968-78* (Rome: Pontifical University of St. Thomas, 1981), pp. 109-148.

38. James Castelli, "Hatch Amendment Still Splits Pro-Life Camp," *Our Sunday Visitor* 70 (January 17, 1982): 6.

39. Th. Deman, "Probabilisme," in *Dictionnaire de théologie catholique* XIII, col. 417-619.

40. "Rome Consultation on Peace and Disarmament," *Origins* 12 (1983): 693.

41. John C. Bennett, "Reinhold Niebuhr's Social Ethics," in *Reinhold Niebuhr: His Religious, Social, and Political Thought*, ed. Charles W. Kegley and Robert W. Bretall (New York: Macmillan, 1956), pp. 67ff.

42. Aquinas, *Summa Theologiae, II^{a}II^{ae}*, q. 184, a. 3.

43. Ramsey, *The Just War*, p. 501.

44. Joan Chittester, "Between Prophetism and Nationalism," *Commonweal* 109 (1982): 429.

45. Pope John Paul II, *Familiaris Consortio: The Role of the Christian Family in the Modern World* (Boston: St. Paul Editions, 1981), n. 29, p. 47.

46. William D. Miller, *A Harsh and Dreadful Love: Dorothy Day and the Catholic Worker Movement* (Garden City, NY: Doubleday Image Book, 1973).

9. Population Control: Methods and Morality

Many people believe that the threat of nuclear war and population growth constitute the two greatest social problems confronting our world at the present time. Earlier chapters have discussed the nuclear-war question, but it is also appropriate to devote considerable attention to the question of the population crisis.

Four United Nations world conferences on population have been held beginning at Rome in 1954, with subsequent meetings at New Delhi in 1965, Bucharest in 1974, and Mexico City in 1984. These conferences have obviously resulted from the general concern about this issue and at the same time have focused world attention on the problem of population growth.

Preparatory discussions for the 1984 conference in Mexico City indicated there was continuing agreement with the World Population Plan of Action adopted by the 1974 meeting in Bucharest. That conference had recognized the population problem but insisted that the crisis in population growth must be seen in the broader context of development. Since 1974 the rate of worldwide population growth has decreased from 1.9% to 1.7%, with forecasts of the total world population rising from 4.7 billion in 1984 to an estimate of more than 6 billion in the year 2000. However, the decline in population growth has not been constant throughout the world. The African population increased in 1984 at a 3.1% rate, with a projected growth from 500 million in 1984 to 877 million in the year 2000. At the 1974 Bucharest meeting the Vatican had been the only participant to vote against the conference plan. The tone of Vatican representatives at United Nations meetings in the last few years has been more tolerant, and they are willing to recognize the existence of some problems caused by excessive population growth; yet no one expected a dramatic change in the Vatican's position at Mexico City.[1]

The 1984 Mexico City meeting produced few surprises. The final document urged increased funding for voluntary birth-control programs. Couples and individuals have a right to decide freely and responsibly the number and spacing of their children, but governments should make sure that all have access to the necessary information, education, and means to limit their fertility. Governmental incentives for population control should be neither coercive nor discriminatory. The Vatican delegation succeeded in having the final document explicitly reject abortion as a means of family planning. However, the Vatican again was the only participant not to support the final statement. Vatican spokespersons at the meeting objected to a number of proposals. The Vatican reaffirmed the immorality of artificial contraception and sterilization, objected to putting individuals on a par with married couples in questions of human reproduction, and insisted that more emphasis be put on development as a means of dealing with population growth.[2]

There is a population problem and the need for population control. This chapter will discuss the problem and the means that have been proposed to deal with it. From the very beginning one must realize that population control and family planning are related but at the same time quite distinct. Population control is implemented by family planning and many other means and involves various organizations and the state itself in planning the optimum population for a given area or for the whole earth. In addition to the moral issues involved in family planning, population control raises moral issues which involve the rights of individuals, families, and nations in the light of broader societal and global needs. From a theological-ethical perspective there are four preliminary considerations that will influence the approach taken to population control.

Preliminary Theological-Ethical Considerations

1. Harmony or Chaos

Does one generally see in the world the possibility of harmony and order among all the component aspects of human existence, or is one more inclined to see these different aspects as competing forces which very often threaten chaos and disorder? An emphasis on harmony and order has generally characterized much of Roman Catholic moral theology. A most fundamental question in Christian ethics concerns the proper relationship involving love of God, love of neighbor, and love of self. The Roman Catholic tradition has tried to harmonize all three of these kinds of love and does not see any opposition among them if they are properly understood. Other traditions in Christian ethics have downplayed the love of self and see self-love as opposed to love for the neighbor, especially the neighbor in need. Some would even accuse the Roman Catholic approach as exemplified in Thomas Aquinas of a eudaemonistic ethic which in the last analysis is seeking the ultimate happiness and fulfillment of the individual person.[3]

Pope John XXIII in the second sentence of his encyclical *Pacem in terris* testifies to the emphasis within the Roman Catholic tradition on order and harmony in the world: "The progress of learning and the inventions of technology clearly show that, both in living things and in the forces of nature, an astonishing order reigns, and they also bear witness to the greatness of man who can understand that order and create suitable instruments to harness those forces of nature and use them to his benefit."[4] Such an approach recognizes two different aspects to this harmony — a basic order in nature itself but also the rational control of human beings over nature. It would constitute a perversion of this understanding to claim that human beings should never interfere and that a laissez-faire approach would be sufficient. Nevertheless, this Roman Catholic approach acknowledges a basic order in nature and assumes that the controlling power of human reason can assure that harmony results.

My own approach modifies and qualifies such an understanding of the order and harmony existing among the various aspects of human existence. From a theological perspective, a greater appreciation of sin and the recognition that the fullness of the eschaton is not yet here call for the existence of stronger opposed forces bringing about a greater tension in the world. From a philosophical perspective, a more historical and process understanding will also introduce more movement and change, thereby not accepting as much order and harmony as in an older, more static approach. From the perspective of human experience, the tragedy of war, the inequities existing in our world, the divisions existing within many nations, the recognition that many people have died because of famine, the pollution of the environment, and many other problems all indicate there are more tensions and possible sources of discord in our world than the first approach is willing to acknowledge.

A third approach sees nature and the world primarily in terms of antagonisms and oppositions so that individuals are opposed to one another, individuals and society are in basic opposition, and the forces at work in all of nature are often antithetical and disharmonious. These three different worldviews affect not only the general understanding of our world, but also the approach to the question of population control. The third approach more easily despairs of finding any harmonious solution. The competing forces involved in the question of population control are so antagonistic that very radical solutions are necessary.

It is significant that the Roman Catholic hierarchical magisterium has at times been very reluctant to admit the existence of a population problem.[5] Since the encyclical *Populorum progressio* of Pope Paul VI in 1967, there have been indications that the hierarchical magisterium is willing to recognize to some degree a population problem;[6] but in his address to the World Food Congress on November 19, 1974, Pope Paul did not even acknowledge that there is a problem calling for population control.[7] As previously noted, Vatican spokepersons before and at the 1984 Mexico City meeting recognized at least in some degree the existence of a population problem but stressed the primacy of development as a solution to it. There is no doubt that a strong factor behind the unwillingness of the Catholic hierarchical magisterium to admit the problem or the gravity of the problem of population stems from its condemnation of artificial contraception. In theory one can separate the two issues (natural family planning can be used to secure a lower birth rate), but in practice it is generally recognized that any effective population control on a worldwide basis in our contemporary society must include the use of artificial contraception. However, the refusal of the hierarchical magisterium of the Roman Catholic Church to admit a population problem or the intensity of the problem is consistent with the world-view which stresses the astonishing order and harmony that exist in the world.

My own position is more disposed to accept the existence of a problem such as population, but it does not readily endorse drastic and radical solutions. There exists a possibility of harmonizing the different values and forces at work without having to sacrifice totally some of these values or some of the persons involved. Practical solutions will always call for some sacrifice but radical solutions should not be that necessary. With education, motivation, socioeconomic development, some important structural changes, and the ready availability of contraception, human beings will begin to respond to cut down on the number of their offspring.

2. The Understanding of the State

In one Christian perspective the state owes its existence primarily to human sinfulness. Sinful human beings will tend to destroy and devour one another unless they are prevented from doing so by a superior force. The state is an order of preservation by which God in accord with the Noachic covenant prevents chaos and preserves some order in this sinful world. The state is understood primarily in terms of coercive power, and the individual's freedom is generally viewed in opposition to the state and to the powers of the state.[8]

Traditional Roman Catholic theology sees the state as a natural society. Human beings are by nature not only social but also political; that is, they are called by nature to join in a political society to work for the common good which ultimately redounds to the good of the individual. Individuals by themselves are not able to achieve some things which are necessary for their good, but by banding together in political society they are able to accomplish these things. A harmony exists between the individual good and the common good. Coercive power is not the primary characteristic of the state because the state has the function of directing and guiding individuals to the common good which ultimately serves for their own good. The state is not viewed as antithetical to the true freedom of the individual.[9]

In practice, there is no doubt that until this present century Roman Catholic theology and philosophy of the state did not give enough importance to the freedom of the individual. With a strong confidence in the ability of the state to discern objective truth and justice, such an approach saw little or no infringement on the freedom of the individual. The freedom of the individual calls for the person to correspond to objective truth and justice.[10] Witness the teaching on religious freedom in the Roman Catholic tradition and the opposition to freedom in general in newer forms of government in the nineteenth century.[11] There is no doubt that the older Roman Catholic approach in the name of objective truth and justice did not give enough importance to the reality of human freedom.

Chapter one has shown that in the twentieth century in the light of totalitarian dictatorships Roman Catholic social ethics has come to give more importance to human freedom and to the human subject.[12] I agree with this approach and with the fact that one cannot so readily insist on objective truth and our ability to know it. In addition, one must also recognize here the effects of the presence of sin because of which the individual will not always be willing to work for the common good and because of which the various powers existing within society might be abused by those who hold them. Such a view of the state recognizes at times the need for coercion and the proper place of coercion in the life of civil society. Free human beings by all means possible should be educated and motivated to work for the common good and the good of society which ultimately redounds to their own good. A proper functioning of society demands a high degree of consensus about the need for willing adherence to the norms of society. In the context of a discussion on population control, Rosemary Ruether makes the point that societies such as China which appear to be very coercive apparently can be perceived by the vast majority of those within them as free and liberated because of their communal elan.[13] Society thus needs a board-based voluntary consent to its guiding norms and principles if it is to be effective.

Applied to the question of the problem of population control, this means that heavy emphasis must be given to the education and motivation of the individuals with a great respect for their freedom to responsibly choose in the light of the total needs of the society. The report of the Commission on Population Growth and the American Future warns that groups which feel deprived and discriminated against by current government policies will be skeptical and resistant to new governmental programs in the population field.[14] This does not exclude at times the possibility that coercion might be necessary, but coercion can never be the first or primary means used by the state.

Another significant aspect of the theory of the state and its functions concerns the principle of subsidiarity and its application to questions such as population control. Subsidiarity declares the larger and higher collectivities should not take over the functions which can be performed by smaller and lesser groups. In population matters, according to André Hellegers, it means that there be no unnecessary curtailment on abrogation of free, individual decision-making.[15] However, a full and accurate picture must also recognize the principle of socialization which emerged in Roman Catholic social ethics in the encyclicals of Pope John XXIII. Pope John points out that one of the principal characteristics of our modern age is an increase in social relationships. This will at times call for greater government intervention and for national and international movements, but these increased social relationships should not reduce human beings to the condition of mere automatons.[16] More so than Hellegers, Joseph Kiernan rightly points out the need to recognize both subsidiarity and socialization (solidarity-justice) in discussing population questions so that considerations of subsidiarity are not absolutized.[17] In practice this means that larger communities including the state may have to intervene in population control if this is deemed necessary.

3. Freedom and the Right to Procreate

One of the most important considerations concerns the freedom of the individual couple in determining family size. Some proposals for population control call for coercion as a necessary means of achieving optimum population. Through one means or another the state would control the number of children that individuals are able to procreate. The World Population Plan of Action adopted by the recent United Nations conferences in Bucharest and Mexico City recommends that all countries respect and insure, regardless of their overall demographic goals, the rights of persons to determine in a free, informed, and responsible manner the number and spacing of their children. This recommendation is in keeping with a traditional emphasis in United Nations literature on the freedom of the individual couple in questions of the size of their family.[18]

From my theological-ethical perspective, the freedom of the couple is very important. Through having children one responds to a very fundamental human desire and need. The freedom of the individual in this matter is very closely associated with human dignity and the basic core freedom of the human person. However, freedom is not the only important moral vaue which is to be considered here. Phrased in another way, this means that the freedom of the couple must be limited and influenced by other factors.

The older Roman Catholic teaching recognized something more than just the freedom of the individuals to do what they choose. The older Catholic teaching so stressed the aspect of the good of the species as to assert that the primary purpose of marriage and sexuality was the procreation and education of offspring, and that every single act of sexual intercourse had to be open to the possibilities of procreation.[19] The prohibition of artificial contraception rests on this understanding of the fact that every act of sexual intercourse involves more than merely the couple and their freedom. The species aspect of human sexuality in the traditional Catholic approach has always had a pronatalist assumption, but logically such an emphasis could also call for a limitation of births if this was required by the needs of the human species. By stressing the primary end of marriage as the procreation and education of offspring, the traditional Roman Catholic theology also recognizes that the upbringing or education of the child is an important factor in the decision of the couple to have a child. This teaching thus recognizes that there are limits placed on couples in terms of their right to procreate offspring.

In keeping with traditional ethical terminology, one can assert that individual couples have the right to procreate offspring, but the exercise of that right is limited. In exercising their rights couples must act responsibly. If individual couples for some reason or other do not act responsibly, then if there is grave harm being done to the public order of society, the state might intervene to insure that individuals act in a more responsible manner. In addition there is a very important distinction between the right of the individual couple to have offspring and the right of an individual couple to have a particular number of children. It is easier to justify limitations restricting the number of children that a particular couple could have since this is not as basic and fundamental a right as the right to procreate children in general. However, the fact that the state can intervene must not be taken for a *carte blanche* authorization, for government coercion remains a last resort. There are many other questions that have to be settled before one could decide that the state should intervene and precisely how it should intervene.

If it is necessary for the state to intervene and curtail the freedom of individuals, then this must be done in accord with justice and other relevant moral principles. This understanding of the right to procreate and its limitations seems preferable to describing it as a social right.[20]

4. Proper Description of the Problem

It is obvious that any solution to the problem of population control must be based on an adequate and objective understanding of the nature of the problem itself. Judgments in moral theology are heavily dependent on empirical data, but the division between facts and values is much more complicated than it might seem at first sight. Today we are more conscious of the fact that it is very difficult if not impossible to speak about something as being objective and value-free. Very often judgments which claim to be purely objective and based on empirical data alone contain concealed value judgments about what is more important and why.[21]

In attempting a proper description and understanding of the population problem one must also honestly recognize one's own presuppositions and prejudices. As a general approach I eschew overly simplistic solutions to human ethical problems. This presupposition arises in theory from a more relational ethical model which sees the individual ethical actor in terms of multiple relationships with God, neighbor, and the world. My insistence on complexity also comes from the recognition that very often erroneous solutions are proposed not because of some error of commission but because of omission — the failure to consider all the elements that must be discussed.

From my perspective I am inclined to accept the analysis of Philip Hauser that human beings are complex culture-building animals, and the population crisis is really a series of four crises or problems. First, the population explosion maintains that, assuming the present trend, by the year 2000 the population of the developing countries will be about the same or as great as the total population of the world in 1960. Second, the population implosion refers to the increasing concentration of people on relatively small portions of the earth's surface, a pheonomenon generally known as urbanization. Third, the population displosion means the increasing heterogeneity of people who share the same geographical space as well as the same social, political, and economic conditions and is exemplified by the current problems in Northern Ireland and many countries in Africa or even in Canada. Fourth, the technoplosion refers to the accelerated pace of technological innovation which has characterized our modern era.[22] Hauser acknowledges that in the developing countries much yet remains to be done before the control of the population explosion is assured.[23] But Hauser also asserts that it is almost certain that problems created or exacerbated by implosion and displosion will create more human misery during at least the remainder of this century than the problems produced by excessive fertility and growth.[24]

Population control cannot be limited merely to providing the means for individuals to control fertility. Under population goals and policies, the World Population Plan of Action mentions in addition to population growth the need for policies and goals in the following areas: reduction of morbidity and mortality; reproduction, family formation and the status of women; population distribution and internal migration; international migration and population structure.[25] The recommendation of the Study Committee of the Office of the Foreign Secretary of the National Academy of Sciences includes these and other considerations.[26]

Personal and national narrowness of perception as well as sinfulness may at times affect the understanding and statement of the problem as well as proposed solutions. In general the developed nations of the world tended to see the problem of population control and most of the problems of the developing nations in terms of the need to cut down on the number of births. In the eyes of the United States government before the Bucharest meeting in 1974, population growth was a problem because it has many effects including retarding economic growth and negatively affecting food resources, the environment, and governmental abilities to meet these needs. Given the causal importance of population growth, massive spending on contraceptive development in family planning programs was the one major solution proposed. A more nuanced view was taken by some American scholars such as Donald Warwick[27] and Arthur Dyck,[28] a Christian ethicist from Harvard, who pointed out that problems such as environmental deterioration, starvation, and poverty as they exist today are not directly and mainly caused by present population growth rates. Neuhaus and others viewed the American emphasis on contraception and family planning as an unwillingness to admit many of the problems caused by the over-consumption of the developed nations and by the inequitable economic structures of modern existence.[29] Even before the 1974 meeting in Bucharest there was a growing realization that a more integral view of the interdependent character of population and social phenomena such as social and economic change, environmental factors, and technological developments was required. Population growth is not the only problem, nor the cause of all the problems, nor the major obstacle to the solution of all problems.[30] Since the Bucharest and Mexico City meetings there is general agreement on the need for multifaceted solutions to the population question.

A final caution in understanding the population problem and its solution stems from the limitations of any one science. The scientific, in general, is not totally identical with the human; also the persective of one science can never be totally identical with the human perspective. One must critically examine various understandings and solutions because of the danger of distortion. Psychology is more interested in the individual, whereas sociology is more concerned about society. The fact that something is genetically possible does not always mean it should be done. In general one must be aware of solutions proposed in the name of only a partial perspective or from the viewpoint of only one science or optique.

Specific Proposals

Having considered four important theological-ethical considerations which inform the ethical judgment about population problems, the following specific proposals will be discussed: (1) a holistic solution; (2) triage; (3) means used by governments to control population; (4) means of fertility and birth control; and (5) the role of the Roman Catholic Church.

1. A Holistic Solution

Solutions for the population problem must be integral and holistic. It is morally wrong merely to propose decreasing the number of births without recognizing the multifaceted nature of the problem which must include other demographic components and social and economic changes. There always remains the danger that the powerful and strong will be tempted to see the solution only in the realm of preventing births and lowering fertility. It is now recognized that many of the problems of the environment are caused as much by the overconsumption of the developed nations as by the birth rate in the developing nations.

There is also good evidence to support the fact that programs aimed at lowering fertility will not be successful unless they are accompanied by social and economic changes. Arthur Dyck relates in a number of articles the poignant story of the ghetto mother which was first told by Robert Coles. To poverty-stricken mothers in the ghettos of the United States a new child is a source of hope, joy, and fulfillment which cannot be had in any other way. The more wealthy people in society may find their fulfillment in many other ways; but for the woman interviewed by Coles, child-bearing and raising was the one source of fulfillment in her life.[31] Many other studies indicate the same result. India's programs based only on massive contraception and sterilization have been a failure.[32]

Here it seems that good morality will have good results in practice — a point which Roman Catholic theology has often been willing to admit in the past. However, one must also point out that narrow efficiency and ethical rightness do not necessarily coincide at all times. In the question of population control, it seems that fertility control is programmatically ineffective, not feasible, and politically and individually unacceptable if there is not the motivation which occurs when societies through socioeconomic development offer their members alternatives that promise an improvement in the future quality of life.[33] Thus one cannot emphasize enough the need for holistic solutions which require not only changes in the birth rate of developing nations but changes in other demographic components, changes in the consumption of developed nations, and changes in the socioeconomic structures in our world.

2. Triage

Even the more popular press has been discussing triage in the light of the population problem.[34] Triage ethics comes to the fore in disaster situations in which there is available a limited supply of medical personnel and/or services so that not all can be cared for. Decisions must be made to care for some and not for others. The hopelessly wounded and those who need greater treatment are left to die without any treatment so that treatment can be given to a greater number of others.

In 1967 William and Paul Paddock in *Famine—1975! America's Decision: Who Will Survive?* pointed to India as the bellwether of what will happen to other nations. It will be impossible to feed and help all the people in the world. The hungry nations of 1967 will become tomorrow the starving nations. Some decisions must be made about giving no further help to certain nations.[35] Garrett Hardin talked about the tragedy of the commons which shows the fundamental error of sharing ethics. In a pasture run as a commons each herder will tend to add more cattle because it is to one's individual benefit. Before long, the common pasture will be overcrowded and deteriorate to the detriment of all. In late 1974, Hardin continued his attack on sharing ethics by invoking the metaphor of lifeboat ethics. The rich nations of this world are comparatively well-stocked boats which are able to survive, but many poor nations with their people cannot survive. If we in the United States today take all or too many others aboard our lifeboat, it will sink. A world food bank and unrestricted immigration exemplify the tragedy of the commons. A sharing ethics will eventually destroy those who unwisely succumb to their humanitarian impulses and will only delay the day of reckoning for poor countries.[36]

Both lifeboat ethics and triage have been discussed by ethicists in the past. Edmond Cahn sees in the lifeboat situation the full force of the morals of the last day. In this situation the individual, stripped of all distinguishing features and special bonds, is left a generic creature embodying the entire genus and having no moral individuality left so that whoever kills another in that situation kills humankind. If none sacrifice themselves of free will, they must all wait and die together.[37]

Paul Ramsey argues that in the lifeboat situation random selection best assures the basic moral principle of the sanctity of the individual in deciding who can be saved and who cannot be saved.[38] Later, Ramsey admits one describable exception to the principle guaranteeing by random selection equal possibility of life when not all can be saved—if and only if a community and its members share a single focus or purpose or goal under now quite extraordinary circumstances.

Ramsey gives as two examples the lifeboat situation in which some are needed because of their special expertise in rowing in order for any to be saved and in triage in disaster medicine where first priority must be given to victims who can quickly be restored to functioning. Thus even a Christian ethicist such as Paul Ramsey, who insists quite strongly on the sanctity (not just the dignity) of the individual, recognizes the moral possibility of triage and some lifeboat ethics.[39]

Although triage and some aspects of lifeboat ethics in my judgment are at times morally acceptable, they are not moral now in the question of population control because the problem, as real and as important as it is, is not now catastrophic or simply focused. We are not in the last days; there is still time for other solutions. Above all the problem is not simply a problem of fertility control but involves many other demographic, social, and economic factors so that the rich nations of the world are also at fault and not just the poor nations. Hardin fails to recognize that the problem is multifaceted and not simply a problem of the poor nations producing too many offspring.

Hardin's proposals do not give the respect for the individual which a Christian understanding of the individual and of Christian love calls for. He is too willing to sacrifice many people when it is not necessary and especially when the proper moral response might call for a more generous action on our part. Not only is it a question of the dignity of the individual human being but also the interdependence of all human beings which Christianity as well as many rational ethics recognize. This interdependence is seen in the numerous ways in which rich and poor countries are related so that the problem cannot be blamed solely on any one group. The irony is that the rich nations of the world have enriched themselves precisely through an exploitation of the poor nations. Lately the energy crisis has made many Americans much more aware of the interdependence of our own human existence. Not only is triage in this situation morally wrong because it does not give enough respect for the meaning of the individual and of the demands of Christian love for those in need, but it also goes against the basic understanding of the interdependent nature of human existence today and therefore even pragmatically is impossible. No one nation or group of nations will be able to go it alone because of our mutual dependencies.

Survival itself is not an absolute or the most important human value and imperative. The moral corollary of this statement is that there are certain things we should not do even if they aid the quest for survival. As Daniel Callahan has pointed out, the need for survival is modified by the need to realize other values such as freedom, justice, and a sense of dignity and worth. There are some means of assuring survival which are themselves morally wrong so that it would be better not to survive than have to survive in such a moral atmosphere.[40]

3. Means Used by Governments

How should the state deal with the problem of controlling population growth? In one of the most comprehensive and synthetic articles on the question of population control, Bernard Berelson lists and summarizes the proposals which have been advanced in the literature — extensions of voluntary fertility control, establishment of involuntary fertility control, intensified educational campaigns, incentive programs, tax and welfare benefits and penalties, shifts in social and economic institutions and political channels and organizations.[41] In my judgment the primary ethical considerations in addition to the proportionality of benefits and harms are freedom and justice, although these elements can be expanded in different ways. The Study Committee of the Office of the Foreign Secretary of the National Academy of Sciences, for example, recommends the ethical criteria for fertility control policies which were first proposed in the above-cited article by Berelson.[42]

As mentioned earlier, freedom is a most important value but cannot be absolutized. On a scale of government interference in a continuum from freedom to coercive policies, the following general approaches can be identified: education, motivation and propaganda for population control together with provision of acceptable means to control fertility to all who want and need them; change of social structures which affect demography; incentives offered to control population;

and coercive methods employed by the government.

Questions of justice arise especially in considerations of incentives and coercion. Robert Veatch elaborates eight criteria which should be used in judging incentive proposals, but he recognizes that the principle of justice creates the gravest difficulty for incentive proposals. The ultimate reasons from justice raised against incentive proposals stem from discrimination. Discrimination exists often toward the poor who are most tempted by monetary inducements and subject to abuse in the process, whereas the wealthy are not put under that same pressure. Likewise, incentives can harm innocent children if certain penalties or lack of services are provided for the nth child born in each family.[43] Veatch proposes as a just incentive a progressive sliding-scale fee which might be called a child welfare fee payable every year for every child.[44] Dyck accepts as the least unjust of all incentive programs the provision of pensions for poor parents with fewer than n children, as a social security for their old age which takes away the insecurity which in some societies is met by the children.[45] Edward Pohlman argues that incentives are not ideal but they are necessary today.[46] In somewhat the same manner Melvin Ketchel says that compulsory fertility control would seem to be the most effective and the least objectionable of any involuntary methods.[47]

In judging the morality of government policy one must again insist on a holistic perspective. Fertility control is not acceptable if it is the only solution because it is necessary also to see the problem in the context of other demographic, economic and social factors. All the lower efforts on the scale from freedom to incentives and coercion must be employed first before one can even think about incentives and coercion. There is an intense need for education, motivation, and the provision of morally acceptable means of fertility control to all who want them as well as the need for changing social structures (e.g., the status of women) which affect demography. At the present time except in extraordinary circumstances, it does not seem that coercion is acceptable. In some situations incentives might be morally acceptable, but here special care should be taken lest fundamental principles of justice are violated. Although perfect justice is never attainable, special concern for the rights of the poor is needed. In addition, the very important pragmatic note should be made that if incentives are employed without all the other means mentioned above, they will apparently be ineffective.

The problem of freedom and coercion does not exist only where there is an attempt by government to cut down the size of populations. There are some countries in the world today (e.g., Brazil and Argentina), which are trying to increase their population; but here, too, the same moral question arises about the means employed by the government to bring about the desired population.[48] The freedom of couples and their right to determine the number of children they want should be protected. The government has the obligation of allowing couples to plan their families and of supplying the poor with the acceptable means they need to be able to achieve the legitimate goals of family planning. Here again the distinction between family planning and population control is significant. In the name of population control the government cannot take away from individuals the right to plan and limit their own families in accord with their understanding of what is right and helpful. However, the government can through education and motivation show the need for an increase in population and appeal to the generosity of families to carry this out. At the present time there is no proportionate reason to justify other measures.

4. Means of Fertility and Birth Control

Contraception, sterilization, and abortion are the principal means which individuals use to prevent conception and birth. What about the morality of these means? From the viewpoint of morality there is general acceptance in the world of the morality of artificial contraception. The official teaching of the hierarchical magisterium of the Roman Catholic Church condemns artificial contraception, but dissent from such official teaching is, in my judgment, both justifiable and widespread in Roman Catholicism.[49] Sterilization from an ethical viewpoint is logically viewed in the same moral category as contraception with the significant difference that sterilization tends to be permanent. The official hierarchical teaching of the Roman Catholic Church continues to condemn all direct sterilization, but here too there is in my judgment justifiable and growing dissent from such teaching.[50] The primary ethical problems connected with contraception and sterilization come from government policies involving incentives or coercion, but these have already been discussed.

Abortion as a means of preventing births and as an instrument of population control raises many more serious ethical problems and objections. The World Population Plan of Action accepted at Bucharest in 1974 shows the tension existing within the world community on the question of abortion. In considering morbidity and mortality the document recommends the reduction of illegal abortions.[51] Proposed amendments to change "illegal" to "induced" and to replace "abortion" with "miscarriage" were both defeated.[52] The Report of the Commission on Population Growth and the American Future made the following recommendation: "Therefore with the admonition that abortion not be considered a primary means of fertility control, the Commission recommends that present state laws restricting abortion be abridged along the lines of the New York State statute. . . ."[53] The Study Committee of the Office of the Foreign Secretary of the National Academy of Sciences recommended that legal and social barriers to fertility control be promptly removed and broad social acceptance and support of fertility control including medically safe abortions should be fostered.[54] However, as mentioned earlier, the United Nations conference in Mexico City in 1984 rejected abortion as a means of family planning.

The Commission on Population Growth and the American Future recognized that it is difficult to make precise quantitative statements concerning the demographic import of abortion.[55] Arthur Dyck, while reporting that permissive abortion generally facilitates a downward trend in population and that restrictive abortion policies do not prevent a downward trend in fertility, concludes that abortion is not needed to solve population problems.[56] Abdel R. Omran maintains that when developing countries are highly motivated to accelerate their transition from high to low fertility induced abortion becomes a popular method of fertility control. Omran concludes his study by emphasizing two major themes for policy formation: (1) there is no question that prevention of pregnancy through effective contraception is much wiser and safer than the termination of pregnancy through abortion; (2) for reasons that vary from country to country, a margin of induced abortion is to be anticipated and provided for.[57] The primary ethical question is not whether or not abortion is an effective means of population control, although it does seem from the evidence mentioned above that Dyck is correct in asserting that abortion is not necessary as a means of population control.[58]

Opposition to abortion on ethical grounds cannot be based merely on its efficacy or inefficacy in terms of population control. It must be pointed out that opposition to abortion on ethical grounds is not limited to Roman Catholicism, as is exemplified in Arthur Dyck's writings. Elsewhere I have discussed the morality of abortion and concluded that individual human life is present between the fourteenth and the twenty-first day after conception, and only the life of the mother or a value commensurate with life morally justifies abortion after that time.[59] Chapter five discussed the question of abortion laws and reactions to the decision of the Supreme Court about abortion. However, my acceptance of some legal abortions in the United States does not mean that I accept abortion as a means of population control to be proposed and promoted by the government. Active promotion of abortion by governments as a means of population control in my judgment is both morally wrong and not necessary. Above all, compulsory abortion is an ethical monstrosity that cannot be accepted.

5. The Role of the Roman Catholic Church

There is no doubt that the Roman Catholic teaching condemning artificial contraception puts the Catholic Church in a difficult posture in terms of population control.[60] I have strongly dissented from such teaching and have urged that it be changed, but unfortunately from a realistic perspective I do not think that the official teaching will be changed in the very near future. In the meantime it seems that many Catholic couples and clergy will continue to dissent so that in pastoral practice most Catholics do not seem to have a problem with the use of artificial contraception. Despite the existing teaching, there is thus a way around the problem in pastoral practice for individual Catholic couples. However, the present official teaching of the Roman Catholic Church continues to condemn artificial contraception as a means of family planning and population control.

Even though I personally go much further, there is a better position that can be taken by the official teaching of the Roman Catholic Church. Couples in a pluralistic society have the right to choose the means (not abortion) by which they will plan their families and respond to the need for population control, and the government can provide them with the help necessary to carry out their decision. Such an approach is both in conformity with developing Catholic teaching on freedom in a pluralistic society as developed in chapter five, and is better than mere opposition to family planning and population control. From the perspective of the official Roman Catholic teaching, one must also insist that the government provide help in nonartificial methods for those who choose to use natural family planning.

There are two interesting anomalies about the present official position of the Roman Catholic Church. First, without the acceptance and provision of artificial contraception there is evidence that in developing countries many people during a transitional period revert to abortion.[61] Second, John Hayes, an Irish Catholic social ethician, has pointed out that by fostering economic development through its social teachings the Roman Catholic Church is also promoting a situation in which the data show that contraceptive practices become more widespread.[62]

It is imperative for official Catholic Church teaching to recognize the existence and gravity of the population problem. In *Populorum progressio* in 1967, Pope Paul did acknowledge to some degree the existence of the problem,[63] but ever since that time there have been many occasions, both official and unofficial, in which the problem was ignored or downplayed. In an address to the World Food Congress in Rome in November 1974, Pope Paul did not recognize the existence of a population problem and the need for population control.[64] The November 1973 statement of the National Conference of Catholic Bishops of the United States is to be applauded, for the American bishops called on Catholic people to take a positive approach to the question of population.[65] Fortunately, Catholic scholars in the United States and abroad have been taking such approaches. Recent statements by Vatican spokespersons in connection with the 1984 Mexico City conference indicate some recognition of the population problem. Official Roman Catholic teaching must not downplay the existence of the problem and should urge governments and people to take steps necessary to deal with it, for the problem will only become more acute in the years ahead. However, the official Church teaching must also help to situate this problem in a broader perspective involving the sharing of food and resources and economic development (as Catholic statements have often done), and must insist on the many ethical values which necessarily enter into the discussion, especially considerations of freedom and justice involving the rights of the poor and innocent.

NOTES

1. Arthur McCormack, "Population and Development," *The Tablet* 238 (July 28, 1984): 714–716; (August 4, 1984): 736-737.

2. "Vatican Objects to Population Plan," *The Tablet* 238 (August 25, 1984): 814; "Population Plan Is Hit by Vatican," *The Catholic Messenger*, August 23, 1984, p. 1.

3. Martin C. D'Arcy, *The Mind and Heart of Love* (New York: Meridian Books, 1956); Jules Toner, *The Experience of Love* (Washington, D.C.: Corpus Books, 1968).

4. Pope John XXIII, *Pacem in Terris* (New York: Paulist Press, 1963). The original is found in *Acta Apostolicae Sedis* 55 (1963): 257-304.

5. Michael J. Walsh, "The Holy See's Population Problem," *The Month* 7 (1974): 632-636; Francis X. Murphy, "The Pope and Our Common Future," *Worldview* 18 (February 1975): 23-28.

6. Pope Paul VI, *On the Development of Peoples (Populorum Progressio)* (New York: Paulist Press, 1967). The original is found in *Acta Apostolicae Sedis* 59 (1967): 257-289.

7. Pope Paul VI, "Address to the World Food Congress, Nov. 9. 1974," *The Pope Speaks* 19 (1975): 208-215. The original is found in *Acta Apostolicae Sedis* 66 (1974): 644-652.

8. Helmut Thielicke, *Theological Ethics*, vol. 2: *Politics* (Philadelphia: Fortress Press, 1969).

9. R. A. Markus, "Two Conceptions of Political Authority: Augustine, *De Civitate Dei* XIX, 14-15, and Some Thirteenth-century Interpretations," *The Journal of Theological Studies* 16 (1965): 69-100; Heinrich Rommen, *The State in Catholic Thought* (St. Louis: B. Herder, 1945).

10. Eric D'Arcy, *Conscience and Its Right to Freedom* (New York: Sheed and Ward, 1961).

11. Pius Augustine, *Religious Freedom in Church and State* (Baltimore: Helicon, 1966).

12. John Courtney Murray, *The Problem of Religious Freedom* (Westminster, Md.: Newman Press, 1965).

13. Rosemary Radford Ruether, "Governmental Coercion and One-Dimensional Thinking," in *The Population Crisis and Moral Responsibility*, ed. J. Philip Wogaman (Washington: Public Affairs Press, 1973), pp. 167-173.

14. "Report of the Commission on Population Growth and The American Future," *Population and the American Future* (New York: New American Library, 1972), p. 91.

15. André E. Hellegers, "Government Planning and the Principle of Subsidiarity," in *The Population Crisis and Moral Responsibility*, pp. 137-144.

16. Pope John XXIII, *Mater et Magistra* (New York: Paulist Press, 1961), n. 59-66. The original is found in *Acta Apostolicae Sedis* 53 (1961): 401-464.

17. Joseph Kiernan, "An Analysis of Certain Population Policies," *The American Ecclesiastical Review* 169 (1975): 118-132.

18 United Nations Economic and Social Council, "World Population Plan of Action," *World Population Conference* (October 2, 1974), E/5585, par. n. 13.

19. John C. Ford and Gerald Kelly, *Contemporary Moral Theology*, vol. 2: *Marriage Questions* (Westminster, Md.: Newman Press, 1963).

20. Yale Task Force on Population Ethics, "Moral Claims, Human Rights, and Population Policies," *Theological Studies* 35 (1974): 105.

21. Daniel Callahan, "Introduction," in *The American Population Debate*, ed. Daniel Callahan (New York: Doubleday, 1971), p. xii; Stanley Hauerwas, "The Moral Limits of Population Control," *Thought* 49 (1974): 240.

22. Philip M. Hauser, "Population Criteria in Foreign Aid Programs," in *The Population Crisis and Moral Responsibility*, pp. 233-239.

23. Philip M. Hauser, "World Population: Retrospect and Prospect," in *Rapid Population Growth* (Baltimore and London: The Johns

Hopkins University Press, 1971), p. 121.

24. Hauser, *Population Crisis and Moral Responsibility*, p. 236.

25. *World Population Conference*, par. nn. 20-67.

26. Study Commission of the Office of the Foreign Secretary, National Academy of Sciences, *Rapid Population Growth* (Baltimore and London: Johns Hopkins University Press, 1971), pp. 77-89.

27. Donald P. Warwick, "Ethics and Population Control in Developing Countries," *The Hastings Center Report* 4 (June 1974): 1.

28. Arthur J. Dyck, "Is Abortion Necessary to Solve Population Problems?" in *Abortion and Social Ethics*, ed. T. Hilgers and D. Horan (New York: Sheed and Ward, 1972), p. 164.

29. Richard John Neuhaus, *In Defense of People: Ecology and the Seduction of Radicalism* (New York: Macmillan, 1971).

30. Peter J. Henriot, "Global Population in Perspective: Implications for U.S. Policy Response," *Theological Studies* 35 (1974): 50.

31. Arthur J. Dyck, "Population Policies and Ethical Acceptability," in *Rapid Population Growth,* p. 633; "Procreative Rights and Population Policies," *The Hastings Center Studies* 1 (1973): 75-76; "American Global Population Policy: An Ethical Analysis." *Linacre Quarterly* 42 (1975): 60

32. John F. X. Harriott, "Bucharest and Beyond," *The Month* 7 (1974): 630

33. Henriot, *Theological Studies* 35 (1974): 58.

34. E. g., Wade Greene, "Triage," *The New York Times Magazine,* December 5, 1975.

35. William and Paul Paddock, *Famine—1975! America's Decision: Who Will Survive?* (New York: Little, Brown and Co., 1967).

36. Garrett Hardin, "The Tragedy of the Commons," *Science* 162 (1968): 1243-1248; "Living on a Lifeboat," *Bioscience* 24 (1974): 561-568.

37. Edmond Cahn, *The Moral Decision* (Bloomington and London: Indiana University Press, 1955, pp. 61-71.

38. Paul Ramsey, *Nine Modern Moralists* (Englewood Cliffs, N.J.: Prentice Hall, 1962), p. 245.

39. Paul Ramsey, *The Patient as Person* (New Haven and London: Yale University Press, 1970), pp. 257-259.

40. Daniel Callahan, "Population and Human Survival," in *The Population Crisis and Moral Responsibility*, pp. 58-59; "Doing Well by Doing Good," *The Hastings Center Report* 4 (December 1974): 1-4.

41. Bernard Berelson, "Beyond Family Planning," *Science* 163 (1969): 533-543.

42. *Rapid Population Growth,* p. 81.

43. Robert M. Veatch, "Governmental Incentives: Ethical Issues at Stake," in *The Population Crisis and Moral Responsibility*, pp. 207-224.

44. Ibid., p.220.

45. Dyck, "Population Policies and Ethical Acceptability," in *Rapid Population Growth,* p. 622.

46. Edward Pohlman, *Incentives and Compensations in Birth Planning,* Carolina Population Center Monograph 11 (1971).

47. Melvin Ketchel, "Fertility Control Agents as a Possible Solution to the World Population Problem," in *The American Population Debate,* p. 295.

48. Warwick, *Hastings Center Report* 4, (June 1974): 1-4.

49. Frederick E. Crowe, "The Conscience of the Theologian with Reference to the Encyclical," in *Conscience: Its Freedom and Limitations,* ed. William C. Bier (New York: Fordham University Press, 1971), pp. 312-332.

50. Charles E. Curran, "Sterilization: Roman Catholic Theory and Practice," *New Perspectives in Moral Theology* (Notre Dame, Ind.: University of Notre Dame Press, 1976), pp. 194-211.

51. *World Population Conference,* par. n. 246.

52. Ibid., par. n. 137.

53. *Population and the American Future,* p. 178.

54. *Rapid Population Growth,* p. 84.

55. *Population and the American Future,* p. 176.

56. Dyck, *Abortion and Social Justice,* pp. 166-168.

57. Abdel R. Omran, "Abortion and Demographic Transition," in *Rapid Population Growth,* pp. 479-532.

58. Dyck, *Abortion and Social Justice,* p. 165.

59. Curran, *New Perspectives in Moral Theology,* pp. 163-193.

60. Denis E. Hurley, "Population Control and the Catholic Conscience: Responsibility of the Magisterium," *Theological Studies* 35 (1974): 154-163.

61. Omran, *Rapid Population Growth,* pp. 486ff.

62. John Hayes, "Aspects of the World Population Problem," *Social Studies* 3 (1974): 243.

63. *Populorum progressio,* par. n. 37.

64. Walsh, *The Month* 7 (1974): 632-636; Murphy, *Worldview* 18 (Feb., 1975): 23-28.

65. National Conference of Catholic Bishops, "Statement on Population," *Origins* 3 (November 29, 1973): 353ff.

10. The Right to Health Care and Distributive Justice

Developments in biomedical research and technology have brought to the fore many new problems. Lately attention has begun to focus on the social aspects of these questions, especially a just distribution. The just distribution of health and medical care has its roots in the problem of dividing up a finite amount of resources.

There are many different aspects of the basic problem of distribution. One aspect concerns the relationship of medical resources to other needed resources — education, food, clothing, defense, transportation, environment. How much should be invested in these different needs? What are the priorities among these different needs?

Even if these priorities were solved, there remains the still-difficult question of a just distribution within health care and medical care themselves. It is impossible to do everything. What should have priority? Should we spend more for exotic lifesaving devices such as artificial hearts or for a better delivery of maternal and prenatal health care? How does one deal with the priorities existing within medicine and health care? A third aspect of distribution concerns the allocation of scarce medical resources. Who shall receive the necessary life-giving resources when only a limited number are available and those who do not receive the resources will probably die?

There is a fourth aspect of distribution which refers to the recipient of medical or health care. On what basis is health care to be obtained by the individual person in our society? There is much discussion in contemporary American society about this aspect of distribution. The problem obviously begins with the fact of the poor distribution of health care in our society; some people even talk about a crisis in the delivery of health care.[1]

Recent developments such as Medicare and Medicaid have tried to insure more just and adequate access to medical care for the aged and the poor, but these programs still fall short of these goals.[2] Other problems of unjust distribution arise from the number and distribution of personnel and facilities in different geographic sections of the country and in urban or rural settings.[3] Existing private insurance programs do not cover all the citizens of our country. Perhaps 20 percent of the population under sixty-five have no private hospital insurance, but this includes a disproportionate number of the working poor, of blacks and of people living in the south. Over a million Americans are uninsurable according to present plans. Many people who are self-employed or who are employed in small firms must pay very large premiums for even limited coverage. Only half the population has any major medical coverage. There are often limits on the amounts to be paid in many insurance policies. Today the middle class is very aware of the financial hardship which can be brought about by prolonged or catastrophic illness in the family.[4]

In addition to these apparent injustices and inadequacies of the present system, one must also mention the problem of the escalating cost of health care in our society. Health care expenses have risen at the rate of about 12 percent per year during the decade of 1966–1975. At the current time 8.3 percent of the gross national product is being spent for health care.[5] A higher percentage of the gross national product in the United States is spent on health care than in most countries which have a system of socialized medicine such as Great Britain or Sweden.[6] Public policy planners are very aware of the need to contain costs.

This chapter will discuss justice and the distribution of health care to individuals in the society, although it is evident that the presence and influence of the other questions of distribution cannot be totally neglected. Legislators have been proposing various bills to deal with the problem. The ethical question underlying the discussion is often phrased in terms of the right to health, the right to medical care or the right to health care. These phrases have become slogans in our contemporary society. The primary focus of our study is the existence of such a right and its grounding. For the moment the precise object of the right will be bracketed, but reference will be made to the right to health care. Is there such a right and what is its basis?

Ethical considerations about the proper distribution of goods in society have also recently been discussed not only in the context of health care but in the broader context of ethical theory and of the proper distribution of all goods in society. Until a few years ago the predominant ethical perspective both in theory and in practice in the distribution of health care in the United States seems to have been a form of utilitarianism. Utilitarianism strives to bring about the greatest good of the greatest number.[7]

In ethical theory in the last few decades there has been strong criticism of the utilitarian approach. Distribution involves not only the total amount of the goods but also the important question of how goods are distributed. The total amount distributed is not the only question. Other considerations most often in terms of justice and rights must enter into the question of proper distribution. The rights of individuals might be violated even though the total amount of goods produced is greater. The greatest good of the greatest number can readily give too little importance to the rights of the individual. The utilitarian canon of distribution seems to neglect the important question of the fairness or justice of the distribution by concentrating only on the total amount produced.[8] Utilitarian theorists are aware of these charges often made against the system and have tried to respond to them.[9]

There is a similarity here with another problem of distribution—the allocation of scarce medical resources when there are not enough to go around. Some advocate a theory based on the contribution to society (especially future contributions).[10] However, others insist on the equal dignity of all human beings and do not want to maintain that some lives are of more value, dignity or importance than others. To protect the equal dignity of all lives, this position proposes a random selection procedure (first come, first served; or lottery).[11]

In more recent ethical writings great emphasis has been given to the language of rights and justice in order to protect the individual (especially the poor) in the distribution of goods within society. Rights' language had been used previously in ethical theory in a very individualistic way (e.g., Thomas Hobbes). In fact, such an individualistic understanding of rights strongly argues against any right to health care. In this conception a right defines a freedom of action. The basic right of the individual is the right to life. To sustain life one produces economic values in the form of goods and services that one should be free to exchange with others. Goods and services are thus owned in order to sustain life by one's own physical and mental effort. Just as the customer has no right to the baker's bread, so the customer has no right to the doctor's services. Medical care is neither a right nor a privilege; it is a service. The concept of medical care as the patient's right is immoral because it denies the most fundamental of all rights—that of the doctor to sell one's own services as the means of supporting her/his life.[12]

Behind such a theory lies a very individualistic concept of society. Robert Sade, whose denial of a right to health care was summarized in the preceding paragraph, logically maintains that the only proper function of government is to provide for the defense of individuals against those who would take their lives or property by force. The state is thus seen as coercive and its function is minimal—to prevent physical harm to individuals. The state should not further impede the liberty of individuals. Sade remarks that it is frequently overlooked that behind every law is a policeman's gun or a soldier's bayonet.[13]

I. Equalitarian Justice

Proponents of a right to health care do not accept such a view of rights. Their primary purpose of establishing a right to health care is to insure the rights of all, especially the poor, to be provided with health care. However, supporters of theories of justice in health care do not all agree on the ultimate meaning of justice and its ramifications. It is impossible to review here all the different theories of justice and their applications to health care. Justice as equality, one of the most significant contemporary theories, will be considered at length and critiqued. Then a different theory of distributive justice, which has been overlooked in the contemporary discussions, will be proposed as theoretically and practically more adequate.

The most simple way of stating the thesis of justice as equality is that similar cases should be treated similarly. Such an approach has many benefits. It has a very sympathetic ring in the popular mind. It is also in keeping with many developments and currents in contemporary ethical theory. Such a theory is formal. The problems connected with the question of what is the proper amount of treatment or of medical care are avoided by merely asserting that equal treatment should be given to all. Such an approach is built upon the fundamental ethical principle of universalizability: No arbitrary exception should ever be made. Whatever is done in this particular situation for this particular sick person should be done in all similar situations. The formal character of such an approach avoids any arguments concerning principles and intuitions. Finally, such a theory is most compatible with the goal of equal access to health care for all. If this is the goal, there is no better way to justify it than by a principle of justice understood in terms of equality. Now two different authors who have developed the concept of justice as equality will be considered.

Gene Outka has made an intriguing argument for what he admits is only a prima facie case that every person in the resident population should have equal access to health care delivery.[14] Outka develops an argument which recognizes that justice as equality (not his words) is a necessary but not sufficient approach. Since the statement of equality is purely formal, it could justify no treatment for all just as much as some treatment.

In any division of distribution within society one must

discuss the various canons or titles of distribution—merit, desert, social contribution, need. Meritarian concerns, for example, are present in the justice governing the teacher assigning grades to a student. The grade should correspond to the quality of the work done by the student. Awards granted within a society are justly distributed primarily by taking account of the contributions made to society. In the area of health care Outka rejects distribution based on merit or on social contribution. The reason for medical care is ill health. An irrational state of affairs is held to obtain if those whose needs are the same are treated unequally when the need (illness) is the ground of treatment.

Outka must prove that the right to health care rests on need and the other canons of distribution such as desert, merit or social contributions do not enter into the picture. To do so Outka emphasizes the distinctive character of health crises. Health crises seem nonmeritarian because they are beyond our control and responsibility. We are equal in being randomly susceptible to disease, for there is little or nothing we can do about these crises. Medical treatment thus differs from other basic needs such as food and shelter, for these latter two factors are at least predictable. One can hold that responsibility increases with the power to predict, but we are not responsible for cancer or the health crises that befall us. Medical need is a classical case of uncertainty.

Outka thereby makes the case for equal access to health care on the fact that need is the governing criterion and that similar cases must be treated similarly. However, he admits this is only a prima facie case. Collisions between equal access and efficiency or insatiable needs do exist, so at times the distribution of medical care in less than optimal situations will not be based solely on the goal of equal access. If all our money were spent on the most ill people in society, there would be nothing to spend for others. In conflict cases actual solutions should be those most compatible with the goal of equal access; for example, random selection when there are not enough resources to go around.

Outka perceptively recognizes the complexity of the problem and the fact that justice as equal access cannot always be obtained. Outka also realizes that meritarian concerns might have some effect on health, but the application of such a recognition is very limited in practice. The author understands that he has made the best case possible for his position by speaking of need in terms of health crises. He purposely excludes speaking about prevention. However, his position is somewhat vulnerable as a result.

By insisting on the crisis aspect of medical care Outka can more readily prove the thesis that need is the only canon of distribution because personal responsibility does not enter in. However, it seems that he actually proves a narrower theory—equal access to medical care in crisis situations. Health care and medical crises are not exactly the same thing. Outka seems to move too readily and too quickly from crisis to care. In addition to the logical difference between crisis and care, many contemporary authors are showing how important personal responsibility is with regard to health care. (This matter will be discussed later at greater length.)

Outka insists on the distinctiveness of health care and both distinguishes and even separates health care from other basic human needs such as food and shelter. He realizes that he is limiting the question and considering the distribution of health care in an isolated context, but justifies considering only one aspect of a complicated question at a time. However, does this not indicate the somewhat formal and too abstract nature of his theory? In reality one cannot abstract from the question of the distribution of all the goods within society. There are significant theoretical and practical benefits in a more unified theory which can be applied to other important goods as well.

The somewhat formal and abstract nature of his approach is also evident in recognizing that some collisions will exist in practice, so that some modifications in the theory of justice as equality are necessary. There is great wisdom in such flexibility, but perhaps it indicates that these other considerations should have been discussed earlier in constructing the theory.

Robert Veatch has also proposed an equalitarian theory of just health care delivery.[15] Veatch does not spend as much effort on justifying the choice of equalitarian justice as does Outka, but he shows how this approach should be modified and applied in practice. Accepting a basic equal claim of all as far as health care goes, Veatch enunciates the principle that justice requires that everyone has a claim to the amount of health care needed to provide an opportunity for a level of health equal, as far as possible, to the health of other persons. Such a formulation avoids the problem that a group of the medically sick who are the most ill could end up with all our health care resources. The neediest have a just claim only when something fruitful can be done. With the recognition that health care does not necessarily produce health, the duty of society is to provide an opportunity of equal health care. Both merit and compensatory justice have been proposed as modifiers of the equalitarian theory, but in general in the area of health Veatch wants to keep these considerations to a minimum.

In the light of the complexity of the problem Veatch recognizes that justice cannot be the only criterion for allocating health care. Often the medically least well-off prefer inequality in order to promote their own medical welfare. Claims of justice may be overturned (although this should be minimized as much as possible) by efficiency, aggregate utility, cost factors and other right-making characteristics.[16] Veatch thus admits that other ethical claims, especially that of efficiency, can modify the claims of justice.

As such the concept of justice as equality is a formal concept which says little or nothing about the real problem of distribution and of priorities within society. Both in theory and in political practice it is not helpful to talk about rights to certain things without seeing the problem in the context of the total question of distribution.[17] Such an approach also ignores the very difficult problem of determining the priorities within health care and medicine. The federal dollar today is paying for much health education, research and service, but the urgent question remains about what should be our priorities. Often the question is addressed today in terms of preventive medicine versus crisis medicine. Veatch explicitly recognizes that something might be unjust but nevertheless right because of other right-making considerations such as efficiency. Such a distinction seems to stem from the failure to integrate the whole question of distribution into justice. Justice is one thing and distribution is another.

In my judgment these problems point to a more serious and underlying defect in the notion of justice as equality—a view of society which is too individualistic and does not give enough importance to the social reality as such. The concept of society presupposed in the justice as equality theory is still too individualistic rather than distributive. If the problem is one of just distribution of goods within society, then it should be impossible to see a contradiction between justice and right distribution. Justice as equality despite its attempts to overcome the charge of individualism and protect the rights of poor individuals in society still suffers from an individualistic concept of justice and of society. To speak about the rights of individuals apart from the question of distribution seems to understand society as the means for individuals to achieve their own good. There is present the notion that society exists only to insure the good of individuals, but this destroys any understanding of society as more than an aggregate of individuals cooperating only to achieve their own good.

The remainder of this chapter will explicate a theory of distributive justice which has been developed within the natural law tradition. In the recent discussions of the right to health care this theory has generally not been represented.[18] However, such a theory seems to overcome some of the problems already mentioned and offers a theoretical framework for grounding, analyzing and applying in practice the right to health care. The theory as proposed here does not accept all the metaphysical presuppositions and historical conditionings surrounding the natural law tradition.

II. The Understanding of Society

A correct understanding of the right to health care and the distribution of resources must rest on a proper understanding of society. The perennial problem in such considerations is to avoid the Scylla of individualism and the Charybdis of collectivism. Society is more than just an aggregate of individuals, and yet society is not merely a collectivity in which the individual is lost or submerged for the good of society or of others. Although its proponents might not advert to it, an equalitarian theory of justice implies too individualistic a view of society. There is an ethical tradition which wants to give more importance and meaning to society and the community without at the same time subordinating the individual to the community. This tradition insists on the common good, not just the private good of individuals, as the purpose of society.

Society and the state as a part of society are not voluntary associations which individuals decide to join merely for their own purposes. Human reality calls us to live in society because human beings must exist in social and political relationships. The state is a natural society based on the social realities of human beings, not something which exists only at the whim and voluntary choice of individuals or something that exists solely or primarily because of the need of individuals to protect themselves and their rights against one another and other outside forces. The human being has a social dimension to one's existence as is illustrated in the many relationships necessary for human living. Both the quest for perfection and weaknesses of the human person call upon the person to live in society, including the political society of the state. The goal of human perfection calls for relationships in reciprocity with others. Human needs and deficiencies require us to work together with others to achieve and accomplish what cannot be accomplished by individuals alone.

The end or purpose of human society is the common good. The common good of human society differentiates the human society from other groupings. In an animal society there is a public good but no common good because there are no persons. Here the animal is merely a part of the whole, and the good of the whole can claim the sacrifice of the individual. However, the good of human society is not merely the individual good or the total aggregate of the individual goods of the persons who constitute the society. In such a conception there is really no society and no truly social fabric.

The distinctive character of human society is the fact that it is a whole containing other wholes. The end of society is the common good, but a common good of human *persons* who are not merely parts of a whole. The common good is common both to the whole and to the persons who comprise it. The common good avoids the extreme of collectivism, because it demands that the good be distributed to the persons who make up society. The common good of a human society ceases to be that when it denies the personhood of its members. The common good not only refers to the various spiritual and material goods existing within society but above all involves the ordered relationships existing in society.

There is a reciprocal and even somewhat paradoxical relationship between the individual and society. In one sense the individual is a part of and subordinated to the community. In another sense the person is transcendent and can never be subordinated to the community. The relationship between individual and community is one of reciprocity; however, precedence is due to the person insofar as all social questions arise and must be resolved in relation to the person.[19] According to Johannes Messner it is wrong to ascribe primary being to society and only secondary being to the individual, but it is equally wrong to ascribe primary being solely to the individual and only secondary being to society.[20] Jacques Maritain recognizes the same tension. On the one hand the person as person, or totality, requires that the common good of the temporal society flow back upon it and even transcends the social whole. On the other hand the person as individual, or part, remains inferior and subordinated to the whole and must serve the common work.[21]

Society thus has a meaning, a significance and a reality which is more than the mere aggregate of individuals. Likewise, the common good of society has a meaning, a significance and a reality which is more than and different from the aggregate of the individual goods. In keeping with this understanding of society and of the common good one can consider the question of rights and justice.

The language of rights is the language of claims—not merely of desires and hopes. In general a right can be described as that which is due someone as one's own. The objective right, or the material, is that which is owed, which might be a thing (money) or an action or even an omission. From the subjective viewpoint a right is the inviolable moral power of an individual to do, to have or to demand something for one's own good. The essential elements of a right are four: the subject of the right, or the person; the object, or the matter, of the right; the title, that is, the fact by reason of which one claims the right; and the term, or the person or persons who are affected by the right and have the corresponding duty.[22]

There are various titles which ground one's rights. Obvious examples include a contract or a law. In addition to the rights which come from legal enactments or from a voluntary contract, there exist fundamental human rights which belong to all persons. The metaphysical grounding of such rights is disputed, but I would see the basis of them in the dignity of the human person, coming ultimately from the fact of creation by a gracious God. These basic human rights are enunciated in political documents such as the Bill of Rights of the Constitution of the United States and the Declaration on Human Rights of the United Nations. The basic principle is that the individual person has a right to life and to those things which are necessary for living a decent human life. Lists of such rights often include the right to life, the inviolability of the person, freedom of conscience, of religion, of speech, of association, the right to marry, the right to earn a livelihood and similar ones.[23] One must note the different objects of rights. The right demands sometimes that others do not interfere or at other times that others positively do something. Within society there are not only rights of individuals vis-à-vis one another but there are also rights and correlative duties of individuals vis-à-vis society.

III. Distributive Justice

How is justice then to be understood? Justice generally deals with giving what is due. Within society there are three basic relationships which must be considered—the relationship of individuals to one another, the relationship of the social whole to individuals and the relationship of individuals to the social whole. These three relationships correspond to the three basic forms of justice. Commutative justice orders the relationship of one individual to another individual. Distributive justice orders the relationship of the community as such to its members; legal justice orders the relationship of the individuals to the social whole.[24]

It is important to notice the differences between commutative justice (one to one) and distributive justice (the society to the individual). Distributive justice has to do with the distribution of the common goods or benefits and burdens of the society equally among the members. Commutative justice can determine quite precisely what is due. Justice and equality in commutative justice consist in an equality of one thing to another; for example, on the basis of the contract it is quite clear what is owed. Distributive justice does not arrive at such preciseness. In distributive justice the ordering of justice is whatever corresponds to a proportional equality of the thing to the person. Distributive justice must consider the subject and not just the thing itself as well as the goods or burdens existing within society. In a true sense there is a subjective aspect involved in distributive justice which is not present in commutative justice. For example, the indemnities given for war damages do not depend only on the damage which was done to the property but must also take into account such factors as whether the person was impoverished by the damage or whether the individual had already suffered from other harm such as physical injury from the war. There exists a different kind of equality in the two cases. Commutative justice involves a quantitative or arithmetical equality based on the one thing's relation to another thing, whereas distributive justice rests on a proportional equality which includes a relationship to the person. Not all, for example, should pay equal amounts of taxes.[25]

There are different kinds of goods to be distributed among the members of society. The distribution will depend to some extent on the type of goods to be distributed. There are basic political rights which must be equal for all because of the equal human dignity of all concerned. Here one thinks of such political rights as freedom of conscience, freedom of religion and the other basic freedoms of the person. Health care belongs to what are often called external goods as differentiated from internal goods such as freedom. There are many types of external goods to be distributed within society, including food, clothing, shelter, education, culture, health. In distributing the common goods of society the community must respect the fundamental human rights of all. The common good can never be in opposition to the fundamental rights of the individual person. The discussion of distributive justice will focus primarily on these external goods in general and then make more specific the right to health care.

As it has already been indicated, there is a lack of precision and exactness in distributive justice as compared with commutative justice. Above all there is the very difficult problem of deciding how distribution should take place. What are the titles, or canons, that should be the basis for the distribution of health care and other goods within society? Some have argued that problems of priorities and distribution are so complex that they are almost, if not altogether, incorrigible to rational determination.[26] However, since the distribution of goods within society is a question of such fundamental importance for human existence, we must make some attempts to come to a rational and just theory of distribution. John A. Ryan in his book on distributive justice mentions five canons for a just distribution of the products of industry—equality, need, efforts, productivity, scarcity. He ultimately chooses a sixth—human welfare, which includes all the others, but with a strong emphasis on needs as determining a decent minimum necessary for human life.[27] Toniolo proposes as a norm for distribution the fact that burdens should be distributed according to capacities and goods or advantages distributed according to needs or necessities.[28] Perhaps such an approach is too simple, but at the very least needs furnish a very significant aspect for the division of goods in society.

The most basic right of the individual in society is the right to life. All individual rights are based on the dignity of human life, which also is a necessary presupposition for all other rights. Society exists to assist the individual to achieve true fulfillment. Although health care is not the most fundamental need of the human person, it is of great significance. Health is necessary for the proper and full functioning of the life of the person. The right to health obviously means that the individual has the right not to have one's health unjustly attacked by others. In addition there exist within society goods and services of health care, and society is thus faced with the distribution of health care. The right of the individual in distributive justice cannot be considered apart from society and all its goods and members. There are many needs that individuals have—housing, education, health, food, culture, clothing. The basic formulation is simple: a person has the right to that minimum which is necessary for living a decent human life. Society has an obligation to provide that which is necessary for a decent human life. Obviously there are many relativities that enter into consideration. Much will depend on the goods which are available at the present time in a given society. We must limit our consideration to the society in which we live, although we cannot forget our obligation to other societies. The human person thus has a right to that basic level of health care which is necessary for decent human living.

The ultimate basis for this right is the dignity of the human person and the fundamental need of the human person. Such a right constitutes a true claim that is obligatory for society to honor. There could be different ways in which society provides for this right, but it is truly a claim and not just a wish or a desire. The right to that level of health care which is appropriate for decent human living is based on the concept of the person and of society which has already been described.

However, there are other factors, especially from a viewpoint of religious ethics, which can bolster the existing right to that level of material goods, including health care, which is necessary for decent human living.

The goods of creation exist primarily to serve the needs of all. In the course of time religious thinkers have unfortunately often forgotten the ramifications of this basic teaching found in the Judaeo-Christian tradition. The acceptance of creation reminds us that we are not the ultimate source of the goods we have, but rather we are stewards of what has been given to all of us by a gracious God. The Judaeo-Christian tradition has recognized this throughout its history in various ways such as the jubilee year, the year of forgiveness, and more recently by recognizing the possibility of expropriating large land holdings for the ultimate benefit of the poor.[29]

One example of the failure to recognize the communal destiny of the goods of creation can be found in concepts of private property. There exists no necessary incompatibility between the common destiny of the goods of creation to serve the needs of all and the acceptance of the right to private property, but at the very least the latter right must always be modified by and subordinated to the common destiny of the goods of creation. Too often the right to private property has been seen as an absolute in itself with no limitations. Perhaps in terms of the language that has already been used, private property and the whole question of property have too often been seen in terms of commutative justice and not in terms of an overarching understanding of distributive justice.[30]

Thomas Aquinas justifies the right to own private property as one's own, but he bases his reason not primarily on the dignity and need of the human person as such but rather on the problems and difficulties that would arise in society if people did not own things as their own. In other words, in a more theological language, the existence of private property is justified by the presence of sin in the world. Aquinas accepted the understanding of some of the fathers of the church that without sin there would have been no need for private property. After justifying the right to own private property,

Aquinas quickly adds that the use of private property is not absolute but is governed by the communal destination of the goods of creation to serve the needs of all creatures. One has the right to keep what is necessary for one's sustenance, but there is an obligation to give superfluous goods to the poor.[31]

In the United States Catholic tradition John A. Ryan proposed a very nuanced theory of the right to private property. As we mentioned in Chapter Three, Ryan carefully distinguishes three kinds of natural rights. First, the object of the right is an end in itself, such as the right to life. Rights of the second category have as their object not ends but rather means which are directly and per se necessary for the majority of individuals to achieve their human end, such as the right to marry. Private property belongs to the third class of rights— those which are only indirectly necessary for the individual because they are necessary for human welfare as a social institution. In a very inductive and a posteriori way Ryan justifies the institution of private property as being the best institution at the present time for social or human welfare in general. His reasoning is pragmatic and practical—private ownership works better for society than any other system. However, if socialism would better serve human welfare, then socialism should be adopted.[32]

The communal destiny of the goods of creation and the stewardship role of human beings remind us that an individual cannot arrogate to oneself the goods of creation at the expense of the truly human needs of the neighbor. The God of creation intends creation to serve the basic needs of all. Another religious support for the fact that the individual person has a claim and right to that basic level of external goods which is necessary for decent human living comes from the Christian concept of love, especially love for those in need. There is a difference between love and justice, but one cannot forget the basic thrust of the Judaeo-Christian message on love for those in need.[33]

The argument thus far has seen health care related to other goods (especially what might be called external or material goods) and argues that every human being has a right to that basic level of goods which is necessary for decent human living. There are many such goods—as health, education, food, shelter, culture. How does health care relate to all these others? What is the level necessary for decent human living? What is the relationship between that level of health care and equal access to health care for all?

This question cannot be considered apart from the broader question of the distribution of goods within a given society. Obviously within a socialistic system it is evident that there should be equal access to health care. In this light one could argue for a complete change in the American system of distribution. From the practical viewpoint of change here and now one must work within the context of a nonsocialist policy of distribution. We accept the existence of such a system and argue within it, although we also recognize that the case could be made for a socialist system.

Even within the present American political and economic system the principle that all have a right to that level of material goods necessary for decent human living must be accepted and put into practice. This principle calls for many changes in our present system as illustrated in the question of welfare reform. Health care differs from many of these other goods (as shelter, food, education, culture) so that there cannot be as great a disparity among people in available health care as there might be in other areas. The basic level of health care, in other words, should be quite high because of some special characteristics of health care itself. There are a number of reasons supporting the case for a comparatively high level of health care available for all. However, all considerations must recognize the finite and limited resources existing within society.

First, the reason for health care is found in ill health or the prevention of ill health. There is the same basic need among all. The provision of health care rests only on this need; other goods such as education or culture require a certain level of ability or of interest among the recipients. Health care is more similar to something like protection or security, a need which is basically the same for all people.

Second, a significant aspect of health care involves prevention of ill health and protection of all people living in society. This protection of all through environmental or public health factors such as inoculations must provide basically the same care for all.

Third, even though it might not be the only or the total aspect, ill health is something that often happens to people. The crisis aspect of ill health, its random character and the fact that for some aspects of ill health there is little or nothing one can do to avoid it argue in favor of a more equalitarian division.

Fourth, since many of the advances in knowledge and technology come through governmentally funded research, then the advantages of this research should be made available to all.

Fifth, whenever it is a question of lifesaving devices, then the basic equal dignity of all human beings should be protected. When those who receive the lifesaving devices will live and those who do not receive them will die, justice demands a random selection process. The availability of lifesaving devices should ordinarily not be based on the ability to pay or on contributions to society.

Sixth, to be truly effective and just the program must embrace at least the vast majority of the citizens. The danger lurks that such a system of health care will be inferior. The participation of most of the citizens in the same program helps to ensure that it does not become a second-class system.

All of these reasons point to the conclusion that the basic level of health care necessary for decent human living must involve a sufficiently high level of quality health care.

IV. Advantages and Disadvantages

There are a number of advantages in an ethical formulation of a right to that level of health care which is necessary for decent human living based on the understanding of society and individual rights proposed above. The canon of distributive justice allows one to consider the more fundamental question of the distribution of all goods within society. Both in theory and in practice health care should not be considered alone as something totally unique.

A theory of distributive justice is not only more wholistic but also more realistic insofar as it considers the question of health care in the light of all the other goods of society and the needs of the individuals. One cannot talk about distribution within society without considering both the existing resources or goods to be distributed and the different needs that must be met.

In distributive justice there is a proportional equality and not a purely numerical or quantitative equality. The need to consider the proportional equality between the individual and the common good as well as the other demands upon the common good should at least in principle help focus public debate on matters of justice and rights. Rights language is one of the strongest possible ethical claims. It is no wonder that political and public rhetoric will often use rights language rather than the language of needs or desires or what is fitting. However, as so often happens, one can merely proclaim certain rights without at the same time considering the basic problem of distribution. The abstract claiming of rights and counterrights tends to produce more heat than light unless one is willing to tackle the whole problem of distribution.

Distributive justice by its very nature raises the question of priorities within society itself. On the basis of what has been said thus far, a minimal criterion of distribution is the satisfaction of basic human needs which are necessary for the decent human livelihood of all citizens. The concept of distributive justice also sheds some light on the difficult problems of priorities within medicine and health care itself. The fundamental concern is to provide the health care necessary for decent human living. Today there is much discussion about the priority between preventive and crisis medicine. Our priorities at the present time are heavily in favor of crisis medicine at least in terms of the money appropriated to the two. However, there is no doubt that preventive medicine (vaccines, changes in environment, better personal health habits) has done in the past and does more today to insure more healthy living than crisis medicine. A theory of distributive justice will insist on the need to give more importance to preventive medicine than we do at present. One word of caution should be addressed to supporters of preventive medicine. We are probably not going to come close to the startling progress made in the last century in terms of life expectancy. The grave, more physical causes of shorter life span have already been thwarted. Now we are dealing with more difficult problems, so that one should never expect to have for the future the same type of progress from preventive medicine that existed in the last century.

Unfortunately, the lure of exotic lifesaving devices often attracts us at the expense of other more basic and more simple forms of preventive medicine. In 1972, for example, Congress made funds available for almost everyone who needed kidney dialysis or kidney transplants. This program by the early 1980s may cost more than one billion dollars each year. Is this such an important priority in medical care? Are there not other aspects which are less sensational but ultimately more significant in contributing to health care?[34] The same problem arises in research in medicine, genetics, biology and their respective technologies. Government funding must recognize the basic priority of fundamental human needs rather than exotic and very costly procedures.

Perhaps the question of priorities is nowhere more evident than in the training of doctors. Doctors are most often taught by researchers who rightly are attempting to expand the boundaries of medical science. However, most patients require only ordinary medical care and attention. Are we training doctors for the real work that needs to be done? This perspective raises the whole question about the need of other health professionals dealing with more ordinary problems of patients. Here, too, distributive justice and the need to satisfy basic human needs should call for a great change in the health care delivery system.

In addition, a theory of distributive justice gives more importance to the societal aspect of human existence and avoids the individualism which seems to be latent in the concept of equalitarian justice. In theory and in practice it is necessary to remember that society is not constituted merely for an individual to achieve self-fulfillment. A theory of distributive justice could never admit that an individual's right could be in conflict with the requirements of proper distribution. Justice does include proportional as well as arithmetical equality. The practical ramifications of the need for society to distribute goods in accord with the basic needs of all its members helps to overcome such an individualism.

Briefly consider two cases in which the social aspect of distributive justice argues against a narrow individualism. The obligation of society to provide basic health care to all its people means that health facilities and personnel have to be distributed in such a way as to make this possible. The individual health care person is not totally free to practice wherever and however one wants to. Services and personnel must be provided for all.

Another significant difference based on proportional equality as distinguished from arithmetical equality is illustrated in the Bakke case. Places in medical school were reserved for sixteen minority students, even though the scores they had on academic tests were less than those obtained by white applicants for the same medical school. Justice as equality often tends to see this type of problem merely in terms of arithmetical or quantitative equality. The white person is being discriminated against because of one's skin. Distributive justice is more open to recognize the need for such approaches because proportional equality takes cognizance of differences in the person and differences in the relationship existing between the society and its different members.[35] Distributive justice as a theory can handle much better what is often called compensatory justice than can a theory of justice as equality.

There are some weaknesses and disadvantages in the theory of distributive justice as outlined. First, proportional equality tends to be a vague measure. Not all can agree on what the proportionality should entail. In this brief treatment no attempt was made to outline a whole theory of distribution and all the canons that should govern a just distribution. However, as a minimum, distributive justice recognizes the right of human beings to that level of health care which is necessary for decent human living. Such a criterion is somewhat vague, but by definition there must be relativity in proportional equality. Additional reasons indicated the need for a comparatively high level of health care as that which is necessary for all.

According to some the proposal of a right to health care necessary for a decent human livelihood does not go far enough even if it does include a comparatively high level of care. It is true that the proposal for equal access to health care is by definition more equalitarian and at the same time more radical (although I think it often rests on a presupposition tinged with individualism, at least as proposed under the rubric of justice as equality). If our society were only to accept the concept of distributive justice as outlined here, significant changes would be required. Our welfare program at the present time falls far below this standard, since many people live well below the official poverty level. Medicare and Medicaid have accepted in some respects the principle enunciated here, but in reality, especially in Medicaid because of the differences from state to state, the basic health-care right is not met. The principle of distributive justice proposed here stands as a critique of our existing system.

In a different society one could more easily argue for equal access for all in one unitary health-care system. I do not want to deny that a case might be made for equal access on the basis of distributive justice, but it would be much more difficult to make the case in theory and especially in practice in the light of American political principles at the present time. I am now arguing for a more reforming approach and not a radically new system. The contemporary American society will not accept a single, publicly financed health-care delivery system for all. Even England and the Scandinavian countries do not have such a system.

From another perspective one could argue that the proposal of distributive justice does not take account of the darker side of human existence—what religious ethicists would call the sinful nature of human beings. However, in practice some of our social programs have already to some degree incorporated the idea of what is due to the individual because of the dignity of the person. In theory what is proposed is not a utopia but something more realistic—what is necessary for a basic level of decent human existence.

One final disadvantage, or negative critique, of the theory of distributive justice goes to the foundation of the theory itself. The natural law basis of such a theory has many shortcomings and is generally not accepted in contemporary discussions. The total metaphysical grounding and the teleological basis of traditional natural law, common good and distributive justice theories do not have to be accepted in order to employ the theory proposed here. There is no doubt that an older natural law theory gave too much importance to organic harmony (e.g., the corporate society) and did not give sufficient attention to historicity, change, diversity and pluralism. The theory of common good and of distributive justice outlined here can stand without some of the philosophical presuppositions and historical limitations of the traditional natural law theory. One important aspect of the traditional natural law theory of the state which should not be forgotten in carrying out the distribution of health care is the principle of subsidiarity, which attempts to avoid overcentralization and the dangers of bureaucracy.

V. Ramifications

Finally some ramifications of distributive justice as applied to health care will be considered. First, our treatment has constantly referred to the right as the right to that level of health care which is required for living a decent human life. Notice the object of the right is health care—not health or medical care. Some have proposed the right to health. The preamble to the Constitution of the World Health Organization states that the enjoyment of the highest attainable standards of health is one of the fundamental rights of every human being. Health is defined as a state of complete physical, mental and social well-being and not merely the absence of disease or of infirmity.[36]

It would be difficult to find a broader understanding either of the right or of the definition of health. No one has a right to a state of complete physical, mental and social well-being. This definition proposes a new messianic kingdom produced by human beings through biomedical science and technology. The empiricist and the metaphysician, the atheist and the believer, all can agree that sooner or later we will all die. No one has a right to such well-being as described here. Unfortunately such excesses indicate a messianic view of medicine which is capable of bringing about such a salvific state. Many have reacted today against such an exaggerated view of human powers as specified in the matter of providing health. A firm antidote to such an exaggerated position can be found in Stanley Hauerwas' insistence on medicine as a tragic profession.[37]

Note too the object of the right is not medical care but health care. We recognize today that there are many factors more important than medical care which influence health care — food, environment, shelter, education, personal habits. Recent studies indicate that following some basic rules about sleep, exercise, diet, and curtailment of smoking and drinking has a very significant effect on health care.[38] Rich Carlson ranks the variables affecting health in the following descending order of importance — environment, life-style, society, genetics and finally medical care, which is said to contribute approximately 6 percent of the total health care.[39] One does not have to be a therapeutic nihilist[40] to recognize that health care and medical care are not the same thing. Our society must give more importance and higher priority to the preventive aspects of health care and to the nonmedical factors influencing health. This priority should also be applied in the area of health research.

Distributive justice recognizes that distribution must consider both what is to be distributed and the cost of distribution, which includes the paying for services. The one question cannot be considered apart from the other in reality, although conceptually it is necessary to consider them separately.

In any finite reality there are limits on the amount of medical care that can be distributed. What are the possible limits and how would a system of distributive justice work out such distribution? Veatch proposes three possible limits on the health care distributed—limits based on the amount paid, limits based on the number of dollars or days of hospital care provided and limits based on excluding certain forms of health care.[41] The question of limits recognizes the problem of the rising cost of health care in our society.

A theory of distributive justice which is based on the need and dignity of the individual person cannot base the level of medical care provided on the amount of money paid. These rights cannot depend on how much one pays. The limit in this theory must come from what medical services and care are included, since the theory talks about a level of medical care which is necessary for decent human livelihood. The criterion is somewhat vague, but certain forms of medical care can readily be seen as outside the range—cosmetic surgery, in vitro fertilization, the provision of exotic lifesaving techniques for *all*, much psychiatric care. Hospital care should not ordinarily involve a private room and other types of extra nursing care beyond the basic level.

Other limits have been suggested in terms of number of dollars spent or days of care provided. If a person is in need of basic medical care and is deprived of it merely because one is suffering from a prolonged illness, an injustice is done. Proponents of such limitations are obviously trying to contain costs. Nevertheless, all people in justice should be protected against the financial difficulties coming from catastrophic illness.

An acceptance of the ethical ramifications of a right to a basic level of health care for all would entail some type of national health insurance. In the last few years many different legislative proposals have been offered as to how this program should be financed.[42] How should such a program be paid for? Distributive justice calls for burdens to be distributed on the basis of capabilities.

The vast majority of the cost must come from some form of taxes, but here distributive justice insists on a progressive tax.

Taxes as burdens should be distributed according to ability to pay.[43] A just tax must be one which progressively requires more of those who have a greater income and cannot merely involve the same dollar amount from all or the same percentage (e.g., 3 percent of total income). In the United States a progressive income tax generally exists, although one must recognize the many loopholes involved. Unfortunately, other taxes are quite regressive. The sales tax requires that rich and poor pay the same; the present social security tax is also regressive. Recently proposed tax changes mean that more of our tax dollars are based on regressive taxation such as social security payments. The taxes for health care must rest on a more progressive taxation. Many health-insurance proposals today do not include this provision since often they are based on a tax somewhat similar to social security payments.

However, in the light of the need to contain costs, to prevent unnecessary use and to help with funding (and thereby provide a higher level of care) some cost sharing by individuals would be appropriate. Two important considerations or conditions should be noted. First, the cost sharing should not be made a burden for the poor. Second, the cost sharing should also be related to income—a certain percentage of one's income. Here again proportionate and not arithmetical equality is required. This cost sharing could take the form of either deductibles or of copayments.

A question arises about increased payments based on meritarian concerns. In general should people who expose themselves to health risks have to pay extra or more than those who do not? Thus far our discussion has excluded meritarian concerns in our theory of distribution. As mentioned earlier, there is wide recognition today of the fact that personal responsibility plays an important role in health care. As a result some have proposed that those who risk health by smoking or excessive drinking, for example, should pay more than those who do not.[44] In general, a total theory of distribution must give consideration to meritarian concerns, but meritarian concerns should be minimal in discussing that level of health care which is necessary for all.

In addition, in the area of health care it is practically impossible to make a case for meritarian concerns in terms of increased costs for some. Why? First of all, the way in which many factors enter into health care is not all that certain. We cannot say, for example, just how much effect proper exercise has on health. Second, there are many factors that are important—exercise, sleep, diet. It is impossible to determine exactly how much each part contributes; consequently it is impossible to work out an equitable system. One might say that smokers should pay more than nonsmokers. But what about those who sleep less than seven hours a day? What about those who do not exercise? And then there is the problem of diet. In practice it would be impossible to monitor all these different aspects and to work out a fair system.

The one possible exception to the exclusion of meritarian concerns might be for those whose job or hobby exposes them to more health risks. Especially if there is significantly higher pay connected with the job because of risk, then some type of greater payment might be equitable. One could also argue that hobbies which involve great risk such as skydiving are generally the preserve of the wealthy who can afford to pay more. However, one could also argue that jobs such as coal mining are very dangerous. It seems somewhat difficult to come up with an equitable plan so that it might be better to do away with all meritarian concerns.

One final aspect stems from the fact that health care and services are goods which must be distributed among the members of society. There are many structural problems in our present health-care delivery system which must be corrected. The problems of cost and of maldistribution are compounded by the existing systems of distribution. The need for more preventive medicine has been pointed out. There is no doubt that more personnel are needed and should be employed. However, the health-care personnel needed above all include health-care professionals and paramedical personnel to provide care and services for which a doctor is not necessary. Hospital care should not be required for those who do not need it. The geographical area in which doctors practice cannot be determined only by the marketplace. Also the fee-for-service approach cannot continue as the only or the primary model of health care delivery. Efforts must be encouraged by society to provide different models. One cannot expect radical change overnight in these areas, but it is necessary to move in the directions indicated.

This chapter has endeavored to provide an ethical perspective on the question of the right to health care. The purpose has been primarily to determine what is this right, what is its grounding and what are its practical ramifications. Ethics and the ethician are not able to supply answers for all the concrete problems facing our society. Questions such as medical care ultimately must be decided by prudential choices in the political realm. However, the principles of distributive justice can well serve as the basis for making political decisions about the provision of health care which are both just and feasible.

NOTES

1. Good summaries of the present discussions can be found in special issues of two significant journals: *Current History* 72, no. 427 (May/June 1977) and 73, no. 428 (July/August 1977) and *Daedalus* 106 (Winter 1977), which has also been published in book form.

2. See, for example, *Medicaid Lessons for National Health Insurance,* ed. Allen D. Spiegel and Simon Podair (Rockville, Maryland: Aspen Systems Corporation, 1975).

3. Christine E. Bishop, "Health Employment and the Nation's Health," *Current History* 72, no. 427 (May/June 1977): 207–210.

4. Karen Davis, *National Health Insurance: Benefits, Costs and Consequences* (Washington, D.C.: The Brookings Institution, 1975), pp. 3–4, 34–41.

5. Herbert E. Klarman, "The Financing of Health Care," *Daedalus* 106 (Winter 1977): 215–234.

6. John H. Knowles, "The Responsibility of the Individual," *Daedalus* 106 (Winter 1977): 75; Joseph G. Simanis, "The British National Health Service in International Perspective," *Current History* 72, no. 428 (July/August 1977): 28.

7. For a contemporary utilitarian theory see Joseph Fletcher, "Ethics and Health Care: Computers and Distributive Justice," in

Ethics and Health Policy, ed. Robert M. Veatch and Roy Branson (Cambridge, Mass.: Ballinger Publishing Co., 1976), pp. 99–109.

8. The most significant recent book espousing a theory of justice in opposition to a utilitarian calculus is John Rawls, *A Theory of Justice* (Cambridge, Mass.: Harvard University Press, 1971). Rawls' work has evoked much comment and discussion. See, for example, *Reading Rawls: Critical Studies on Rawls' A Theory of Justice,* ed. Norman Daniels (New York: Basic Books, 1974). Rawls does not discuss health care distribution in this book, but his theory has been applied to health care distribution by Ronald M. Green, "Health Care and Justice in Contract Theory Perspective," in Veatch and Branson, *Ethics and Health Policy,* pp. 111–126.

9. J.J.C. Smart and Bernard Williams, *Utilitariansim: For and Against* (Cambridge: Cambridge University Press, 1973).

10. Nicholas Rescher, "The Allocation of Exotic Medical Lifesaving Therapy," *Ethics* 79 (1969): 178.

11. James F. Childress, "Who Shall Live When Not All Can Live?" *Soundings* 43 (1970): 339–355; Paul Ramsey, *The Patient as Person* (New Haven, Conn.: Yale University Press, 1970), pp. 239–275.

12. Robert Sade, "Medical Care as a Right: A Refutation," *New England Journal of Medicine* 285 (December 2, 1971): 1288–1292. Sade has published his basic theory in other articles: e.g., "Is Health Care a Right? Negative Response," *Image* 7, no. 1 (1974): 11–19; "Medical Care: Not a Right," *Massachusetts Physician* 35, no. 6 (June 1976): 5–26.

13. Sade, "Medical Care as a Right," p. 1289.

14. Gene Outka, "Social Justice and Equal Access to Health Care," *The Journal of Religious Ethics* 2 (1974): 11–32. Page references will be made in the text to this journal, but the article has been published in many anthologies.

15. Robert M. Veatch, "What Is 'Just' Health Care Delivery?" in Veatch and Branson, *Ethics and Health Policy,* pp. 127–153.

16. Ibid., p. 142.

17. For opposition to the theory of equalitarian justice in health care and a proposal for the right to a decent minimum see the writings of Charles Fried: "Rights and Health Care: Beyond Equality and Efficiency," *New England Journal of Medicine* 293 (July 31, 1975): 241–245; "An Analysis of Equality and Rights in Medical Care," *The Hastings Center Report* 6, no. 1 (February 1976): 30–32.

18. *Ethics and Health Policy,* for example, does not discuss this theory. For one discussion which incorporates some of this theory see Joseph M. Boyle, "The Concept of Health and the Right to Health Care," *Social Thought* 3 (Summer 1977): 5–17.

19. Eberhard Welty, *A Handbook of Christian Social Ethics I: Man in Society* (New York: Herder and Herder, 1960), pp. 101–113.

20. Johannes Messner, *Social Ethics: Natural Law in the Western World*, 3rd ed. (St. Louis: B. Herder, 1965), p. 107.

21. Jacques Maritain, *The Person and the Common Good* (Notre Dame, Indiana: University of Notre Dame Press, 1966), p. 70.

22. Marcellino Zalba, *Theologiae moralis summa II: tractatus de mandatis dei et ecclesiae* (Madrid: Biblioteca de Autores Cristianos, 1953), pp. 425-432.

23. E.g., Messner, *Social Ethics*, pp. 326-330.

24. Josef Pieper, *The Four Cardinal Virtues* (Notre Dame, Indiana: University of Notre Dame Press, 1966), pp. 81-103. There is no need here to enter into the discussion about the meaning of social justice and its relationship to the other kinds of justice.

25. A. Vermeersch, *Quaestiones de justitia* (Bruges: Beyaert, 1901), pp. 49-69.

26. Paul Ramsey, *The Patient as Person*, pp. 240, 268.

27. John A. Ryan, *Distributive Justice* (New York: Macmillan, 1916), pp. 243-253.

28. Cited in Vermeersch, *Quaestiones de justitia*, p. 52.

29. E. Lio, *Morale e beni terreni: la destinazione universale dei beni terreni nella 'Gaudium et spes' e in alcuni fonti* (Rome: Città Nuova Editrice, 1976).

30. J. Diez-Alegria, "La lettura del magistero pontificio in materia sociale alla luce del suo sviluppo storico," in *Magistero et morale: atti del 3°congresso nazionale dei moralisti* (Bologna: Edizioni Dehoniane, 1970), pp. 211-256.

31. Thomas Aquinas, *Summa theologiae: Pars II^a II^{ae}* (Rome: Marietti, 1952), q. 66, a. 1 and 2. See also Odon Lottin, "La nature du devoir de l'aumône chez les prédécesseurs de Saint Thomas d'Aquin," *Ephemerides Theologicae Lovanienses* 15 (1938): 613-624; L. Bouvier, *Le precepte del l'aumône chez saint Thomas d'Aquin* (Montreal: Collegium Immaculatae Conceptionis, 1935).

32. Ryan, *Distributive Justice*, pp. 56-66.

33. Outka makes references to this throughout his article and refers to his earlier work, *Agape: An Ethical Analysis* (New Haven: Yale University Press, 1972). For a monograph from the perspective of Christian ethical warrants see Earl Edward Shelp, "An Inquiry into Christian Ethical Sanctions for the 'Right to Health Care' " (Ph.D. dissertation, Southern Baptist Theological Seminary [Ann Arbor, Michigan: University Microfilms, 1976, no. 76-23, 963]).

34. James F. Childress, "Priorities in the Allocation of Health Care Resources," in *No Rush to Judgement: Essays in Medical Ethics*, ed. David H. Smith (Bloomington, Indiana: The Poynter Center, 1977), pp. 135-144. For other references indicating the primacy of preventive health care see footnote 38.

35. Daniel C. Maguire, "Unequal but Fair," *The Commonweal* 104 (October 14, 1977): pp. 647–652.

36. *World Health Organization: Basic Documents,* 26th ed. (Geneva: World Health Organization, 1976), p. 1. This preamble was originally adopted in 1946.

37. Stanley Hauerwas "Medicine as a Tragic Profession," in *No Rush to Judgement: Essays on Medical Ethics,* pp. 93–128.

38. N. B. Belloc and L. Breslow, "The Relation of Physical Health Status and Health Practices," *Preventive Medicine* 1 (1972): 409–421; Belloc and Breslow, "Relationship of Health Practices and Mortality," *Preventive Medicine* 2 (1973): 67–81. See also Leon R. Kass, "Regarding the End of Medicine and the Pursuit of Health," *The Public Interest* 40 (Summer, 1975): 11–42; John H. Knowles, "The Responsibility of the Individual," *Daedalus* 106 (Winter, 1977): 59–80.

39. Rich J. Carlson, "Alternative Legislative Strategies for Licensure: Licensure and Health." This paper was presented at the Conference on Quality Assurance in Hospitals, Boston University, Program on Public Policy for Quality Health Care, November 21–22, 1975. Quoted by Walter J. McNerney, "The Quandary of Quality Assessment," *The New England Journal of Medicine* 295 (December 30, 1976): 1507.

40. Paul Starr, "The Politics of Therapeutic Nihilism," *The Hastings Center Report* 6, no. 5 (October, 1976): 24–30.

41. Veatch, "What Is 'Just' Health Care Delivery," pp. 142–150.

42. For overviews and comparisons of the major different legislative proposals see *Current History* 73, no. 428 (July/August 1977): 48–49; Veatch, "What Is 'Just' Health Care Delivery," pp. 142–152.

43. E.g., Ryan, *Distributive Justice,* pp. 102–117, 296–302.

44. For a discussion pro and con on a tax on smoking and other harmful behavior which would be paid to help meet health-care expenses under a system of national health-care insurance see Robert M. Veatch and Peter Steinfels, "Who Should Pay for Smokers' Medical Care?" *The Hastings Center Report* 4, no. 5 (November 1974): 8–10.

Index